Can Unlike Students Learn Together? Grade Retention, Tracking, and Grouping

A Volume in
Research in Educational Productivity

Can Unlike Students Learn Together? Grade Retention, Tracking, and Grouping

Edited by

Herbert J. Walberg
University of Illinois at Chicago

Arthur J. Reynolds
University of Wisconsin-Madison

The Late Margaret C. Wang
Temple University

INFORMATION AGE
PUBLISHING

80 Mason Street
Greenwich, Connecticut 06830
www.infoagepub.com

Published in cooperation with

Library of Congress Cataloging-in-Publication Data

Can unlike students learn together? : grade retention, tracking, and grouping / edited by Herbert J. Walberg, Arthur J. Reynolds, Margaret C. Wang.
 p. cm. — (Research in educational productivity)
 Includes bibliographical references.
 ISBN 1-59311-114-2 (pbk.) — ISBN 1-59311-115-0 (hardcover) 1. Grade repetition—United States. 2. Ability grouping in education—United States. I. Walberg, Herbert J., 1937- II. Reynolds, Arthur J. III. Wang, Margaret C. IV. Series.
 LB3063.C32 2004
 371.2'52—dc22

2004001327

Copyright © 2004 Information Age Publishing Inc.

All rights reserved. No part of this publication may be reproduced, stored in a retrieval system, or transmitted, in any form or by any means, electronic, mechanical, photocopying, microfilming, recording or otherwise, without written permission from the publisher.

Printed in the United States of America

The Mid-Atlantic Regional Educational Laboratory, the Laboratory for Student Success (LSS), is one of 10 regional educational laboratories funded by the Institute of Education Sciences (IES) of the U.S. Department of Education. LSS seeks to significantly improve the capacity of the region—including Delaware, Marlyand, New Jersey, Pennsylvania, and Washington, DC—and the nation to enact and sustain systemic educational reform. LSS aims to transform research-based knowledge into useful tools that can be readily integrated into the educational reform process.

CONTENTS

Preface	vii
1. Introduction and Overview *Herbert J. Walberg*	1
2. Dropout in Relation to Grade Retention: An Accounting of the Beginning School Study *Karl L. Alexander, Doris R. Entwisle, Susan L. Dauber, and Nader Kabbani*	5
3. Grade Retention and School Dropout: Another Look at the Evidence *Judy A. Temple, Arthur J. Reynolds, and Suh-Ruu Ou*	35
4. Is Grade Retention Educational Malpractice? Empirical Evidence from Meta-Analyses Examining the Efficacy of Grade Retention *Shane R. Jimerson*	71
5. Race-ethnicity, Social Background, and Grade Retention *Robert M. Hauser, Devah I. Pager, and Solon J. Simmons*	97
6. Race Effects on Ability Group Outcomes *Maureen T. Hallinan*	115
7. Classroom Organization and Instructional Quality *Adam Gamoran*	141
8. Grouping, Tracking, and De-tracking: Conclusions from Experimental, Correlational, and Ethnographic Research *James A. Kulik*	157
9. Understanding Research on the Consequences of Retention *Lorrie A. Shepard*	183
10. Recommendations and a Personal View *Herbert J. Walberg*	203
About the Contributors	209

PREFACE

For the first time, this book brings together three controversial topics: homogeneous grouping of students within classrooms by ability or achievement criteria, tracking of students into courses of study by the same criteria, and retention of students in their present grade so that they repeat a year's work instead of being promoted. The editors solicited syntheses of research on these topics from outstanding scholars with a variety of views.

Initial versions of the chapters were discussed at a national invitational conference sponsored by the Laboratory for Student Success, the Mid-Atlantic Regional Educational Laboratory, at Temple University Center for Research in Human Development and Education (CRHDE) through a contract with the former Office of Educational Research and Improvement (OERI), now the Institute of Education Sciences (IES) of the U.S. Department of Education.

At the conference, the chapter authors benefited from discussions with one another, other scholars, policymakers, educators, and parents. Their recommendations are reported in the last chapter.

Julia St. George, Robin Neal, and Marilyn Murphy helped plan and coordinate the conference to ensure it was well managed and productive. Lydia Hoag provided splendid editorial service in preparing the manuscript for publication.

The late Margaret C. Wang, former director of LSS and the Center, approved the selection of authors and participants in the conference. She provided much of the energy that initiated this conference and its initial chapter manuscripts. Even though she was unable to participate in the conference and subsequent editing of the book, we have retained her name as editor because of her inspiration of the project. We thank JoAnn Manning, former Executive Director of LSS and Kent McGuire, Dean of the College of Education at Temple University, for their support of this project and the continuation of Margaret's leadership in working for the educational success of the nation's children.

Herbert J. Walberg

CHAPTER 1

INTRODUCTION AND OVERVIEW

Herbert J. Walberg and Arthur J. Reynolds

With the federal No Child Left Behind act and new education legislation in all 50 states, educators are pressed to raise academic standards and raise achievement test scores. These developments make the central issues of this book—tracking, ability grouping, and grade retention—all the more salient. They are obviously timely topics for research and comment, and this book, for the first time, considers them together since they bear on the central question of the book's title, *Can Unlike Children Learn Together?* Reasonable people of good will, including policy makers, scholars, and K–12 educators, have differing views of the possible benefits, costs, and problems of these issues. What are some of the issues?

Tracking, most often practiced in secondary school, groups students into courses or sequences of courses of various levels of difficulty suited to their levels of achievement. Ability grouping, most often practiced in primary schools, assigns students within classrooms to homogeneous groups of like ability. Grade retention requires students who have not attained achievement standards to repeat one or more grades. All three practices are based on the theory that children of like abilities or levels of achievement can learn together more efficiently than can heterogeneous students. Tracking, grouping, and retention are widely practiced in the United States and in many other countries, and they are founded on both theory and research.

Yet other theory and research suggest that these practices may be inefficient and unwise. Some scholars argue, for example, that students retained in grade may suffer declining self-esteem, which may deter their progress so that they are less likely to catch up with grade level standards. This may be attributable, in part, to the fact that by itself, grade retention does not address the causes of academic failure. Others argue that, to the contrary, such students would eventually fall further behind and drop out whether or not they were retained. To "socially promote" ill-prepared students would depreciate the value of the high school diplomas of those who meet rigorous standards.

Similarly, some argue that it is more efficient to teach subjects such as mathematics when students are similar in initial mastery. It may seem difficult, for example, to simultaneously teach consumer mathematics, algebra, and calculus to a group of students who are variously prepared for these subjects. Still, it may be argued that, in some cases, faster students may benefit from helping slower students. Schools might also provide more classroom time and intensified instructional services to at-risk students for remediation or to prevent them from falling behind in the first place.

Written by national authorities who do not necessarily agree on these issues, the chapters in this book summarize the most recent theories and research emerging from the analysis of tracking, ability grouping, and grade retention. The authors are diverse in their views and both sides of the most important issues are represented.

In their chapter, Karl Alexander, Doris Entwisle, Susan Dauber, and Nader Kabbani use the Beginning School Study (BSS), a panel of Baltimore school children who began first grade in the fall of 1982 in 20 city public schools, to examine the relationship between grade retention in the primary grades and high school dropout. The authors explore the question, "When children are not keeping up, is it better to hold them back or move them ahead?"

Judy Temple, Arthur Reynolds, and Suh-Ruu Ou discuss their findings from the Chicago Longitudinal Study (CLS), an ongoing study of 1,539 low-income, minority students who attended kindergarten at various Chicago public schools in 1980. The study sample for the chapter includes the 1,267 students who were in Chicago public schools for at least six years and whose dropout status was known by age 20. The authors compared the dropout rates of students who were retained, those who were not, those who were retained and received academic intervention/remediation, and those who were not retained and received intervention/remediation.

Shane Jimerson's chapter reviews research on the effects of grade retention as presented in studies in the last half of the twentieth century.

He focuses on four seminal meta-analyses: Jackson's 1975 systematic review, Holmes' and Matthews' 1984 meta-analysis, Holmes' 1989 meta-analysis, and his own 2001 systematic review and meta-analysis.

Robert Hauser, Devah Pager, and Solon Simmons explore race-ethnicity, social background, and grade retention. The chapter reports analyses of race-ethnic differences in grade retention, or enrollment below the modal grade level for a child's age, using data from the October Current Population Surveys (CPS) from 1972 to 1998. Their analyses focus on children at selected ages from 6 to 17—ages that span the period between entry to elementary school and the later years of high school. The authors observed typical developmental patterns of retention and of differentials in retention by looking at several ages. By combining data from the 27 annual surveys, trends in retention practices across three decades are identified.

Maureen Hallinan, on the other hand, responds to claims that ability grouping is discriminatory because of data demonstrating that a disproportionate number of minorities are assigned to lower ability groups. She questions the claims that race is used as an indicator of assignment and suggests many other verifiable determiners of group placement. To further illuminate the effects of ability grouping on the achievement gains of Black and White students, she examines whether race affects the amount of change in a student's achievement if the student moves to a higher ability group.

Adam Gamoran offers an insightful literature review of the studies exploring the tracking and de-tracking of students. He discusses many studies, most of which suggest that tracking and grouping are associated with unequal classroom instruction that results in unequal student achievement. Gamoran also explores alternatives to either strict tracking or de-tracking and offers evidence that finding a middle ground is the most ideal solution for students' optimal achievement. In order for progress to be made, Gamoran implores researchers to move beyond "existence proofs" to a more generalizable conclusion about the real advantages and disadvantages of policy choices.

In his chapter on grouping, tracking, and de-tracking, James Kulik describes and evaluates experimental, correlational, and ethnographic evidence on the effectiveness of grouping and tracking systems. The experimental evidence comes from studies that examined educational outcomes for possibly equivalent students assigned to grouped and non-grouped classes. The correlational evidence draws from studies of performance differences in upper and lower tracks when characteristics of students selecting the tracks are statistically controlled. Finally, Kulik summarizes qualitative observations of upper and lower track classrooms for ethnographic evidence.

While explaining the potential for invalid inferences, Lorrie Shepard summarizes research findings that show links between repeating a grade and dropping out of school. She reviews comparatives studies that evaluate the effect of grade repetition on student achievement, and she considers several recent large-scale studies on retention. Shepard concludes her chapter by using a model of the Federal Drug Administration's requirements for safe and effective treatment to consider how evidence of effectiveness should be weighed in making decisions about retention policy.

The original versions of the chapters were commissioned for a National Invitational Conference "Can Unlike Students Learn Together? Grade Retention, Tracking, and Grouping," sponsored by the Laboratory for Student Success and the National Center on Education in the Inner Cities at Temple University Center for Research in Human Development and Education. The papers discuss research findings and point out the implications for policy, programs, and practices.

We, the conference organizers, brought together education leaders and scholars known for their differing views. Also represented were teachers, principals, superintendents, and state and federal officials. In addition to addressing the key issues framed by the commissioned papers, the conferees devoted much of the conference time to small work groups, which discussed what is known from research, its practical applications, and next-step recommendations for raising achievement and closing the achievement gap between slower and faster learners. Their recommendations are presented in the last chapter of this book.

CHAPTER 2

DROPOUT IN RELATION TO GRADE RETENTION:

An Accounting from the Beginning School Study[1]

Karl L. Alexander, Doris R. Entwisle,
Susan L. Dauber, and Nader Kabbani

This paper examines the relationship between retention in the primary grades and high school dropout from the perspective of the Beginning School Study (BSS), a panel of Baltimore school children who attended first grade in 20 city public schools in the fall of 1982.[2] It extends our earlier work on effects of grade retention (e.g., Alexander, Entwisle, & Dauber, 1994), which investigated consequences for children's academic performance and socioemotional development through the middle school years.

When children are not keeping up, is it better to hold them back or move them ahead? That is the question addressed in our earlier work. For answers, we examined the experience of 1st grade repeaters, 2nd grade repeaters, 3rd grade repeaters and, as a group, children held back in grades four through seven, monitoring their academic progress and attitudes from the beginning of first grade, before anyone had been held back, to the end of seventh grade (in the case of repeaters) or eighth grade (in the case of children never retained). The time frame was eight years in both instances, but with repeaters a grade (or more) behind their never retained age-mates.

Retention rates in the BSS panel are quite high—almost 17% of the cohort was held back at the end of first grade, and over 5 years (ordinarily the end of elementary school), 40% of the group had repeated, including many double retentions. The BSS has been monitoring these children's academic and socioemotional standing for almost 20 years now, with fieldwork commencing at the very start of their formal schooling in first grade. "Pre-post" research designs that span many years are uncommon in the retention literature, and the panel's experience, we felt, could shed light on how repeating a grade affects children's subsequent development—personal as well as academic.

The analyses reported in our 1994 volume tracked the group's progress into middle school, focusing on achievement test scores and report card marks in the academic arena. The present paper extends the time frame to the end of high school and to a rather different outcome: high school dropout. Our earlier study generated considerable interest, as well as some controversy. Retention's effects were assessed in a whole host of ways, and though the results were complex, we concluded that repeaters, in most instances, were doing better in elementary school after retention than they had been doing before, and that these advances generally held up for a number of years (although in diminishing measure) into middle school. The experience certainly did not set them back academically, and often it seemed to provide a boost. Nor did we see evidence of great stigma being attached to grade retention. Instead, repeating a grade in most of our comparisons was associated with improved, not depressed, attitudes toward self and school.

This conclusion that grade retention has mainly salutary or neutral effects put us at odds with many in the research community, both then (e.g., Holmes & Matthews, 1984; House, 1989; Smith & Shepard, 1987) and since (e.g., Hauser, 1999b; Reynolds, Temple, & McCoy, 1997). That obliged us, among other things, to review the research ourselves. The evidence holding grade retention harmful, we concluded, was neither as consistent (e.g., a scattering of positive findings) nor as compelling (e.g., much of the research was old and methodologically suspect) as critics of the practice claimed. Since then, positive achievement effects of grade retention have been reported in several additional studies. These have used local (Pierson & Connell, 1992), state-level (Sociology of Education Research Group, 1999), and national (Karweit, 1999) samples and varied modes of analysis.

Grade retention, in these studies, is not the *source* of poor-performing children's academic difficulties, and sometimes its effects are salutary.[3] These conclusions, in our view, fairly characterize the balance of evidence, and indeed sentiment seems to have shifted in recent years toward a more neutral middle ground. For example, in her chapter, Lorrie Shepard, one of the more prominent critics of traditional grade retention, adopts "a working summary that retention 'does not improve achievement,' rather than the prior summary, which was that it 'harms achievement'." But any such softening is hardly warranting for wholesale grade retention as a remedy for below-par school performance. There are many reasons for preferring alternatives to retention. Here we mention five (for additional comment, see Alexander, Entwisle, & Kabbani, 2003):

1. Not all studies find positive effects. The evidence is mixed, which means that holding children back does not always help. At a programmatic level, the conditions that maximize retention's benefits and minimize its harm are not well understood, and without good "best practice" guidance, blanket prescriptions (or proscriptions) would be ill advised.
2. Related to the first point, the studies currently available tell us what happens "on average," but "on average" is not good enough for making decisions in individual cases. To commit to a course of action assumes an understanding of what is behind a particular child's difficulties, and the available research does not offer that level of detail. Whether or not retention helps or hurts students must be highly dependent on the specifics of context. Effects of retention on youths' psychological well-being are bound up with neighborhood, school, and family. In schools with high retention rates, for example, repeaters are not "singled out" or conspicuous to the same extent as in schools with low retention rates.
3. In none of the studies that have favorable retention findings does repeating a grade bring repeaters' performance up to the level of the average student. At best, it provides some help, but that help still leaves repeaters performing far off the standard we want for our children.
4. Grade retention is an expensive intervention—at a minimum, the cost of an extra year's schooling—and in general there ought to be better, cheaper, and less disruptive ways to realize its benefits.
5. Finally, and most immediately relevant, to date, the literature that reports positive effects, ours included, has not undertaken a comprehensive evaluation of how grade retention impacts children's long-term schooling, and major gaps leave major questions. The gap that concerns us presently is the connection between grade retention and high school dropout.

THE RETENTION-DROPOUT CONNECTION

Early grade retention is perhaps the most extensively documented school-based risk factor for dropout (e.g., Brooks-Gunn, Guo, & Furstenberg, 1993; Grissom & Shepard, 1989; Rumberger, 1995; Rumberger & Larson, 1998; Temple, Reynolds, & Miedel, 2000). Indeed, the grade retention-dropout connection is so prominent a concern that an entire section is devoted to it in the 1997 edition of the Department of Education's annual series on high school dropout. This is noteworthy, as these descriptive reports rarely address "causes."

So how strong is the connection? Against a 1995 (status) dropout rate of 12% for never retained 16–24-year-olds, repeaters weigh in at 24.1% (U. S. Department of Education, 1997, pp. 46–47),[4]—a pattern that aligns in general terms with much other research. Hauser's review (1999a, pp. 21–22), for example, cites studies in which grade retention increases dropout risk by 12 percentage points, 70 percentage points, and 2.5 times, all after adjusting statistically for relevant characteristics that distinguish dropouts from nondropouts.

The grade retention-dropout association is thus well established, but still there are reasons to examine the connection from the vantage point of the BSS panel. First, the BSS found positive or neutral effects of grade retention on "near-term" outcomes—achievement scores, marks, and attitudes. Thus far, the link between retention and dropout has not been assessed in any of the studies that report positive effects for other outcomes. To find that grade retention pushes children out of school in a context where it does not impede their academic progress or assault their self-esteem would be a stringent test of the proposition.

In addition, few studies provide compelling evidence that the link, in fact, is causal. The uncertainty inheres in what econometricians refer to as the "endogeneity problem." A shared history of poor school adjustment and low levels of school achievement often is the backdrop to both retention and dropout. Our earlier work on determinants of grade retention shows this "shared history" for repeaters (Alexander et al., 1994; Dauber, Alexander, & Entwisle, 1993) and it is evident as well for dropouts in the BSS (e.g., Alexander, Entwisle, & Kabbani, 2001). Under such circumstances, the seeming effect of grade retention on dropout could instead reflect a common history of academic difficulty.

To achieve clarity, the standard remedy is to adjust statistically for presumed common causes that predate both retention and dropout, and the more complete the coverage, the greater the clarity achieved. As noted, there are many studies, but owing to research design constraints these typically do not provide broad coverage of preretention confounds,[5] a limitation noted by the Goals 2000 panel on high school dropout (Goal 2

Work Group, 1993, p. 18): "Few retention studies follow students throughout their school careers, especially studies beginning in the early elementary grades where retention is most likely to occur." As noted, data gathering for the BSS began at the start of first grade, and this timing puts us in a position to pursue the matter of causal priority with a measure of authority.

What confounds might be at issue? The BSS panel evidences a "high risk" profile, personally and contextually. Regarding context, when our study youngsters were in school, conditions in Baltimore exemplified all the urban problems associated with de-industrialization, job loss, white flight and suburbanization (e.g., Wilson, 1987, 1996; see Rusk, 1996, for an assessment of how these transformations have impacted Baltimore specifically). For instance, Baltimore has one of the highest dropout rates in the country (Annie E. Casey Foundation, 1997; Bomster, 1992; S. P. Kelly, 1988); in 1990, its childhood poverty rate was 32.5% for children 18 and under (39.1% among African Americans) as against 15.2% for the nation's 200 largest cities (Children's Defense Fund, 1992). That same year Baltimore also ranked eleventh among the nation's 100 largest cities in terms of poverty concentration (Kasarda, 1993, Table A.1), while in 1997 it placed second highest among U.S. cities in the percentage of births to teen mothers, near the top in percentage of low birth weight babies and infant mortality, and its juvenile arrest rate led the nation (Annie E. Casey Foundation, 1997).

Such community conditions add onto academic risk that attaches to children's personal and family attributes. A majority of the BSS panel is African American (55%), two thirds were living in low-income families as first graders (many with just one parent in residence),[6] and 40% of their parents lacked high school degrees. These are all well-documented "risk factors" (e.g., Kaufman, Bradby, & Owings, 1992), and many of our study participants indeed stumbled along the way. That is reflected in the panel's high level of grade retention. It is reflected, too, in the group's statistics on high school dropout: 42% overall, rising to 54% for those from low-income families and to 60% for those from families we classify more generally as low socioeconomic status (about half the panel).[7]

Low-income minority youth in high-poverty school systems discontinue school at an alarming rate (e.g., for overview, see Bryk & Thum, 1989; Chen, Kaufman, & Frase, 1997; Pallas, 1987; Rumberger, 1987; Wagenaar, 1987; Wehlage & Rutter, 1986) and the risk elevates further when they arrive in high school with a history of poor school performance and low-level track placements (e.g., Alexander et al., 2001; Catterall, 1998). This sort of risk profile fits many retainees and it puts them at grave risk of dropout *apart from* their standing as repeaters. Does being a repeater give an extra "push," or, as the National Education Goals Panel

(Goal 2 Work Group, 1993, p. 18) puts it, "were these students ... more likely to drop out even if they had not been retained?" The question, then, is whether being held back in the years before high school *elevates* dropout risk in the BSS panel of mainly low-income youth or whether the academic benefits observed for other outcomes carry over to dropout also?

HIGH SCHOOL DROPOUT AS A CONTINUING CONCERN

Are concerns about high dropout exaggerated, as some have argued (e.g., Finn, 1987; McLaughlin, 1990)? High school completion among young adults age 18–24 stood at 84.8% in 1998. Completion figures over the ten years prior all fell within a percentage point or two of this level, and even as far back as 1972 the *lowest level* of high school completion for youth in this age group was 82.3% (U. S. Department of Education, 1999, p. 42). The figures fall short of the 90% target for high school completion enunciated in Goals 2000 (e.g., National Education Goals Panel, 1999), but with high school completion plateauing at historically high levels, is there still a need for vigorous efforts at dropout prevention? Absolutely.

For one thing, the relatively low levels of high school dropout and non-completion that have been achieved in recent years still leave too many young people without degrees—3.2 million 18–24-year-olds in 1997 (U. S. Census Bureau, 1999, p. 191). That is a big number by any standard, and the problem weighs heavier on some than on others. That year, over 90% of non-Hispanic White 18–24 year-olds were "credentialed," compared to 82% of non-Hispanic Blacks in that age range and 66.7% of Hispanic youth (U. S. Department of Education, 1999, p. 42).

And what of consequences? For those who fail to finish high school, job prospects in today's high-technology/high-service economy probably are as bleak as they ever have been. Gone are the well-paying manufacturing jobs that not long ago provided steady employment and a comfortable living for much of the blue-collar work force. Dropouts suffer high levels of unemployment and depressed earnings (Markey, 1988; U. S. Department of Education, 2001, pp. 137–139). To illustrate, in October 2000, 51% of 16- to 24-year-olds who dropped out during the 1999–2000 school year were unemployed, not looking for work, and not in college. The corresponding figure for that year's high school graduates was 11% (U. S. Bureau of Labor Statistics, 2001). And in 1999, male dropouts ages 25–34 who worked full-time year-round earned 30% less than their counterparts with high school degrees and general equivalency degrees (GEDs); for female dropouts, the shortfall was comparable, 28% (U.S. Census Bureau, 2000, pp. 36–39). Extrapolated over a lifetime's work, a one-year disparity of this magnitude projects to a huge difference in dropouts' and graduates' cumulative earnings (Mishel & Bernstein, 1994; Peng, 1985).

There are social costs to dropout as well, and these spread inexorably like the ripples on a pond. Dropouts constitute about half of all welfare recipients and half of the prison population (Educational Testing Service, 1995; National Research Council, 1993), for example. This incurs huge service expenditures, and losses to the treasury in terms of taxes forgone are likewise huge. Catterall (1987) estimates that high school dropouts from the class of 1981—a single graduating class—will pay almost $69 *billion* less in taxes over their lifetimes than if they had graduated. And for a single dropout class (1985) for a single school district (Los Angeles), he puts the cost for *extra* municipal services (e.g., police, health) at $500 million (lifetime).

Catterall's figures from the 1980s represent large increases over similar calculations from the early 1970s (Levin, 1972), and if carried forward to today they surely would be larger still. And beyond such dollar costs are additional costs that are harder to calculate, but which are no less important—costs in terms of wasted potential, human suffering, and diminished self-regard. Clearly, high school dropout, even at the relatively low levels that have prevailed for the last 20+ years, remains costly—for those who leave school early *and* for the rest of us, who are its victims once-removed.

National statistics on dropout, moreover, mask huge differences at the local level. In 1989, for example, over a fourth of Baltimoreans age 25–29 were out of school and without degrees (U.S. Census Bureau, 1992), but even that figure does not tell the whole story as it mixes together regular high school degrees and GEDs. Nationally, about half of all dropouts eventually obtain high school certification (U. S. Department of Education, 1998), but most dropouts who later finish high school do so by way of the GED. Indeed, reliance on the GED for high school certification has increased in recent years—from 4.2% of all degrees among 18–24-year-olds in 1988 to 10.1% in 1998 (U. S. Department of Education, 1999, p. 23). Unfortunately, though, the GED does not have the same economic value as a regular high school degree (e.g., Cameron & Heckman, 1993; Murnane, Willett, & Boudett, 1995).

As mentioned, 42% of the BSS panel left school without degrees, a figure in line with other estimates for Baltimore (e.g., Bomster, 1992) and for other high-poverty cities like it (Council of Great City Schools, 1994; *Education Week*, 1998). In these places, the dropout "crisis" is of the present, not the past. Details on the experience of the BSS panel follow.

THE TIMING AND EXTENT OF DROPOUT IN THE BSS

"Dropout" here means leaving school for an extended period of time prior to graduation. The withdrawal could be temporary or permanent, and whether dropouts later get certified by way of the GED is a separate matter—it is the distinction between "high school dropout" and "high school noncompletion" alluded to above. We identify dropouts through self-reports, with questions first posed of BSS students in the spring of 1991 (ninth grade for those not held back) and repeated annually thereafter through fall 1999 (five years after the group's expected high school graduation in spring 1994). Questioning covered the fact and timing of dropout, as well as subsequent degree completion. Weaving together information from many sources, dropout status was determined for 92.3% of the original cohort (729 of 790).[8] These self-reports identify 41.6% of the BSS cohort ($N = 303$) as having dropped out at least once.

And what of high school completion? Through Fall 1999, 9.2% of BSS dropouts had returned to school and completed regular high school degrees. Another 30.4% obtained the GED, putting high school completion among dropouts at 39.6%.[9] This is close to the 44% figure registered by dropouts nationally (U.S. Department of Education, 1998, p. 10), despite very different baseline levels of dropout in the two instances (42% in the BSS versus 21% nationally).[10] With GEDs factored in, overall high school completion in the BSS stands at 76% and noncompletion 24%, the latter being about the same level as indicated in 1990 Census data for the city as a whole. This is a vastly better showing than when later certification is overlooked, but it still leaves a fourth of Baltimore's young people trying to make their way in the world without high school degrees.

The timing of dropout in the BSS is organized in matrix format in Table 2.1. The two dimensions of the matrix are *year* of dropout and *grade* of dropout. The two distributions differ and how they intersect is revealing.

In the left-most column of the matrix we see that three dropouts left during or just after eight years in school, but only one of the three was at grade level at the time (i.e., in eighth grade). One of the others had completed sixth grade and the other seventh grade. The diagonal elements in Table 2.1 (bolded entries) show, year by year, the number of dropouts who were "on-time" when they left school, while entries above and to the right of the bolded diagonal reflect the retention histories of the others who dropped out in a given year. For example, of the 53 dropouts who left school during or just after year 10 (third column from the left), only 13 had completed 10th grade at the time, that is, they were "on-time." Thirty-two others were behind one year, five were behind two years, and three were behind three years.

Table 2.1. Timing of First Dropout

Grade Level Attained	Year Left School								Total	
	8	9	10	11	12	13	14	15	N	%
6	1								1	0.3
7	1		3						4	1.3
8	**1**	9	5						15	5.0
9		**11**	32	36	2	1			82	27.2
10			**13**	37	30	7	1		88	29.2
11				**22**	31	12	4	1	70	23.2
12					**18**	16	6	1	41	13.6
Total N	3	20	53	95	81	36	11	2	301	100.0
%	1.0	6.6	17.6	31.6	26.9	12.0	3.6	0.7	100.0	
On-Time	1	11	13	22	18	0	0	0	65	21.6
Off-Time	2	9	40	73	63	36	11	2	236	78.4
% Off-Time	66.6	45.0	75.5	76.8	77.8	100.0	100.0	100.0		
	52% On-Time		23% On-Time			0% On-Time				

According to the entries above the bolded diagonal in Table 2.1, *through* year 12 the vast majority of dropouts were repeaters. Students still in school *after* 12 years are "off-time" by definition, so the 49 students who left during years 13, 14, and 15 all had repeated at some point—these youth comprise 16% of all dropouts. Altogether, just 22% of dropouts were at grade level when they left. Tenth grade, for example, is the modal *grade* for dropping out, but year 11 is the modal *year* for dropping out.

The table also clarifies the perplexing pattern of dropout during students' twelfth year in school, when graduation would seem close. Of the 81 students who drop out during year 12, only 18, or less than a fourth, are on-time. These late dropouts demonstrate impressive commitment to school, but having already repeated at least one grade, they apparently decided it was time to try another course.

Elsewhere (Entwisle, Alexander, & Olson, 2000b) logistic regression models that control on demographics and school performance show that the odds of dropout for retained students are anywhere from 6 to 10 times the odds for the nonretained. The detailed display in Table 2.1 enriches the notion of "odds" by incorporating a time dimension for understanding these odds. In the BSS panel one third of those who drop out have less than a 10th grade education although most of them have spent at least 10 years in school. Roughly another third of dropouts have only a 10th grade education, which most have achieved by spending 11 or more years in school. These youth are staying in school longer than their age-mates, but still not getting degrees—the extra time, it seems, is not working.

The scheduling of dropout in Table 2.1 shows that many students leave at the earliest opportunity,[11] while others persevere but leave eventually anyway. The scheduling of dropout in relation to "push-pull" considerations has received scant attention in the literature, but one suspects the circumstances surrounding early and late dropout must differ (see Entwisle et al., 2000b). Here, though, we are more interested in commonalities than differences. Grade retention lurks behind the time-line of dropout in the BSS; that is clear from Table 2.1. But to ascertain its role as an impetus to dropout requires a different approach. In the next section we evaluate risk factors for dropout, and in particular whether early grade retention plays a distinctive role in elevating dropout risk.

GRADE RETENTION AS AN IMPETUS TO DROPOUT IN THE BSS

The likelihood of dropping out is distinctly nonrandom. We know that from much research, including several BSS studies, which thus far have mainly examined early precursors. Children's conduct and school performance *as first graders* forecast dropout risk, for example (e.g., Alexander, Entwisle, & Horsey, 1997), as do later academic experiences (Alexander et al., 2001). The context of children's early schooling is implicated as a predictor of dropout in non-BSS research also (e.g., Brooks-Gunn et al., 1993; Ensminger & Slusarcick, 1992; Garnier, Stein, & Jacobs, 1997).

Family background also weighs heavily on graduation prospects in the BSS, including family socioeconomic status (SES), family structure, mother's age, family stress, and maternal employment (Alexander et al., 2001)—a listing similar to that documented in numerous other studies (e.g., Pallas, 1987; Rumberger, 1987; Wagenaar, 1987).[12] All are important, but in the BSS, family SES dominates the list, with a four-fold difference in dropout rates across the socioeconomic "extremes": 60% of children from lower SES households (half of the sample) drop out at some point, as against 15% of those in the upper-SES fourth of the sample (Alexander et al., 2001).

Dropout risk is nonrandom by retention status also. Table 2.2 shows the basic data using the distinctions drawn in our 1994 volume to assess retention's effects on test scores, marks, and affective outcomes. Two criteria are reported: dropout (i.e., leaving school without a degree) and high school noncompletion (failure to obtain certification by any route as of age 22/23). Trends are similar for the two, although at much lower levels for noncompletion.

The relevant figures sample-wide are 42% dropout and 24% noncompletion (or permanent dropout). Against those standards, the experience of repeaters is bleak. Two thirds of them leave school at some point, and even as young adults almost half still are without degrees. By way of comparison, a fourth of the never-retained group drops out and only 10% remain degreeless at age 22/23.

According to these figures, then, repeaters in the BSS drop out at a rate approximately 2.8 times the never retained, and the noncompletion disparity is larger still, amounting to more than a four-fold difference. This establishes disproportionality, but are all classes of repeaters at similar risk? Apparently not. Differences among repeater groups are not as large as disparities across the retainee/nonretainee divide, but in Table 2.2 children held back after second grade are more prone to drop out than are 1st and 2nd grade repeaters, and those held back in grades 4–7 evidence an especially high rate of noncompletion (54.4%). The situation of children held back in the upper grades is especially intriguing, as their school performance ranks quite a bit above the level of 1st and 2nd grade repeaters (see Alexander, Entwisle, & Dauber 1994). Higher rates of dropout are seen for later repeaters in national data also (e.g., U.S. Department of Education, 1997, p. 41).

Table 2.2 Dropout Risk by Retention Status

	% Dropout[a]	% Noncomplete[b]
All Rets[c]	67.3	45.5
	(287)	(286)
All Never Ret	24.2	10.3
	(430)	(429)
Ret 1	67.8	43.0
	(115)	(114)
Ret 2	58.1	46.0
	(62)	(63)
Ret 3	73.8	36.6
	(42)	(41)
Ret 4–7	70.6	54.4
	(68)	(68)
DEC Only	53.1	38.8
	(49)	(49)
DEC & Double Ret	61.5	47.4
	(39)	(38)
Double Ret (No DEC)	88.6	58.3
	(35)	(36)
Double Ret	74.3	52.7
	(74)	(74)

a. "Dropout" means left school at some point without a degree.
b. "Noncompletion" means has not obtained high school certification by any route as of age 22/23.
c. "All Rets" are children held back through Year 7; "All Never Ret" are children not held back through Year 7; children held back in years 1, 2, 3, and 4–7 are identified, respectively, as "Ret 1," "Ret 2," "Ret 3," and "Ret 4–7"; "DEC Only" are children assigned to separate special education classes at some point over years 1–7 but not held back (DEC stands for "Division of Exceptional Children"); "DEC and Double Ret" are double repeaters who also were assigned to special education classes at some point; "Double Ret (No DEC)" are double repeaters who were not assigned to special education; "Double Ret" includes all double repeaters.

Double repeaters are also at high risk. Almost 90% of them drop out when special education students are excluded; the figure is 74% when special education pupils are included, and for over half of these youngsters dropout is permanent.[13] About half of all double retainees received special education services at some point,[14] so separating effects of the two is not easy. However, dropout stands at 71.4% among repeaters who never receive special education services versus 50.0% among special education students who manage to avoid retention,[15] which seems to implicate grade retention over special education.

Is the "excess" dropout observed for repeaters in Table 2.2 due to their status as repeaters or is it due to other "risk" attributes that predate, and perhaps prompt, their retention? That question is addressed in Table 2.3, which uses statistical means to adjust the comparisons for possible confounds. The same repeater distinctions and control variables are used here as in our earlier work (Alexander et al., 1994) to adjust retention effects for students' preretention academic status and background characteristics. However, because dropout and noncompletion are measured as categorical outcomes (i.e., "0" – "1"), logistic regression is used in Table 2.3 to estimate repeater-promoted differences, whereas previously OLS regression was used.

Results are reported separately for dropout and noncompletion. The table entries are odds ratios. These estimate the conditionality of dropout for a particular repeater group as the ratio of their odds of dropping out to the odds for children never retained (the latter constitute the frame of reference throughout). To illustrate, Table 2.2 shows that roughly two thirds of repeaters leave school without degrees. Accordingly, their odds of dropping out given retention are about 2.030 to 1 (i.e., .67/.33). The corresponding odds for children not held back are .316 to 1 (i.e., .24/.76). The ratio of these two odds (i.e., 2.030/.316) gives the difference in the relative risk of dropout associated with grade retention: repeaters are about 6.42 times as likely to drop out as are never-retained students.

Note that the ratio is derived by dividing the comparative odds. From that, it follows that a value of 1.0 signifies "no difference." Also, retention, dropout, and noncompletion are assigned a value of "1.0" versus values of "0" for their respective contrasts (i.e., nonretention, nondropout, high school completion). Accordingly, odds ratios above 1.0 indicate higher odds of dropout and noncompletion for repeaters compared to the never retained. It is worth mentioning too that the odds ratio conveys *relative prospects*. Level of dropout cannot be inferred or derived from them—such as, for an odds ratio of 2.0, the underlying odds could be 6/3, 2/1, .6/.3, .2/.1, or any other numbers that stand in a 2-1 ratio to one another. Hence, to judge whether dropout levels are high or low in an absolute sense requires going to the actual figures, as in Table 2.2—in the BSS they are high in general, but much higher for some than for others.

Table 2.3, then, reports estimated odds ratios for the several repeater groups relative to the never retained, both before and after adjusting for other related risks. The first set of statistical adjustments takes account of California Achievement Test (CAT) scores from first grade and relevant demographic factors (e.g., race/ethnicity, gender, mother's age, lunch subsidy status, number of siblings, household type, and age as of the fall of first grade). The second set highlights the experience of one-time repeaters who managed to avoid assignment to special education.

**Table 2.3. Odds Ratios Predicting Dropout and
High School Completion:
Repeaters vs. Never Retained, With and Without Controls**

	HS Dropout[a]	HS Noncomplete[b]
With No Adjustments[c]		
Ret 1	8.89**	9.29**
Ret 2	5.47**	8.52**
Ret 3	6.58**	3.33*
Ret 4-7	6.74**	12.08**
With Fall CAT and Demographic Adjustments[d]		
Ret 1	4.79**	4.33**
Ret 2	3.15**	4.83**
Ret 3	3.29**	1.49
Ret 4-7	4.30**	8.18**
With Double-Ret and Special Ed Adjustments[e]		
Ret 1	4.32**	3.64**
Ret 2	2.96**	4.29**
Ret 3	2.65*	1.28
Ret 4-7	4.03**	7.78**
DEC Only	.64	1.02
DEC & Double Ret	.95	1.42
Double Ret	6.63*	1.84

*$p \leq .05$. **$p \leq .01$.
[a]"Dropout" means left school at some point without a degree.
[b]"Noncompletion" means has not obtained high school certification by any route as of age 22/23.
[c]These regressions adjust for differences among the several retainee groups and between retainees and those never retained.
[d]These regressions adjust additionally for CAT scores from the fall of Year 1 and for demographic factors: race/ethnicity, gender, mother's education, lunch subsidy status (eligible or not), number of siblings, age as of the fall of first grade, and whether or not the child was living in a two-parent household at the start of first grade.
[e]These regressions adjust additionally for differences associated with special education alone, double retention alone, or both.

To do this, it adjusts additionally for double retention and receipt of special education services. Entries in the *top panel* of Table 2.3 implement no such controls, however. They adjust only for the scheduling of retention, and so are akin to the comparisons in Table 2.2 (although in terms of odds rather than percentages). These "effect estimates" show all classes of repeaters at elevated risk of dropout relative to the never-retained.[16] Almost all the estimated differences are significant and sizeable, although they seem a bit larger for noncompletion than for dropout (the exception being 3rd grade repeaters) and for the earliest and latest retainees (as opposed to 2nd and 3rd grade repeaters). These details notwithstanding, the disadvantage suffered by repeaters is both broad-based and substantial.

"Effect estimates" is in quotes for a reason, however: these results simply describe the association between retention and dropout in the BSS. To gauge retention's role as an *impetus* to dropout requires a more refined approach that takes account of possible confounding factors. Estimates in the second panel implement the relevant adjustments and so constitute our best evidence on retention's effects in the "impetus" sense—they equate repeaters and the never retained in terms of first grade CAT scores and sociodemographic risk factors.

These adjustments indeed moderate retention's effects some, but not so much as to alter the essential conclusion: grade retention continues to stand out as a distinctive risk factor for dropout. In the case of 1st grade repeaters, for example, an unadjusted nine-fold difference in the odds of dropping out reduces to about a five-fold difference after adjustment. Most of the other adjusted differences in Table 2.3 remain robust also, and similar results are obtained in analyses we have performed with even more expansive sets of controls, including measures of school performance closer in proximity to the time of dropout (e.g., Alexander et al., 2001; Alexander, Entwisle, & Kabbani, 2003). According to all these results, grade retention indeed takes many children off the path to high school graduation, and at least in terms of noncompletion, it is late retainees, those held back in grades 4–7, who are most set back by the experience.

The last panel of results separates effects of double retention and receipt of special education services. Three points stand out. First, these further adjustments do not have much effect on estimates of risk for the four repeater groups. The figures from the middle panel attenuate somewhat, but not much, indicating that even one-time repeaters who have been spared special education interventions evidence higher than expected levels of dropout and noncompletion (3rd grade retainees are an exception). Second, double repeaters are at especially high risk of dropout (although they are not noticeably disadvantaged with respect to high school completion). Third, when allowance is made for levels of test performance and background risk factors, receipt of special education services does not elevate dropout risk, nor do special education children, whether repeaters or not, fall noticeably short in terms of eventual degree completion. This contradicts others studies of special education students (e.g., McDonnell, McLaughlin, & Morison, 1997, pp. 95–96), but in the BSS there is no *added* risk that traces specifically to placement in special education. Not so with respect to retention, though, as repeaters drop out and fail to obtain high school certification at rates far in excess of those predicted by their risk profile.[17]

DISCUSSION

The present results for dropout and high school completion identify longer-term adverse consequences of grade repetition in the BSS that were not apparent for achievement and attitudinal outcomes. Retention's effects on achievement and attitude ranged from modestly positive to neutral, but certainly not harmful. But repeating a grade in the BSS increases dropout risk, and later, the risk of noncompletion, anywhere from three- to eight-fold, and this in a group already at high risk.

The standards for judging an educational intervention's efficaciousness often are left implicit, as though the appropriate criteria were self-evident. In fact, the issue is far from straightforward—is improvement sufficient, for instance, even if that improvement does not bring poor-performing students up to desired levels?[18] One principle or standard seems fundamental: an intervention intended to help should do no harm, and there can be no doubt that elevated dropout risk of the magnitude seen in these results qualifies as "harm." This challenges our earlier conclusions on the merits of grade retention, but before revisiting those matters, we first offer an accounting of the present results in light of those earlier findings.

Age-Grading and the Dropout Dynamic

The results in Table 2.3 identify children held back in the upper grades and multiple repeaters as especially prone to leave school without degrees. However, with single repeaters also at elevated risk, grade retention alters children's school trajectories across the board. Our 1994 volume concluded that double repeaters and 1st grade repeaters were helped least by repeating a grade, so for them to have elevated levels of dropout and noncompletion is not surprising. But single repeaters who were held back in second grade also drop out in numbers greater than expected and, in at least one instance, so do 3rd grade repeaters, whereas before we concluded that those children profit from an extra year in grade. If repeating a grade in elementary school boosts children's school performance and shores up their self-regard, as we believe it does in the BSS, why would it later increase dropout risk?

The fact that this risk is especially pronounced among repeaters held back in grades 4–7 holds a clue. When these children were held back, they were not as academically behind their promoted classmates as were children held back earlier (e.g., Alexander et al., 1994, ch. 3 & 6). If retention were simply a proxy for relevant academic difficulties, then repeating first or second grade, and not grades 4–7, would pose the greatest problems later, but that is not the case for dropout.

If not academics, then what? The social side of schooling seems a likely candidate. Grade retention takes children off the prescribed timetable of grade progressions in a rigidly age-graded system. This makes them conspicuous and complicates their social integration. Being "off-time" in school can cause problems at any age, but conditions peculiar to adolescence, the onset of puberty, and the impending transition to middle school very likely heightens them (e.g., Simmons & Blyth, 1987).

The early adolescent years (typically age 12–14) are a time of heightened self-consciousness, when "fitting in" is paramount, but for late repeaters, "fitting in" is not easy. The separation from their friends is still fresh when the time comes to change levels of school, and the disruption of peer groups they suffer is two-fold—their age-peers move on to middle school, while they are left behind with younger classmates, whom they may well view as lower on the age/status hierarchy. The numbers work against these children also. Repeating is less common in the upper elementary years than in first and second grade (e.g., Shepard & Smith, 1989), which means there are relatively few age-peers available in late repeaters' classes to help ease their adjustment.

Earlier (Alexander et al., 1994), we saw repeaters' academic standing begin to slide when they moved from elementary to middle school. Reflecting transition shock, their marks and test scores began to trail off at that point, and although usually they remained ahead of where they had been before, there was little room for them to absorb additional academic setbacks—their marks, on the whole, were barely passing.

Repeaters' situations in middle school thus were precarious, and no doubt even greater challenges awaited them at the transition into ninth grade. Changing schools is hard on children generally (Belsky & MacKinnon, 1994; Dunn, 1988; Eccles, Lord, & Midgley, 1991; Entwisle & Alexander, 1989; Simmons & Blyth, 1987), and the middle grades to high school transition is no exception. Relative to middle schools, high schools typically are larger, more bureaucratic, more impersonal and more academically demanding. Under such circumstances, even high-achieving, well-integrated students often experience difficulty. And what of repeaters? Their academic and social standing are both low, which leaves them especially vulnerable. Consider this one "symptom": in their ninth year of school, future dropouts in the BSS averaged 46.8 absences compared with an average of 13.5 absences among nondropouts. With 47 *recorded* absences, these students were missing about one day out of every four, which we interpret as a signal that the dropout process already has begun.

The timetable and social context of schooling in these ways magnify problems for late repeaters, but the differences between them and early repeaters are matters of degree, not kind. All the retentions evaluated in Table 2.3 precede high school, and so have the effect of putting children off-time when they make the transition into middle school, and then later into high school. Late retentions may be more problematic because their recency makes them more salient and because they involve double disruption of the peer group, a known factor in increased dropout risk (e.g., Entwisle, 1990), but the underlying age-grading dynamic holds generally for children held back in the primary and middle school grades.[19] Roderick (1993, 1994), for example, finds so-called "academic redshirts" (i.e., children who are over-age for grade because they started school late, not because of retention) at high risk of dropout, and this interpretation also makes sense of double-repeaters' poor showing in the present results.[20]

Some Thoughts on Policy and Practice

We said at the outset that we are not enthusiasts for retention—that should be clear from the concluding chapter of our book on the practice (Alexander et al., 1994; Alexander, Entwisle, & Dauber, 2003). The new evidence presented here showing that grade retention elevates dropout risk certainly reinforces our conviction that holding back children ought to be a last resort (see commentary in Alexander, Entwisle, & Kabbani, 2003). We still believe that repeating a year may be appropriate when extra time is needed to consolidate skills and master material missed the first time through—"additional learning time for misplaced students," as Jim Grant puts it (quoted in K. Kelly, 1999, p. 1)—but for most children under most circumstances, traditional retention (i.e., grade repetition without supplemental services) ought to be rare. However, candidates for retention typically are far behind academically and often evidence serious behavior problems. Absent an effective intervention, many of these children are on a path that will lead to dropout whether they are held back or not. Ignoring the problem (i.e., simply moving them ahead to the next grade level) and hoping for the best certainly is not the corrective we have in mind. That is a formula for failure: children who are far behind and struggling do not suddenly spurt ahead, but a spurt is what is required for them to catch up.

The obvious first priority should be to keep children from reaching the point where they are candidates for retention in the first place. Many poor and minority children start school already behind (U.S. Department of Education, 2000), but we know that high-quality preschool programs can enhance school readiness (e.g., Barnett, 1995; Ramey, Campbell, & Blair, 1998; Schweinhart & Weikart, 1998). We need more such programs, and more disadvantaged children need to have access to them (for further comment, see Entwisle, Alexander, & Olson, 2000a). Likewise, there is a need for high-quality, full-day kindergarten (e.g., Entwisle, Alexander, Cadigan, & Pallas, 1987), and then supplemental services afterward to help preserve the gains realized as a result of those early interventions (Reynolds, 1994; Reynolds & Temple, 1998; Temple et al., 2000).

Chicago's reform program surely is not optimal,[21] but the experience there demonstrates that a coordinated package of "best practice" interventions can help many struggling children get back on track. Mandatory summer school with small classes, a highly structured curriculum and intensive instruction are the core of Chicago's reforms, along with other support elements, including after-school enrichment programs and small transition schools for overage ninth graders who fall short of promotion standards (see Toch, 1998). An evaluation of the first two years of the Chicago reforms (Roderick, Bryk, Jacob, Easton, & Allensworth, 1999) found pass rates in grades 3, 6, and 8 up overall (compared against prereform benchmarks), with the largest gains registered by the poorest-performing children. It also concluded that summer school helped many children avoid retention (on the order of half overall). However, children held back despite these interventions were not faring well, a result that is reminiscent of the achievement findings from our own study: in the BSS 1st grade repeaters, double repeaters, and children moved into special education after being held back were helped least by repeating a grade, and sometimes not at all.

These children had the most severe academic deficiencies before being earmarked for retention, as well as the most depressed family backgrounds. They are the neediest children in the BSS, and nationally there are many others like them. Most of their problems can be traced to conditions outside school—problems associated with deep and persistent poverty and community decay—but we look to our schools for solutions and indeed there is good news on the schooling front: we know enough to help many of these children achieve success at school.

But there is another side to Chicago's experience, one that is evident also in the struggles evidenced by many repeaters in the BSS, as well as in results obtained under even the best designed and implemented intervention models (e.g., Farkas, Fischer, Dosher, & Vicknair, 1998; Pinnell, Lyons, DeFord, Bryk, & Seltzer, 1994; Ross, Smith, Casey, & Slavin, 1995): achieving "success for all" has proven an elusive goal. There are some children, and in high poverty settings perhaps many, whose academic problems run deeper than our current repertoire of well-drafted programs can reach. To help them will require even more far-reaching reforms. According to Larry Cuban (1989), nothing less than the dismantling of graded schooling will do the job, and he may be right. We developed this idea in an earlier paper (Alexander, Entwisle, & Kabbani, 2003) and the highlights bear repeating here.

We commented above on how rigid age-grading complicates life in middle school and high school for children who are older than their classmates. These challenges involve the social side of schooling, but age-grading has far-reaching consequences in the early grades also, although of a rather different character.

All children are expected to be "ready" for first grade at age six; they are expected to move in lockstep annually thereafter from one grade to the next; and within the year, they are expected to master the curriculum in roughly the same time frame—nine months, fall to spring. However, that is not the way children learn. The National Education Commission on Time and Learning puts it this way:

> Decades of school improvement efforts have foundered on a fundamental design flaw, the assumption that learning can be doled out by the clock and defined by the calendar.... Some students take three to six times longer than others to learn the same thing. Yet students are caught in a time trap—processed on an assembly line to the minute. Our usage of time virtually assures the failure of many students. (1994, p. 7)

Our current calendar-driven model of schooling sets a severe pace: children who are not caught up when the teacher is obliged to move to the next lesson fall behind, and if they are far behind at year's end, then what? Should these children be moved ahead even though they are not ready; or should they be held back knowing that most will not be helped enough for them to keep up later? Either way, they are trapped in the same structure and many, it seems certain, will simply slip farther and farther back.

The set of options clearly needs to be expanded, and organizational reforms like multi-age classes, ungraded classes, and partial promotion (e.g., Goodlad & Anderson, 1987; Gutierrez & Slavin, 1992; Lloyd, 1999; Veenman, 1995) give more options. The challenge—a daunting one—is to build more flexibility into the system without the stigma and other problems that come with being "off-time" for one's age.

Most such interventions are targeted at the primary grades, but similar issues arise in the upper grades, where youngsters who are older than their classmates are made to feel out of place. At issue is the four-year, full-time schedule, along with the expectation that high school is a place for "kids," not adults. In point of fact, many high school students today are over 18 owing to retention: 27% of the BSS panel was still in school beyond their "expected" graduation, including 16% of [eventual] dropouts (see also Portner, 1996).

Thus far, schools have done little to adapt to this age heterogeneity, but does it have to be this way? Perhaps experience at the postsecondary level holds lessons about how to accommodate the needs of "mature" students. Colleges too once labored under the "four-year program" fiction,[22] but that fiction was impossible to sustain once the 1980s "baby-bust" created financial pressures to make the sector more accommodating to so-called nontraditional students—such as, mature adults who had to juggle work and school and "re-entry" women seeking to upgrade their skills after a spell at full-time parenting. Part-time programs proliferated, and suddenly it was not so odd to have 30 year-olds studying alongside traditional college-age students. Just 36% of students receiving their BA degree in 1992–1993 finished within four years of their initial enrollment and one in six was age 30 or older at graduation (National Center for Education Statistics, 1996)—hardly the "traditional" college profile.

Is the secondary landscape really all that different from the postsecondary? Today almost all high school students juggle school and work at some point (e.g., Entwisle et al., 2000b; Light, 1995; Steinberg & Cauffman, 1995) and many shoulder heavy family responsibilities. These students already have begun to fill adult roles in many respects, but programs to help them balance their in-school and out-of-school obligations are rare (for additional comment see Entwisle et al., 2000b).

Most school systems have not been especially imaginative in addressing the needs of over-age students, and some of the more popular approaches risk making matters worse rather than better. So-called alternative schools for over-age, pregnant, or parenting students often suffer an "image" problem and with typically only one or two in the area, there may be logistical problems also. But beyond that, it is asking a great deal of someone shouldering heavy work or parenting responsibilities, as many repeaters do, to commit to the traditional school schedule, and even then he or she still will be in the company of a student body preoccupied with the traditional concerns of adolescence.

Current arrangements segregate and marginalize these youth. To break down these barriers requires somehow relaxing the overly tight link between "age" and "grade." Doing so very likely would improve the graduation prospects of children who are a year or two behind, and it certainly would give educators more options for addressing their needs. Under this accounting, the problem is not so much grade retention as it is the structure within which grade retention is embedded, a structure that makes deviants of otherwise perfectly normal children (e.g., Tyack & Cuban, 1995; Tyack & Tobin, 1994).

NOTES

1. This paper draws heavily from a work-in-progress chapter that is intended for the second edition of our book *On the Success of Failure* (Alexander, Entwisle, & Dauber, 2003). It also adds to, and borrows liberally from, a series of BSS papers on precursors to dropout, including retention: Alexander, Entwisle, and Horsey (1997); Alexander, Entwisle, and Kabbani (2001, 2003); and Entwisle, Alexander, and Olson (2000b).
2. The study schools were randomly selected, as were the children sampled from within them. For detail on the BSS research design, see the appendix in Entwisle Alexander, and Olson (1997).
3. To be sure, not all recent research finds in favor of retention (e.g., Jimerson, Carlson, Rotert, Egeland, & Sroufe, 1997; McCoy & Reynolds, 1999). Our point, rather, is that the evidence is mixed and not uniformly negative.
4. This breaks down to 22.4% dropout for single repeaters and 39.3% for multiple repeaters.
5. Exceptions include Cairns and Cairns (1994); Garnier, Stein, and Jacobs (1997), and Temple et al. (2000).
6. Families are identified as low income (or not) from school records indicating participation in the government's reduced price/free school meal program for low-income households.
7. Family SES is measured as a standardized composite, derived from five items: mother's education, father's education, mother's occupational status, father's occupational status, and family income, as indicated by participation in the federal program that subsidizes the cost of school meals for low-income households. Mother's education in the lower SES group averages 10 years and 95% of lower SES families qualify for subsidized school meals; in the higher SES group, mother's education averages 14.6 years and 13% receive reduced price meals. These distinctions capture the range of family standing in Baltimore's public school enrollment, but that range embraces few genuinely upper SES, wealthy households. The "lower"/"higher" descriptors in that sense are context bound.
8. Not all children were interviewed each year, so dropout histories had to be constructed with care. However, with questions posed nine times, often responses could be checked for consistency. Members of the cohort ($N = 61$) whose graduation status could not be determined resemble dropouts more than graduates across a range of criteria. This suggests more dropouts have been missed than graduates, but *patterns* relating risk factors to dropout are robust in attrition analyses (Alexander et al., 1997).
9. These figures exclude 10 dropouts for whom re-enrollment could not be determined. Accordingly, the base N is 293.
10. The national figure is for the NELS88 panel. It represents certification obtained as of 1994, or two years after the group's expected graduation in spring 1992. The corresponding figure in the earlier High School and Beyond project (U.S. Department of Education, 1989, pp. 35–36) was 30%, but high school completion increased to 46% after four years.
11. Thirty-five percent of BSS dropouts (amounting to 14% of the entire cohort), left school *before* 10th grade, the standard in the literature for

identifying "early leavers" (e.g., Rumberger, 1995; Schneider, Stevenson, & Link, 1994). This is about the same percentage as in national estimates (in this instance for 16–24-year-olds; U.S. Department of Education, 1997, p. 15).

12. Race/ethnicity is an exception. In the BSS the Black/White difference in dropout rates is not significant. However, African American and White dropout rates are close nationally also (e.g., Day & Curry, 1998) and in other localized longitudinal studies (e.g., Cairns & Cairns, 1994). Keeping in mind that Whites who attend Baltimore's public schools (just 13.6% of the city system enrollment in 1998; Maryland State Department of Education, 1999) are mostly low income, the parity seen here could well be characteristic of disadvantaged urban populations generally (McDonald & LaVeist, 1999).

13. High levels of dropout among double-repeaters are seen in other studies also (Cairns & Cairns, 1994; Fine, 1991).

14. The intersection of various "problem placements" is reviewed in detail in Chapter 8 of Alexander et al. (1994).

15. The latter figure is a bit different from the DEC ONLY entry in Table 2.2, which screens on double-retention, not any retention.

16. However, the odds ratios themselves are not identical to those that could be calculated from Table 2.2. Case coverage differs in the two instances because Table 2.3 screens out cases with missing data on any of the control variables used in the analysis.

17. Similar results are reported by Temple et al. (2000), in their panel study of low-income Chicago school children: no net effects associated with special education placements; large differences associated with grade retention.

18. See, for example, the recent exchange between Slavin and Madden (2000) and Pogrow (2000) over the effectiveness of "Success for All"—much hinges on what constitutes "success."

19. Others too have implicated age-grading in the dropout dynamic—see especially Grissom and Shepard (1989) and Roderick (1994).

20. Although why double-repeaters are not also disadvantaged in terms of high school completion is not obvious. More generally, practically nothing is known about "recovery" from dropout, that is, why it is that some dropouts and not others manage to avail themselves of second chance opportunities (see Alexander et al., 2001; U. S. Department of Education, 1998).

21. Chicago's first "promotional gate," for example, is not until third grade, by which time many children already are far behind.

22. Eckland (1964), for example, reports that only about 30% of a sample of college freshmen in 1952 graduated four years later from the same institution in which they enrolled initially.

REFERENCES

Alexander, K. L., Entwisle, D. R., & Dauber, S. L. (1994). *On the success of failure: A reassessment of the effects of retention in the primary grades.* Cambridge, MA: Cambridge University Press.

Alexander, K. L., Entwisle, D. R., & Dauber, S. L. (2003). *On the success of failure: A reassessment of the effects of retention in the primary grades* (2nd ed.). New York: Cambridge University Press.

Alexander, K. L., Entwisle, D. R., & Horsey, C. (1997). From first grade forward: Early foundations of high school dropout. *Sociology of Education, 70*, 87–107.

Alexander, K. L., Entwisle, D. R., & Kabbani, N. (2001). The dropout process in life course perspective: Early risk factors at home and school. *Teachers College Record, 103*, 760–822.

Alexander, K. L., Entwisle, D. R., & Kabbani, N. (2003). Grade retention, social promotion and "third way" alternatives. In A. J. Reynolds, M. C. Wang, & H. J. Walberg (Eds.), *Early childhood programs for a new century* (pp. 197–238). Washington, DC: CWLA Press.

Annie E. Casey Foundation. (1997). *Kids count data book: State profiles of child wellbeing.* Baltimore: Author.

Barnett, W. S. (1995). Long-term effects of early childhood care and education on disadvantaged children's cognitive development and school success. *The Future of Children, 5*(3), 25–50.

Belsky, J., & MacKinnon, C. (1994). Transition to school: Developmental trajectories and school experiences. *Early Education and Development, 5*(2), 106–119.

Bomster, M. (1992, September 18). City's dropout rate ranked 9th-worse in nation in 1990. *The Baltimore Sun*, pp. C1–4.

Brooks-Gunn, J., Guo, G., & Furstenberg Jr., F. F. (1993). Who drops out and who continues beyond high school? A 20-year follow-up of Black urban youth. *Journal of Research on Adolescence, 3*(3), 271–294.

Bryk, A. S., & Thum, Y. M. (1989). The effects of high school organization on dropping out: An exploratory investigation. *American Educational Research Journal, 26*, 353–383.

Cairns, R. B., & Cairns, B. D. (1994). *Lifelines and risks: Pathways of youth in our time.* Cambridge, UK: Cambridge University Press.

Cameron, S. V., & Heckman, J. J. (1993). The nonequivalence of high school equivalents. *Journal of Labor Economics, 11*(1), 1–47.

Catterall, J. S. (1987, October/November). On the social costs of dropping out. *The High School Journal, 20*, 19–30.

Catterall, J. S. (1998). Risk and resilience in student transitions to high school. *American Journal of Education, 106*, 302–333.

Chen, X., Kaufman, P., & Frase, M. (1997). *Risk and resilience: The effects on dropping out of school.* Paper presented at the annual meeting of the American Educational Research Association, Chicago, IL.

Children's Defense Fund. (1992). *City poverty data from 1990 census.* Washington, DC: Author.

Council of Great City Schools. (1994). *National urban education goals: 1992–93 indicators report.* Washington, DC: Author.

Cuban, L. (1989). The "at-risk" label and the problem of urban school reform. *Phi Delta Kappan, 70*(10), 780–801.

Dauber, S. L., Alexander, K. L., & Entwisle, D. R. (1993). Characteristics of retainees and early precursors of retention in grade: Who is held back? *Merrill-Palmer Quarterly, 39*(3), 326–343.

Day, J., & Curry, A. (1998). *Educational attainment in the United States: March 1997* (#P20-505). Washington, DC: U.S. Census Bureau.

Dunn, J. (1988). Normative life events as risk factors in childhood. In M. Rutter (Ed.), *Studies of psychosocial risk: The power of longitudinal data* (pp. 227–244). New York: Cambridge University Press.

Eccles, J. S., Lord, S., & Midgley, C. (1991). What are we doing to early adolescents? The impact of educational contexts on early adolescents. *American Journal of Education, 99*, 521–542.

Eckland, B. K. (1964). Social class and college graduation: Some misconceptions corrected. *American Journal of Sociology, 70*(1), 36–50.

Education Week. (1998, January). Quality counts, '98: An Education Week Pew Charitable Trust report on education in the 50 states. *Education Week, 17.*

Educational Testing Service. (1995). *Dreams deferred: High school dropouts in the United States*. Princeton, NJ: Author.

Ensminger, M. E., & Slusarcick, A. L. (1992). Paths to high school graduation or dropout: A longitudinal study of a first-grade cohort. *Sociology of Education, 65*, 95–113.

Entwisle, D. R. (1990). Schools and the adolescent. In S. S. Feldman & G. R. Elliott (Eds.), *At the threshold: The developing adolescent* (pp. 197–224). Cambridge, MA: Harvard University Press.

Entwisle, D. R., & Alexander, K. L. (1989). Children's transition into full-time schooling: Black/White comparisons. *Early Education and Development, 1*(2), 85–104.

Entwisle, D. R., Alexander, K. L., Cadigan, D., & Pallas, A. M. (1987). Kindergarten experience: Cognitive effects or socialization? *American Educational Research Journal, 24*, 337–364.

Entwisle, D. R., Alexander, K. L., & Olson, L. S. (1997). *Children, schools and inequality.* Boulder, CO: Westview Press.

Entwisle, D. R., Alexander, K. L., & Olson, L. S. (2000a). Summer learning and home environment. In R. D. Kahlenberg (Ed.), *A notion at risk: Preserving public education as an engine for social mobility* (pp. 9–30). New York: Century Foundation Press.

Entwisle, D. R., Alexander, K. L., & Olson, L. S. (2000b, August). *Urban teenagers: Work and dropout.* Paper presented at the annual meeting of the American Sociological Association, Washington, DC.

Farkas, G., Fischer, J., Dosher, R., & Vicknair, K. (1998). Can all children learn to read at grade-level by the end of third grade? In D. Vannoy & P. J. Dubeck (Eds.), *Challenges for work and family in the twenty-first century* (pp. 143–165). New York: Aldine de Gruyter.

Fine, M. (1991). *Framing dropouts: Notes on the politics of an urban public high school.* Albany, NY: State University of New York Press.

Finn, C. E., Jr. (1987, Spring). The high school dropout puzzle. *The Public Interest, 87*, 3–22.

Garnier, H. E., Stein, J. A., & Jacobs, J. K. (1997). The process of dropping out of high school: A 19-year perspective. *American Educational Research Journal, 34*, 395–419.

Goal 2 Work Group. (1993). *Reaching the goals: Goal 2, high school completion*. Washington, DC: U.S. Department of Education, Office of Research and Improvement.

Goodlad, J. I., & Anderson, R. H. (1987). *The nongraded elementary school*. New York: Teachers College Press.

Grissom, J. B., & Shepard, L. A. (1989). Repeating and dropping out of school. In L. A. Shepard & M. L. Smith (Eds.), *Flunking grades: Research and policies on retention* (pp. 34–63). London: Falmer Press.

Gutierrez, R., & Slavin, R. E. (1992). Achievement effects of nongraded elementary schools: A best evidence synthesis. *Review of Educational Research, 62*, 333–376.

Hauser, R. M. (1999a). *How much social promotion is there in the United States?* (CDE Working Paper No. 99-06). Madison, WI: University of Wisconsin, Madison, Center for Demography and Ecology.

Hauser, R. M. (1999b, April 7). What if we ended social promotion? *Education Week on the Web* [On-line], *18*(30). Available: http://www.edweek.org

Holmes, C. T., & Matthews, K. M. (1984). The effects of nonpromotion on elementary and junior high school pupils: A meta-analysis. *Review of Educational Research, 54*, 225–236.

House, E. R. (1989). Policy implications of retention research. In L. A. Shepard & M. L. Smith (Eds.), *Flunking grades: Research and policies on retention* (pp. 202–213). London: Falmer Press.

Jimerson, S., Carlson, E., Rotert, M., Egeland, B., & Sroufe, L. A. (1997). A prospective, longitudinal study of the correlates and consequences of early grade retention. *Journal of School Psychology, 35*, 3–25.

Karweit, N. L. (1999). *Grade retention: Prevalence, timing, and effects* (Report No. 33). Baltimore: CRESPAR.

Kasarda, J. D. (1993). Inner-city concentrated poverty and neighborhood distress: 1970 to 1990. *Housing Policy Debate, 4*(3), 253–302.

Kaufman, P., Bradby, D., & Owings, J. (1992). *National Education Longitudinal Study of 1988: Characteristics of at-risk students in NELS:88* (Contractor Report, NCES 92-042). Washington, DC: U.S. Department of Education, National Center for Education Statistics.

Kelly, K. (1999). Retention vs. social promotion: Schools search for alternatives. *Harvard Education Letter, 15*(1), 1–3.

Kelly, S. P. (1988, February 8). 46% of Baltimore 9th-graders drop out before graduation. *The Evening Sun*, pp. A1, A5.

Levin, H. M. (1972). *The costs to the nation of inadequate education. Report to the Select Committee on equal educational opportunity in the United States*. Washington, DC: U.S. Government Printing Office.

Light, A. (1995). *High school employment* (Report No. NLS 95-27). Washington, DC: U.S. Department of Labor, Bureau of Labor Statistics.

Lloyd, L. (1999). Multi-age classes and high ability students. *Review of Educational Research, 69*(2), 187–212.

Markey, J. P. (1988). The labor market problems of today's high school dropouts. *Monthly Labor Review, 111*(6), 36–43.

Maryland State Department of Education. (1999). *The fact book, 1998–99*. Baltimore: Author.

McCoy, A. R., & Reynolds, A. J. (1999). Grade retention and school performance: An extended investigation. *Journal of School Psychology, 37*, 273–298.

McDonald, K. B., & LaVeist, T. A. (2002). Black educational advantage in the inner city. *Review of Black Political Economy, 29*, 25-48.

McDonnell, L. M., McLaughlin, M. J., & Morison, P. (1997). *Educating one and all: Students with disabilities and standards-based reform*. Washington, DC: National Academy Press.

McLaughlin, M. J. (1990, August 3). High school dropouts: How much of a crisis? *Backgrounder* [On-line], *781*. Available: www.heritage.org/library/archives/backgrounder

Mishel, L., & Bernstein, J. (1994). *The state of working America*. New York: Economic Policy Institute.

Murnane, R. J., Willett, J. B., & Boudett, K. P. (1995). Do high school dropouts benefit from obtaining a GED? *Educational Evaluation and Policy Analysis, 17*(2), 133–147.

National Center for Education Statistics. (1996). *A descriptive summary of 1992–93 bachelor's degree recipients one year later* (NCES 96-158). Washington, DC: U.S. Department of Education, National Center for Education Statistics.

National Education Commission on Time and Learning. (1994). *Prisoners of time*. Washington, DC: Author.

National Education Goals Panel. (1999). *The National Education Goals report: Building a nation of learners, 1999*. Washington, DC: U.S. Government Printing Office.

National Research Council. (1993). *Losing generations: Adolescents in high-risk settings*. Washington, DC: National Academic Press.

Pallas, A. M. (1987). *School dropouts in the United States* (Issue Paper CS87-426). Washington, DC: U.S. Department of Education, National Center for Education Statistics.

Peng, S. S. (1985). *High school dropout: A national concern*. Washington, DC: U.S. Government Printing Office.

Pierson, L. H., & Connell, J. P. (1992). Effect of grade retention on self-system processes, school engagement and academic performance. *Journal of Educational Psychology, 84*, 300–307.

Pinnell, G. S., Lyons, C. A., DeFord, D. E., Bryk, A. S., & Seltzer, M. (1994). Comparing instructional models for the literacy education of high-risk first graders. *Reading Research Quarterly, 29*(1), 9–39.

Pogrow, S. (2000). Success for All does not produce success for students. *Phi Delta Kappan, 82*, 67–80.

Portner, J. (1996, September 18). Older students make presence felt in classes. *Education Week* [On-line], *16*. Available: http://edweek.com/ew/vol-16/03older.h16

Ramey, C. T., Campbell, F. A., & Blair, C. (1998). Enhancing the life course for high-risk children: Results from the Abecedarian Project. In J. Crane (Ed.), *Social programs that work* (pp. 163–183). New York: Russell Sage Foundation.

Reynolds, A. J. (1994). Effects of a preschool plus follow-on intervention for children at risk. *Developmental Psychology, 30,* 787–804.
Reynolds, A. J., & Temple, J. A. (1998). Extended early childhood intervention and school achievement: Age thirteen findings from the Chicago Longitudinal Study. *Child Development, 69*(1), 231–246.
Reynolds, A., Temple, J., & McCoy, A. (1997, September 17). Grade retention doesn't work. *Education Week on the Web* [On-line], *17*(3). Available: http://www.edweek.org
Roderick, M. (1993). *The path to dropping out: Evidence for intervention.* Westport, CT: Auburn House.
Roderick, M. (1994). Grade retention and school dropout: Investigating the association. *American Educational Research Journal, 31,* 729–759.
Roderick, M., Bryk, A. S., Jacob, B. A., Easton, J. Q., & Allensworth, E. (1999). *Ending social promotion: Results from the first two years.* Chicago: Chicago Consortium on School Research.
Ross, S. M., Smith, L. J., Casey, J., & Slavin, R. E. (1995). Increasing the academic success of disadvantaged children: An examination of alternative early intervention programs. *American Educational Research Journal, 32,* 773–800.
Rumberger, R. W. (1987). High school dropouts: A review of issues and evidence. *Review of Educational Research, 57,* 101–121.
Rumberger, R. W. (1995). Dropping out of middle school: A multilevel analysis of students and schools. *American Educational Research Journal, 32,* 583–625.
Rumberger, R. W., & Larson, K. A. (1998). Student mobility and the increased risk of high school dropout. *American Journal of Education, 107*(1), 1–35.
Rusk, D. (1996). *Baltimore unbound: A strategy for regional renewal.* Baltimore: The Abell Foundation.
Schneider, B., Stevenson, D., & Link, J. (1994, April). *Social and cultural capital: Differences between students who leave school at different periods in their school careers.* Paper presented at the annual meeting of the American Educational Research Association, New Orleans, LA.
Schweinhart, L. J., & Weikart, D. P. (1998). High/Scope Perry Preschool Program effects at age twenty-seven. In J. Crane (Ed.), *Social programs that work* (pp. 148–183). New York: Russell Sage.
Shepard, L. A., & Smith, M. L. (1989). Introduction and overview. In L. A. Shepard & M. L. Smith (Eds.), *Flunking grades: Research and policies on retention.* London: Falmer Press.
Simmons, R. G., & Blyth, D. A. (1987). *Moving into adolescence: The impact of pubertal change and school context.* Hawthorn, NY: Aldine de Gruyter.
Slavin, R. E., & Madden, N. A. (2000). Research on achievement outcomes for Success for All: A summary and response to critics. *Phi Delta Kappan, 82,* 38–40, 59–60.
Smith, M. L., & Shepard, L. A. (1987). What doesn't work: Explaining policies of retention in the early grades. *Phi Delta Kappan, 69,* 129–134.
Sociology of Education Research Group. (1999). *Elementary school retention and social promotion in Texas: An assessment of students who failed the reading section of the TAAS.* Houston, TX: University of Houston.

Steinberg, L., & Cauffman, E. (1995, April). The impact of employment on adolescent development. *Annals of Child Development, 11*, 131–166.

Temple, J. A., Reynolds, A. J., & Miedel, W. T. (2000). Can early intervention prevent high school dropout? Evidence from the Chicago child-parent centers. *Urban Education, 35*(1), 31–56.

Toch, T. (1998, October 5). Making the grade harder. *U.S. News and World Report, 125*(13), 59.

Tyack, D., & Cuban, L. (1995). *Tinkering toward Utopia: A century of public school reform.* Cambridge, MA: Harvard University Press.

Tyack, D., & Tobin, W. (1994). The grammar of schooling: Why has it been so hard to change? *American Educational Research Journal, 31*, 453–479.

U.S. Bureau of Labor Statistics. (2001). *College enrollment and work activity of year 2000 high school graduates* (News release No. USDL 01-94). Washington, DC: Author.

U.S. Census Bureau. (1992). *Census of population and housing, 1990: 5% public use microdata samples U.S.* Washington, DC: Author.

U.S. Census Bureau. (1999). *Statistical abstract of the United States: 1999.* Washington, DC: Author.

U.S. Census Bureau. (2000). *Money income in the United States: 1999* (Current population reports No. P60-209). Washington, DC: U.S. Government Printing Office.

U.S. Department of Education. (1989). *Dropout rates in the United States: 1988* (NCES 89-609). Washington, DC: U.S. Department of Education, National Center for Education Statistics.

U.S. Department of Education. (1997). *Dropout rates in the United States: 1995* (NCES 97-473). Washington, DC: U.S. Department of Education, National Center for Education Statistics.

U.S. Department of Education. (1998). *National Education Longitudinal Study of 1988 (NELS:88) base year through second follow-up: Final methodology report* (Working Paper No. 98-06). Washington, DC: U.S. Department of Education, National Center for Education Statistics.

U.S. Department of Education. (1999). *Dropout rates in the United States: 1998* (NCES 2000-022). Washington, DC: U.S. Department of Education, National Center for Education Statistics.

U.S. Department of Education. (2000). *American's kindergartners: Findings from the Early Childhood Longitudinal Study, kindergarten class of 1998–99, fall 1998* (NCES 2000-070). Washington, DC: U.S. Department of Education, National Center for Education Statistics.

U.S. Department of Education. (2001). *The condition of education 2001* (NCES 2001-072). Washington, DC: U.S. Government Printing Office.

Veenman, S. (1995). Cognitive and noncognitive effects of multigrade and multiage classes: A best-evidence synthesis. *Review of Educational Research, 65*, 319–381.

Wagenaar, T. C. (1987). What do we know about dropping out of high school? In A. C. Kerckhoff (Ed.), *Research on sociology of education and socialization* (Vol. 7, pp. 161–190). Greenwich, CT: JAI Press.

Wehlage, G. G., & Rutter, R. A. (1986). Dropping out: How much do schools contribute to the problem? *Teachers College Record, 87,* 374–392.

Wilson, W. J. (1987). *The truly disadvantaged: The inner city, the underclass, and public policy.* Chicago: University of Chicago Press.

Wilson, W. J. (1996). *When work disappears: The world of the new urban poor.* New York: Knopf.

CHAPTER 3

GRADE RETENTION AND SCHOOL DROPOUT

Another Look at the Evidence

Judy A. Temple, Arthur J. Reynolds, and Suh-Ruu Ou

INTRODUCTION

Grade retention has become an important practice in school reform. In response to increased demands for accountability by taxpayers, parents, and policymakers, school districts across the country now rely more heavily on grade retention (also called grade repetition) and associated remedial services to improve student achievement (Heubert & Hauser, 1999; Rothstein, 1998; Temple, 1998). One of the most well-known of these efforts is in the Chicago Public Schools (Roderick, Bryk, Jacob, Easton, & Allensworth, 1999; Roderick, Jacob, & Bryk, 2002), but others include New York, Philadelphia, and Houston. In addition, state legislators from coast to coast have also adopted state-wide accountability initiatives that include the related goal of ending social promotion.

Despite the current emphasis on grade retention as an educational policy designed to help low-achieving students, the majority of empirical studies suggest that grade retention typically does not benefit the students it is designed to help. With few exceptions, the existing literature finds moderately strong associations between grade retention and lower levels of later school achievement (Byrd & Weitzman, 1994; Heubert & Hauser,

1999; Holmes, 1989; McCoy & Reynolds, 1999). Years after being made to repeat a grade, retained students have significantly lower achievement than similar students who were not retained. Many retained students never catch up to their promoted same-age peers with similarly low test scores. Whatever performance advantage retained students have over their younger, same-grade peers is short-lived, as they typically fall behind these students after 1 or 2 years.

Even more striking is the strong positive correlation between grade retention and the probability of dropping out of high school. A recent review of such findings from retrospective and longitudinal studies is presented in Jimerson, Anderson, and Whipple (2002). Researchers using longitudinal data have the advantage of being able to control for individual preretention achievement. These studies (Alexander, Entwisle, & Dauber, 2003; Alexander, Entwisle, & Kabbani, 2003; Anderson, 1994; Ensminger & Slusrick, 1992; Grissom & Shepard, 1989; Jimerson, 1999; Roderick, 1994; Temple, Reynolds, & Miedel, 2000) indicate that relative to low-achieving students who are promoted to the next grade, students who are retained are significantly more likely to drop out of school. After accounting for socioeconomic status and prior performance, dropout rates for retained students often exceed comparable promoted students by 50% or more. The link between grade retention and school dropout has been so consistent across a wide range of samples, model specifications, and settings that it is unlikely to be a statistical artifact.

Given this cumulative evidence of ineffectiveness and potential long-term harm, why does grade retention continue to be such a popular and desirable strategy for school improvement? Three explanations are apparent. First, retaining students is a relatively straightforward educational policy to enact and, if implemented without additional remediation services, can be done without a noticeable impact on current school budgets. All that is needed is a set of promotion standards that can be uniformly applied across schools. Retention policies do not require substantial innovation, school reorganization, or the introduction of comprehensive programs designed to impact the root causes of underachievement.

The second explanation for the continued popularity of retention is that the evidence base on the effects of grade retention rests exclusively on correlational data that are open to alternative interpretations. This is especially relevant in the politically charged arena of education policy. Experimental studies of retention with random assignment have not been conducted in six decades (i.e., Cook, 1941). As frequently noted in reviews of the literature (Alexander, Entwisle, & Dauber, 2003; Jackson, 1975; Karweit, 1992; Reynolds, 1992), most studies fail to control for basic predictors of retention such as preretention achievement, let alone most observed and unobserved differences between retained and promoted students that are associated with school performance. Until methodologically stronger studies are conducted, findings of evaluations of the effects of grade retention may continue to be contested.

Absent a true experiment, the preferred way to address this issue is to measure students' achievement growth (rate of learning) prior to the decision to retain. This test of selection bias is possible only if two or more measures of preretention achievement at different occasions are available. If achievement growth is different between groups but not taken into account, estimated effects of grade retention may mistakenly indicate harm when retained students may be more academically disadvantaged than promoted students prior to retention (e.g., they have lower rates of learning).

The third reason for grade retention's current popularity is that in contrast to the retention policy of the past, newer retention policies frequently pair grade retention with remedial education in the form of summer school, after-school programs, tutoring, and smaller class sizes. These "retention-plus" policies were rarely implemented in the past 2 decades. Even if the cumulative evidence that simple grade retention is ineffective or harmful to students' educational success is valid, most research does not address the question of whether retention-plus policies are more effective than retention-only or promotion-plus policies. The success of these efforts will depend, of course, on the quality, duration, and intensity of the remedial help that students receive.

THE PRESENT STUDY

This paper investigates the latter two explanations as justifications for the continued use of retention policies to promote student achievement. The authors discuss methodological drawbacks of previous studies and investigate whether "retention-plus" policies are more effective than past policies that simply retain children in grade, or that promote children and provide remedial help. Using data in the Chicago Longitudinal Study (CLS), we address the following questions:

1. After children's growth rates in achievement prior to retention (and other factors) are taken into account, is grade retention associated with significantly lower levels of school achievement and higher rates of school dropout?
2. Among children who are retained during the early school years, is participation in a comprehensive instructional intervention associated with improved school achievement and a lower likelihood of

school dropout by age 20? Does this participation lead to better performance than promotion with remediation?

An answer of "yes" to the first question would provide evidence to refute the claim that the link between grade retention and low achievement or school dropout is spurious. It would further validate the existing knowledge base against the routine practice of grade retention. An answer of "yes" to the second question would help to validate, at least in part, the potential effectiveness of new retention-plus policies being implemented around the country. An answer of "no" to the second question would raise questions about the current high level of investments in retention-plus policies.

THE CHICAGO LONGITUDINAL STUDY

The Chicago Longitudinal Study (Reynolds, 1994, 1999; Reynolds & Temple, 1998) is an on-going investigation of a cohort of 1,539 low-income, minority (93% African American) children born in 1980 and who attended kindergarten programs in 25 Chicago public schools in 1985–1986. The main early childhood program that children attended was the Title I Child-Parent Center Program, a comprehensive preschool and school-age preventive intervention for children from high-poverty neighborhoods. The sample consisted of the entire kindergarten classes of the Child-Parent Centers (989 students) and five randomly selected schools that offered an alternative intervention for disadvantaged children called the Chicago Effecitve Schools Project (550 students). Although children in the CLS completed the elementary grades in 1995 (eighth or ninth grade) before the new policy in Chicago was enacted in 1996, a study based on CLS data has several unique features that advance the knowledge base on the effects of retention.

Study Participants

Study participants, who grew up in high-poverty neighborhoods in Chicago, represent children who are most likely to be retained and are thus most likely to be impacted by retention policies ending social promotion (Alexander, Entwisle, & Dauber, 2003; McCoy & Reynolds, 1999). Moreover, students who attend urban schools in poor neighborhoods are at high risk of school dropout (U.S. Department of Education, 1996). Because many reforms are justified on the basis of improving the school achievement of urban schools, documenting the long-term effects of retention and retention-plus policies is an important test of the success of these efforts. Many previous studies of retention are based on relatively small samples of students from middle-income families, few of whom are retained. The schools in which they attend also have more resources than typical urban schools to implement remedial education programs.

Family and School Experiences

As a prospective investigation that began when children were age 5, a comprehensive set of family and school experiences were collected to determine the consequences of retention. The most important of these for investigating the effects of retention are achievement test scores (Iowa Tests of Basic Skills, ITBS), which have been collected beginning at kindergarten entry in 1985 and continuing every spring until high school. Thus, unlike previous studies of retention, at least three years of achievement test scores are available (start and end of kindergarten, end of first grade) before any students were retained in first grade. Although a few other studies (e.g., Alexander, Entwisle, & Dauber, 2003) have at least one measure of preretention achievement and extensive data on child and family background, researchers using national data sets such as High School and Beyond and the National Education Longitudinal Study (e.g., Eide & Showalter, 2001; Meisels & Laiw, 1993) are unable to control for pre-retention achievement. Even researchers attempting to use more recent data obtained from the Chicago Public Schools (and other districts) would face difficulties with data availability because students younger than third grade no longer take standardized tests.

School Progress of Students

The school progress of students in the sample has been traced up to age 20. The educational attainment of 1,281 of the original sample (83.2%) was determined by January 2000 so that the link between grade retention and school dropout can be investigated. Given the scope of the measures collected in the study, other predictors of retention and school dropout also can be investigated.

Child-Parent Center Program (CPC) Participation

Regardless of their retention status, children had the opportunity to participate in the early school-age component of the Child-Parent Center (CPC) Program. The CPC program provides educational and family-support services to low-income children from ages 3 to 9 in 24 sites. The

CPC school-age component provides services in the following areas: (a) Class sizes are limited to 25 students, and each class is staffed by a teacher aide resulting in student to teacher ratios of 25 to 2; (b) The curriculum parent-resource teacher in each school coordinates instructional activities for children in the classroom and organizes activities for parents in the parent resource room. These activities range from running workshops for parents to volunteering in the classroom; (c) Extra instructional resources and materials are provided for more individualized instruction in the classroom. Students can participate in the school-age intervention for 1 to 3 years, although only 2 years are possible in 14 sites.

Notably, the duration, intensity, and comprehensiveness of services far exceed what most students receive under current promotion-plus policies. The Chicago Public School's promotion policy enacted in 1996, for example, requires that students at risk of being retained enroll in summer school. In the retention year, students have the opportunity to receive special instruction (during the school day or after-school) or enroll in classes with fewer students, but the availability of these options varies widely across schools (Roderick et al., 1999; Roderick, Nagaoka, Bacon, & Easton, 2000). One consequence of retention is class sizes in some schools are increased if the number of students in third or sixth grade exceeds the number expected because of high numbers of retainees.

Sample and Measures in the Chicago Longitudinal Study

The study sample for this paper includes 1,267 students who were enrolled in the Chicago public schools for at least six years (beginning in kindergarten) and whose school dropout status was known by age 20 (January 2000). Children who have left the study or cannot be located are similar to those that remain in the sample on measures of kindergarten achievement and socioeconomic status (see Temple et al., 2000).

Since 1986, the CLS has collected data from multiple sources. Information on grade retention and high school completion as of January 2000 were obtained from school records. School records provided descriptive information on children including gender, race, and name of the school in which the student is enrolled at the end of each school year. Standardized test scores in reading and math were obtained annually from the beginning of kindergarten (1985) through ninth grade (1995). Teacher and parent surveys were used to obtain information on classroom adjustment, parent involvement, and family background.

Two measures of educational attainment were used in analyzing the effects of retention. Data were collected from school records, surveys, and interviews from youth and, if necessary, their parents. School dropout measured whether youth left their formal education or diploma-granting high school prior to graduation for any reason other than death or school transfer. Youth who enrolled in a GED or equivalent program also were coded as dropouts. Students who graduated from high school or were active in high school were defined as nondropouts. High school completion measured whether youth completed their secondary education with an official diploma or were awarded a GED. All others, including those who remained in high school by January 2000, were coded as noncompleters.

Grade retention was measured by school records from kindergarten to eighth grade. A child was coded as retained if he/she had identical grade codes in consecutive years. At the time the study sampled enrollment in elementary school, the policy of the Chicago Board of Education stated that "a student shall not be promoted from one grade to the next if the student has not met the minimum levels of performance from the assigned grade levels" but Chicago school policy also stated that grade retention should be used as a last resort and that "decisions must be made on an individual level" (Easton & Storey, 1990, p. 2). In practice, retention decisions were made in a decentralized fashion and there was variation across schools in the propensity to retain. Beginning in 1996, Chicago policy requires grade retention if students (excluding some bilingual and special education students) in grades 3, 6, or 8 do not meet specified cut-offs on standardized tests after being given a second chance to improve their scores at the end of summer school. Note that the policy was recently revised in 2000 to allow teachers to take into account other indicators of school performance such as grades and attendance.

A comprehensive set of predictors of both grade retention and school achievement and dropout included the following: sex of child, minority status, overage at kindergarten, parent education, eligibility for a subsidized lunch, residence in a high-poverty neighborhood (60% or more children in school attendance area from low-income families), and years of participation in the Child-Parent Center Program. Early adjustment indicators were included as preretention measures as well as intervening school-based factors that would be associated with retention. These included standardized test scores on the ITBS on several occasions prior to retention, teacher-reported grades in reading and math, school mobility, teacher ratings of parent participation in school, and placement in special education (see also McCoy & Reynolds, 1999).

Characteristics of Retained and Promoted Students

Of the 1,267 youth for whom school dropout status was known, 360 were retained at least once from kindergarten to eighth grade. This resulted in a cumulative rate of grade retention of 28.4%. Table 3.1 presents descriptive information on the characteristics of the total sample of retained and promoted students. Importantly, the retained students had higher dropout rates and lower completion rates than promoted students. Table 3.1 also indicates that the two groups of students are different in other ways. Students who participated in the Child-Parent Center Program were less likely to be retained, and this relationship was stronger for students who had the most intervention. Students who were retained had lower achievement levels both before retention occurred and years later (as of age 14). Controlling for many of the preretention observable differences across the two groups will be important for obtaining a precise estimate of the effect of grade retention.

Figure 3.1 provides descriptive information on the timing of grade retention. Relatively few kindergartners were made to repeat a grade, while the single largest group of students was retained in first grade ($n = 134$; 12 also were retained in kindergarten), followed by third grade ($n = 71$), second grade ($n = 76$), and fourth grade ($n = 48$). Fewer numbers of students were retained in fifth to eighth grades.

Predictors of Grade Retention

Before investigating the association between grade retention and high school completion or dropout, we examined a comprehensive set of predictors of retention as described above, including child and family background, early adjustment indicators (kindergarten and first-grade academic performance and achievement), and intervening school experiences (e.g., school mobility and special education placement). Because of our interest in controlling for achievement in more than 1 year before the students were retained, our regression analysis excludes the small number of students who were retained at the end of kindergarten. While these students are included in the summary statistics reported in this paper, they are not included in the regression analysis because only one observation on preretention achievement is available for them. We estimated the odds ratios (probability of being retained) in a logistic regression analysis. In order of magnitude, the following factors *increased* the odds of being retained: low family income (2.22; children eligible for a subsidized lunch had twice the risk of retention than those not eligible); sex of child (2.04;

Table 3.1 Means (*M*) and Standard Deviations (*SD*) for Retained, Promoted, and All Children

	Retained (N = 360)			Promoted (N = 907)			All Children (N = 1,267)		
	M	N	SD	M	N	SD	M	N	SD
Educational Attainment									
Dropout as of 1/00	.67	342	.47	.43	834	.49	.50	1,176	.50
High school completion as of 1/00	.25	325	.44	.55	820	.50	.46	1,145	.499
Program Participation									
Preschool participation	.57	360	.50	.69	907	.46	.65	1,267	.48
Follow-on participation	.48	360	.50	.63	907	.48	.59	1,267	.49
Total years of CPC participation	2.32	360	1.87	3.15	907	1.99	2.91	1,267	1.99
Sociodemographic Factors									
Sex of child (1 = girl)	.35	360	.48	.57	907	.49	.51	1,267	.50
Overage for kindergarten (older than 69 months with a 12/1 cutoff)	.01	360	.12	.03	907	.18	.03	1,267	.16
If parent completed high school by child age 12	.41	360	.49	.57	907	.50	.52	1,267	.50
Ever reported receiving free lunch by age 14	.97	325	.17	.91	850	.28	.93	1,175	.26
School Performance									
Mathematics achievement at age 14	131.9	359	15.84	153.6	905	15.4	147.4	1,264	18.4
Reading achievement at age 14	128.0	359	18.09	151.7	905	19.63	145.0	1,264	22.0
Intervening School-based factors									
Number of years of school move (year 4–8)	1.26	360	1.08	.80	907	.93	.93	1,267	1.0
Number of years parent participation average or above grades 1–6	1.34	360	1.24	2.39	907	1.50	2.1	1,267	1.51
Any special education placement year 1–8	.29	360	.46	.10	907	.30	.16	1,267	.36
Ever retained (year 1–8)	.99	360	.11	.00	907	.00	.28	1,267	.45

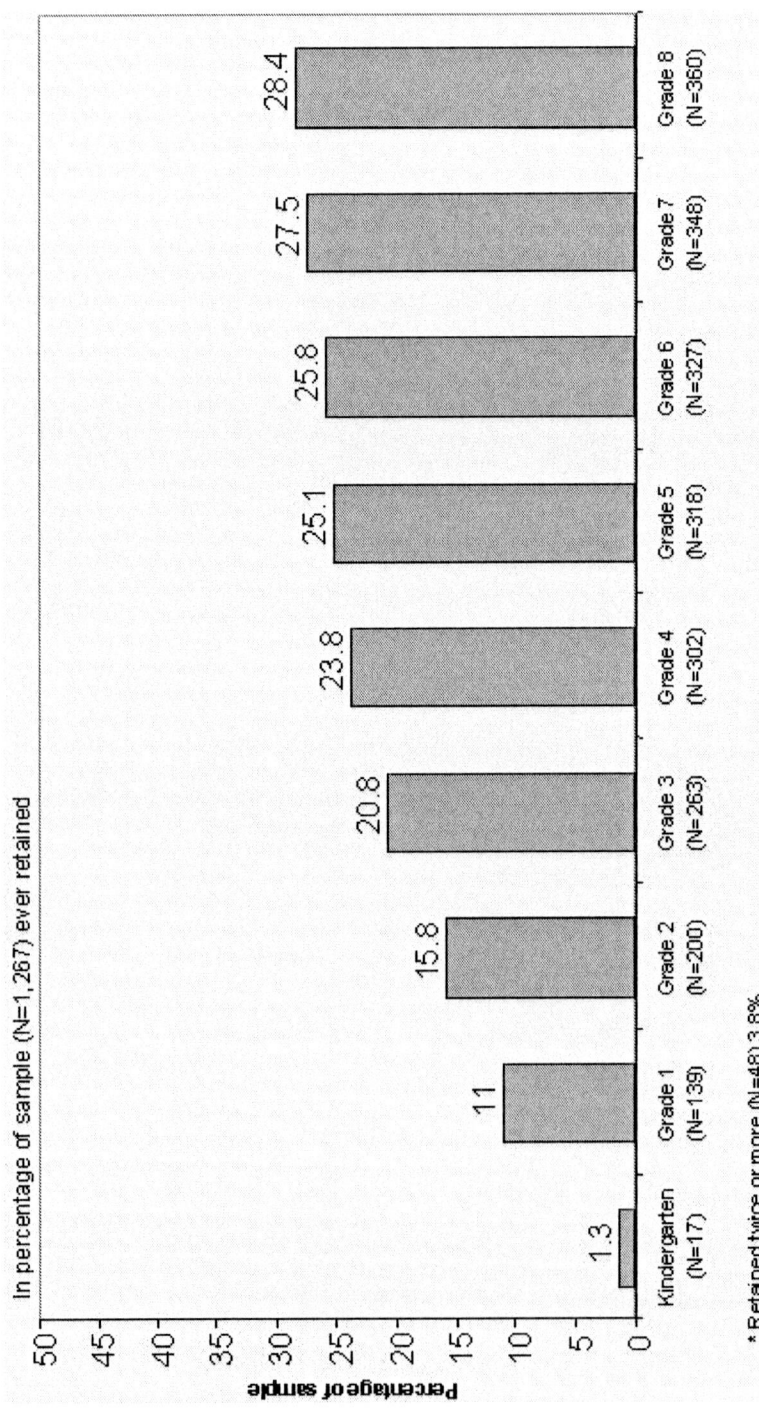

Figure 3.1. Cumulative retention in the Chicago Longitudinal Study.

boys had twice the risk of retention than girls), and number of school moves from ages 10 to 14 (1.28).

The following factors *decreased* the odds of being retained: overage at kindergarten entry (0.17; overage children had an odds of retention that was one sixth of other children), number of years of average or better parent involvement in school (0.76), reading and math achievement in first grade (0.97), grade in reading in first grade (0.67), and math achievement in kindergarten (0.99). Findings that the number of school moves increases the risk of retention and parent involvement in school decreases the risk are relatively new, and especially significant. Variables such as race/ethnicity, parent education, years of CPC intervention, residence in a high-poverty school attendance area, and special education placement were not associated with retention.

Reading Achievement and Growth Before and After Retention

Figure 3.2 shows the achievement trajectories from the beginning of kindergarten (age 5) to ninth grade (age 15) for students who were retained in each of grades 1 to 8 and two comparison groups. Appendix A shows the achievement trajectories for those students retained in kindergarten. The first comparison group consists of promoted students who are the same age as retained students but one grade ahead (i.e., same-age comparisons of test scores in the same academic year). The second comparison is made by contrasting the achievement of the retained students to the achievement of the promoted students a year earlier when they were in the grade of the currently retained students (i.e., same-grade comparisons of test scores in different academic years). The vertical line in each chart is when retention occurred. The scores are reported in ITBS developmental standard scores, which have a mean of 100 in the fall of third grade and a mean of 160 in the fall of eighth grade. One point is roughly equal to 1 month on a grade-equivalent scale. Three findings are evident.

Mean Reading Scores

With one exception (sixth grade), the mean reading scores of retained students diverged significantly from those of promoted students up to the school decision of retention. This is shown by the nonparallel lines in the years before students were retained in a particular grade. The largest divergence of scores occurred for students retained in the first three grades, which is not surprising given that the most academically disadvantaged are identified earliest. Compared to other grades, the prereten-

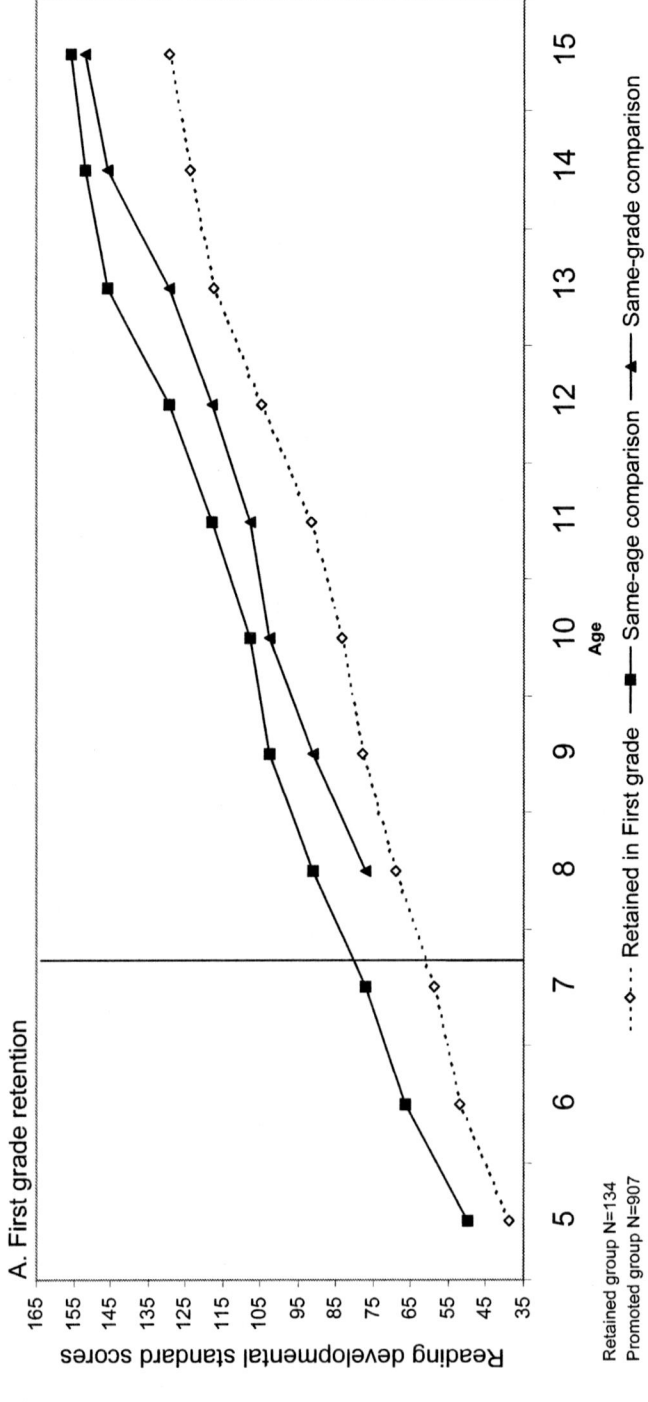

Figure 3.2. Patterns of ITBS reading achievement for retained and promoted students in the CLS.

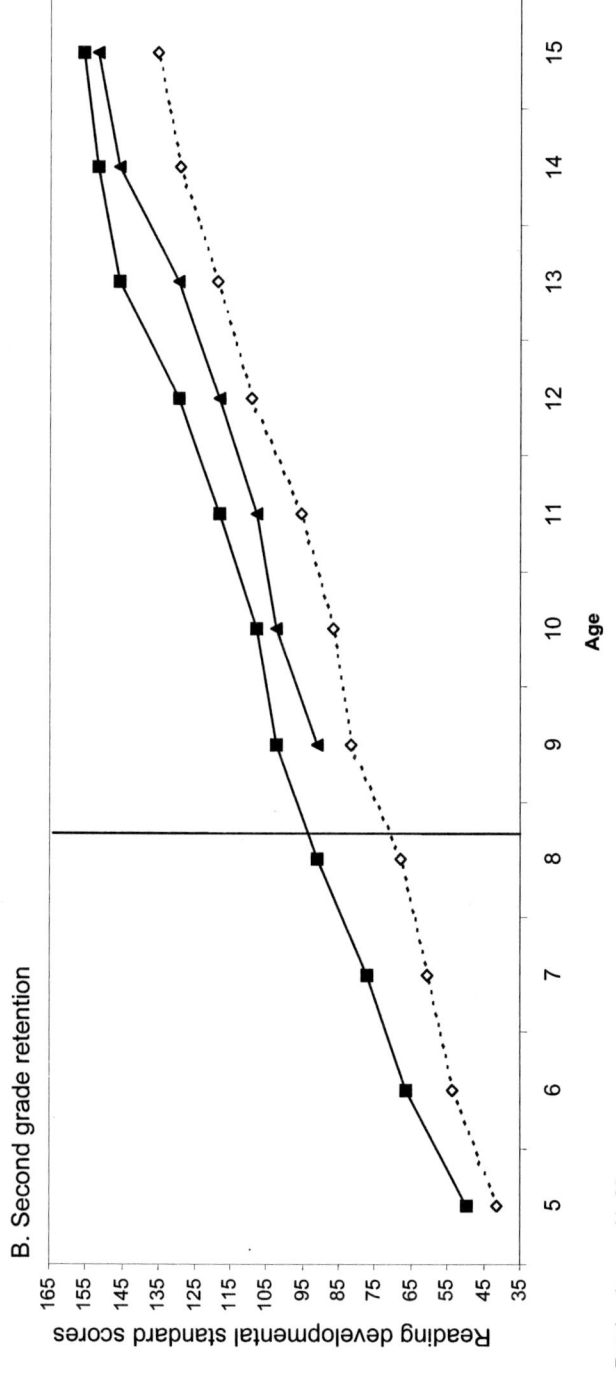

Figure 3.2. Continued

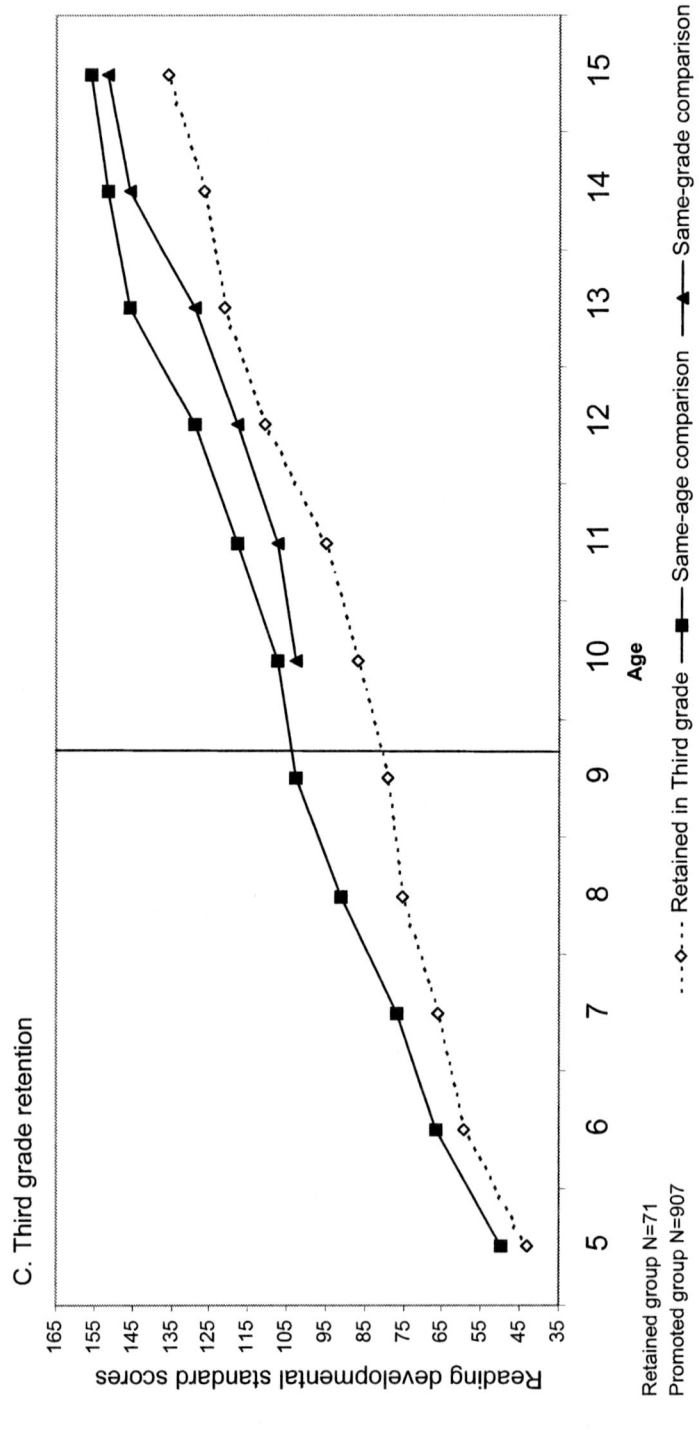

Figure 3.2. Continued

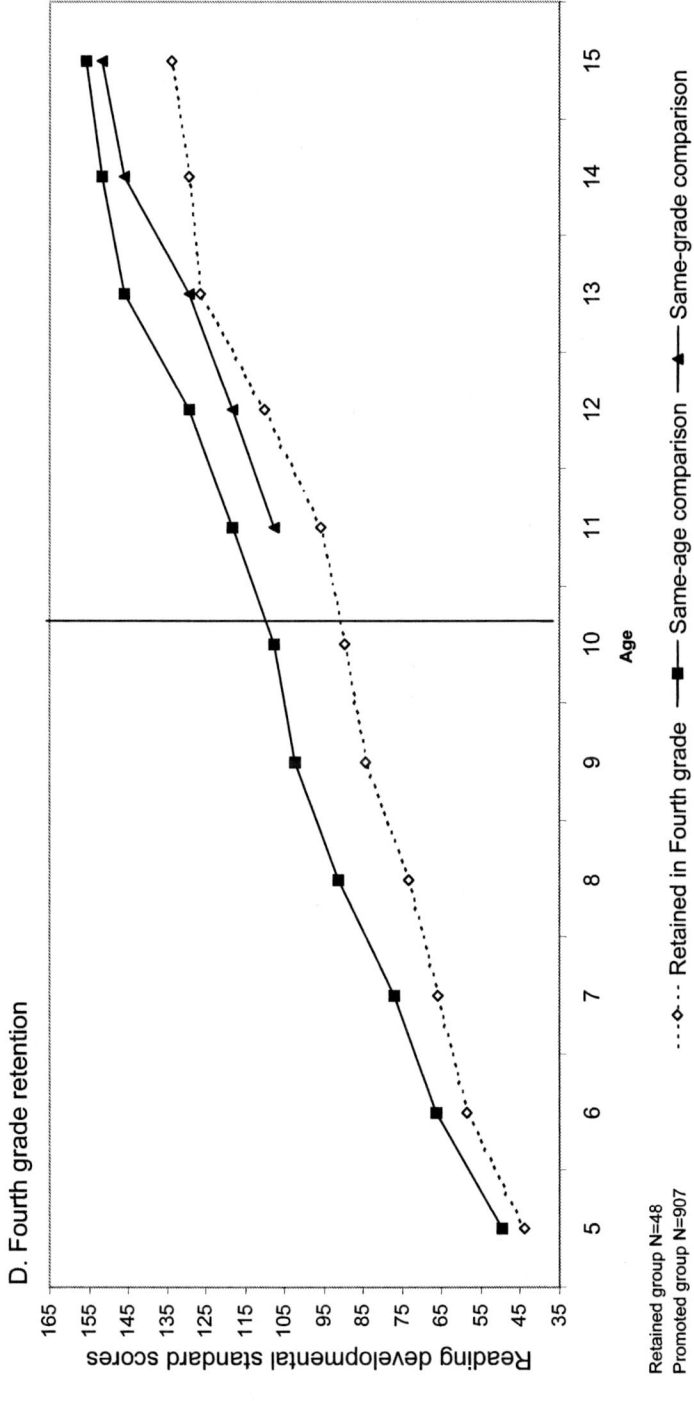

Figure 3.2. Continued

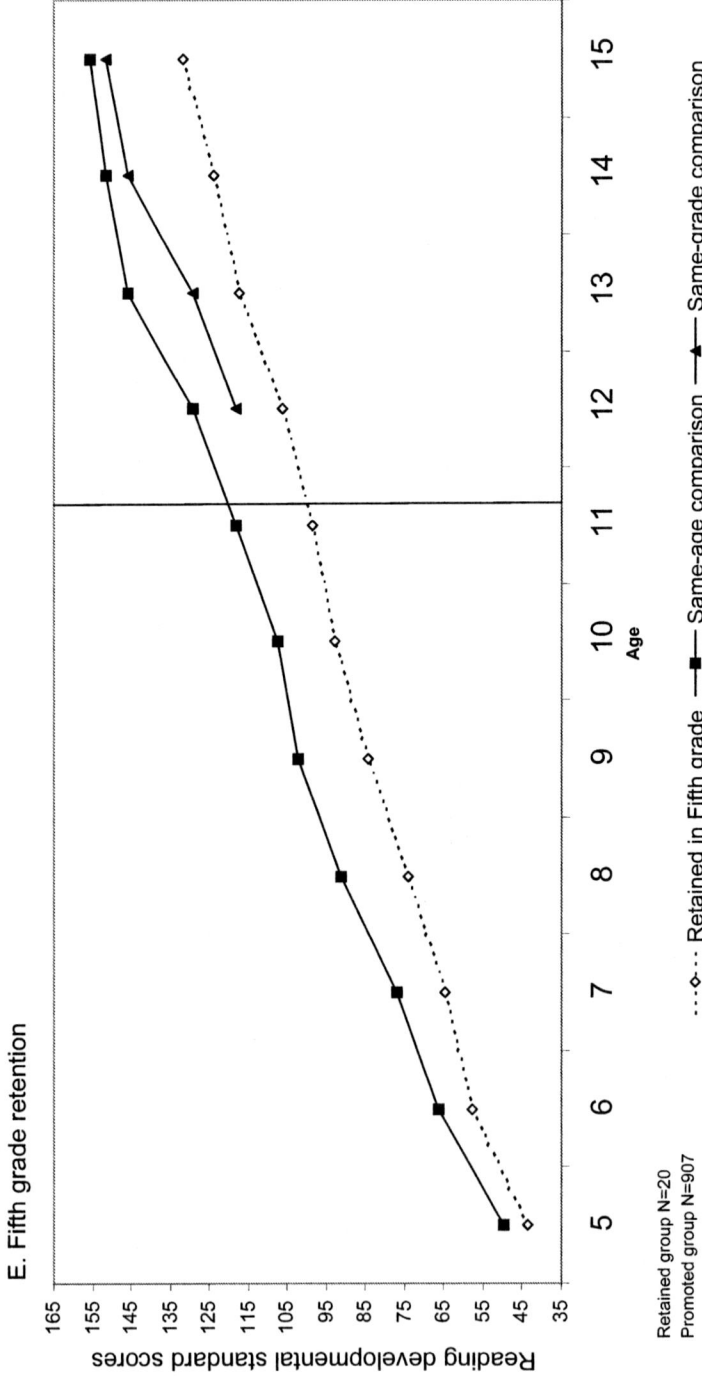

Figure 3.2. Continued

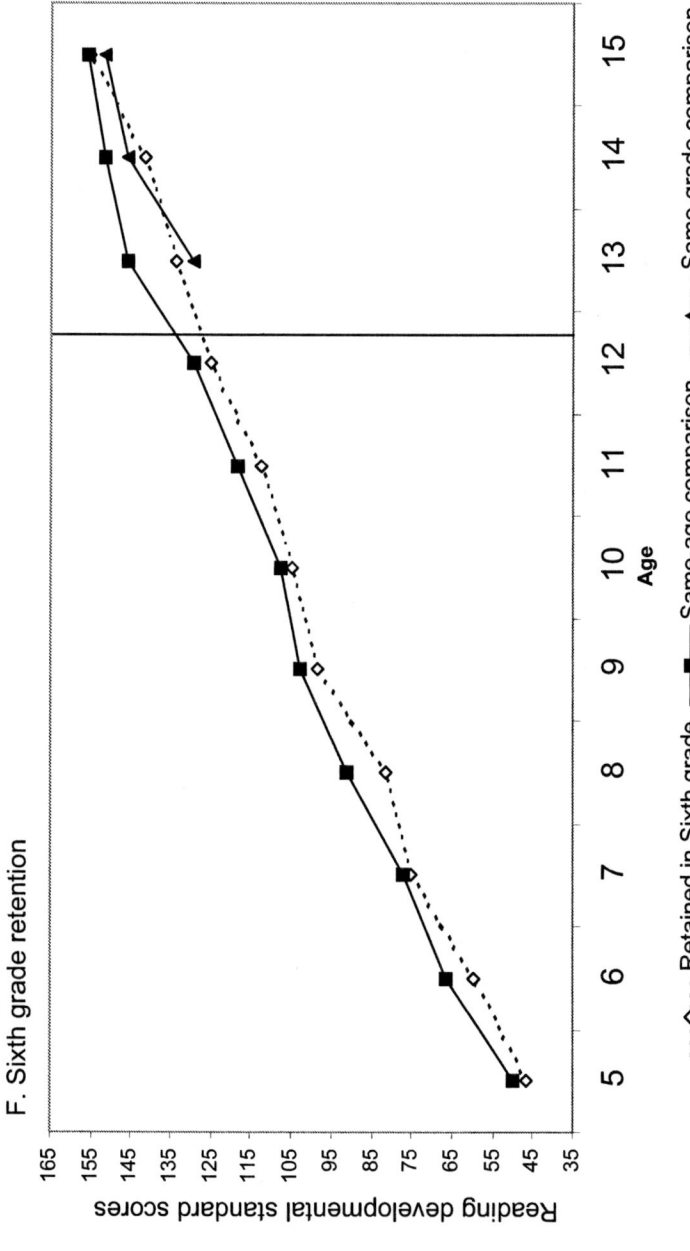

Figure 3.2. Continued

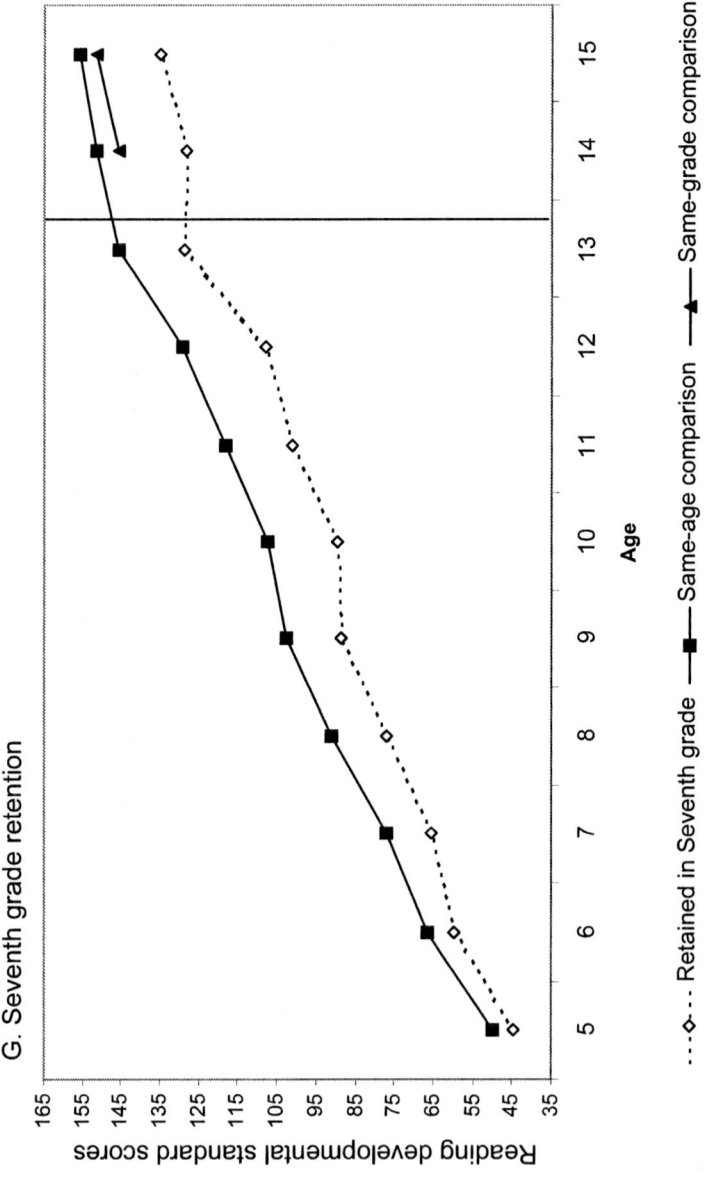

Figure 3.2. Continued

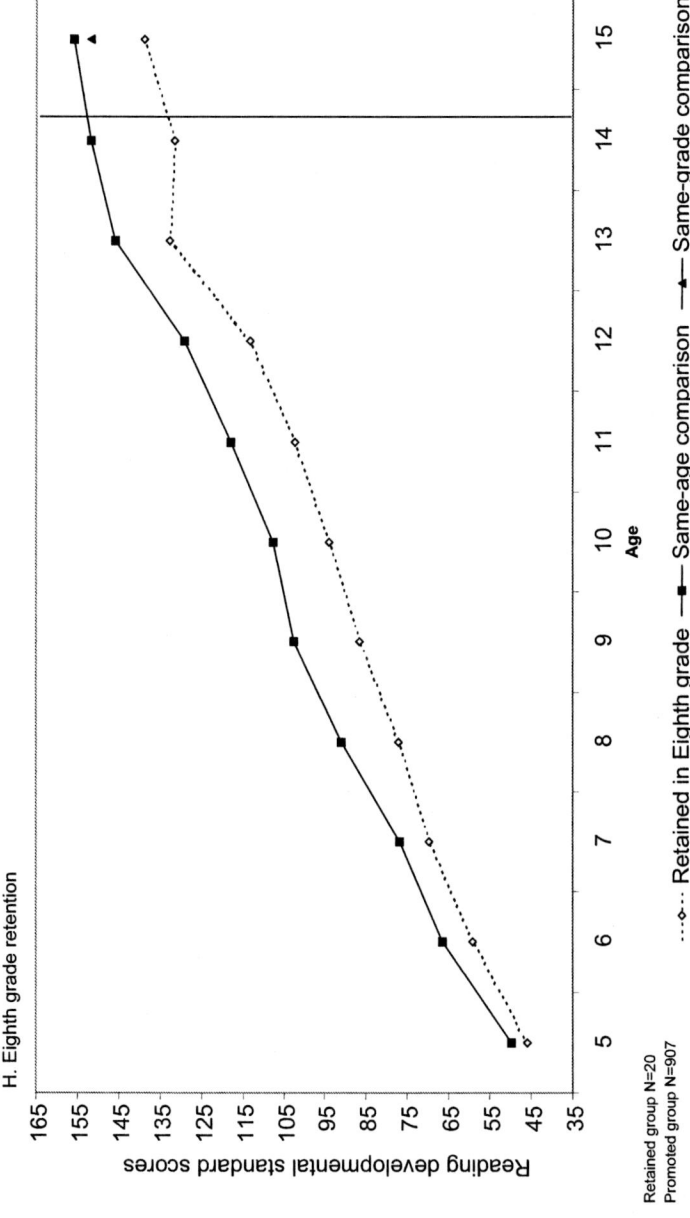

Figure 3.2. Continued

tion achievement of students retained in sixth and seventh grades was closer to the promoted students. This pattern suggests that most of the retention groups were experiencing lower rates of learning prior to the decision to retain. These different rates must be taken into account in properly estimating the effect of retention.

Same-age Comparisons

Regardless of the preretention growth rates in reading, the gap between the retained and nonretained students continued to widen throughout the elementary grades until the first year of high school (age 15). Thus, grade retention did not help narrow the achievement differences between the retained and promoted groups. By the end of the eighth grade year (age 14), for example, the original mean difference in achievement test scores prior to retention nearly doubled in the years after retention for students retained in first grade, fourth grade, and seventh grade. This pattern of results suggests that programs and policies to help underachieving students must alter the rate of achievement growth in order to be effective. A temporary change in the mean level of performance is insufficient. Nevertheless, the reading scores of promoted students also are substantially below (by more than a year) the national average of 168 and 178, respectively, for eighth (age 14) and ninth (age 15) graders.

Same-grade Comparisons

In all retention groups except one (the 10 students retained in grade 7), retained students not only fail to narrow the gap in reading achievement with their same-age peers, but with their same-grade peers as well. This latter comparison is the most conservative test of the effects of retention because retained students at the end of their second year in the same grade would be expected to perform at the level of their younger peers who are going through the grade for the first time. As reported by McCoy and Reynolds (1999), the average performance of retained students did not meet or exceed that of same-grade comparison groups by age 14 even after accounting for the preretention school performance and adjustment. Retained students scored an average of five months lower in reading than their same-grade comparison group in reading achievement and about 1 month lower in math achievement.

Two questions are raised by the patterns of achievement in Figure 3.2. Does retention continue to be associated with later school dropout and completion after differential rates of reading growth prior to retention are taken into account? Given the recent interest in retention-plus policies, does participation in the CPC school-age intervention during or after the retention year help deflect achievement patterns in a more positive direction?

Grade Retention and School Dropout and Completion

Grade retention and high school dropout are highly correlated for students in the Chicago Longitudinal Study. Figure 3.3 shows that 67% of the retained students have dropped out of school by age 20, while only 43% of the continuously promoted students dropped out. Additional information comes from the relation between high school completion and retention. Of the retained students, 25% have completed high school by age 20 while 55% of promoted students have completed high school. These percentages are shown in Figure 3.3 (unadjusted model).

Because retained and promoted students differ with respect to a number of individual and family characteristics that may also predict educational attainment, Figure 3.3 also shows the rates of dropout and completion for retained and promoted students after controlling pre-retention achievement on two occasions (as suggested in Figure 3.2), subject grades, child and family background variables, and early adjustment variable of parent involvement, school mobility, and special education placement. The adjusted model indicates that students who were retained in the elementary grades had a 24.6% higher rate of school dropout than promoted students (57.7% vs. 46.3%) and a 26.8% lower rate of high school completion than their promoted age peers (50.3% vs. 36.8%), even

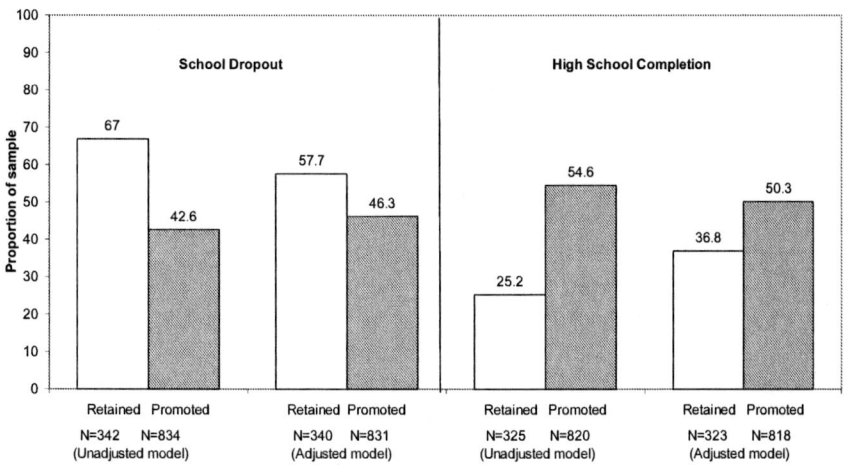

Figure 3.3. Educational attainment by age 20 for retained/promoted groups.

Table 3.2. Odds Ratios and Estimated Rates of Dropout and High School Completion for Retention/Promotion Groups by Model Specification

	Dropout Odds Ratio		High School Completion Odds Ratio	
	Unadjusted Model	Adjusted Model	Unadjusted Model	Adjusted Model
1. Any retention	2.8*	1.9*	.28*	.43*
2. Number of retentions one/two/three/none	2.1*	1.6*	.36*	.52*
3. a. 1–3 retention	2.2*	1.4*	.35*	.55*
b. 4–8 retention	4.2*	2.8*	.16*	.26*
c. Multiple retention	2.2*	1.3	.28*	.49

Note. Adjusted model was adjusted for sex, race, overage in kindergarten, parent education, ever reported free lunch, income level is 60%+ poverty for school area, missing data from parent education or free lunch report, years of CPC intervention, and early achievement. For 1–3 retention, kindergarten and first grade achievement are controlled. For 4–8 retention, third grade and fourth grade achievement are controlled.
*$p < .05$.

after taking into account differences in achievement growth prior to retention.

Table 3.2 shows these most important results of the negative impact of retention on educational attainment in odds ratios—the probability of dropout/completion for being retained at different grades. We estimated these probabilities through logistic regression analysis controlling for child and family background, 2 years of achievement prior to retention, and school mobility, parent involvement, and special education placement (the coefficients of the full regression models are reported in Appendixes B and C). Findings show that grade retention was associated with lower rates of educational attainment regardless of model specification. Model 2 for "any retention," for example, indicates that the risk of school dropout for students retained in any of the elementary grades was 1.9 times (nearly double) that for students not retained when controlling for child and family characteristics, preretention achievement growth, and school-based factors. The risk of school dropout for students retained in grades 4 to 8 was 2.8 times that for promoted students. The bottom half of Table 3.2 shows that grade retention was significantly associated with lower rates of high school completion by age 20. For example, the odds of completion for the total retention group was about one half (odds ratio = .43) that of the promoted group. Students retained in grades 4 to 8 had the smallest odds of high school completion (odds ratio = .26).

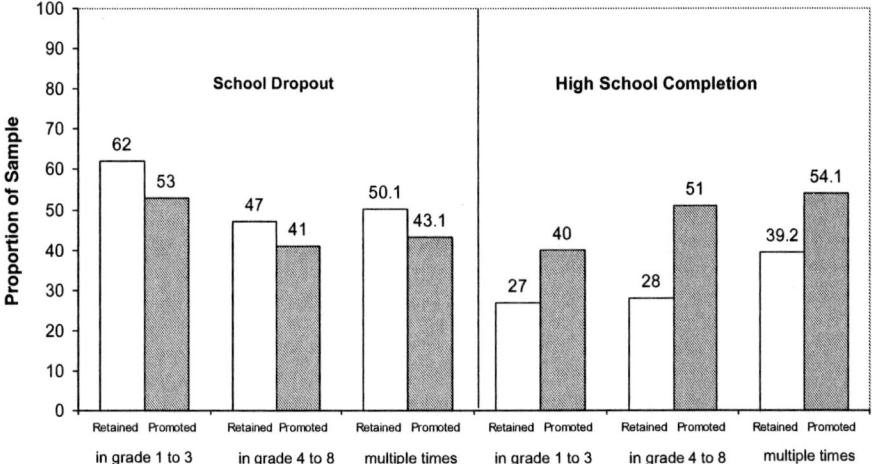

Figure 3.4. Educational attainment by age 20 for retained/promoted groups.

Figure 3.4 displays the rates of high school dropout by timing of retention (adjusted for the full set of predictors of retention and dropout). Grade retention in first to third grades and in fourth to eighth grades was associated with significantly higher rates of school dropout. Relative to promoted students, students with two or more retentions also were more likely to drop out of school.

Impact of Retention Plus Remediation on Achievement and School Dropout

Given the new emphasis in some school districts on retention accompanied by remediation services, we also investigated whether the performance of retained students is aided by the provision of extra educational support services beginning in the repeated grade. To conduct our analysis, we focus on several smaller subgroups drawn from our large sample. We compare the performance of students who were retained in any of the first three grades but participated in the school-age intervention offered by the Child-Parent Center program during those first three grades ($n = 65$) to that of retained students who did not receive school-age intervention after being retained ($n = 180$), to low-achieving, promoted students who received the school-age intervention for 1 to 3 years ($n = 157$), and to low-achieving, promoted students who did not participate in the intervention ($n = 131$). Low-achieving students were defined as those with a reading grade equivalent under 2.8 (standard score of 92 or lower) in the spring of third grade (more than 1 year under the national average).

The school-age intervention is located in the elementary schools serving Child-Parent Centers preschool and kindergarten programs. Children may participate for 1 to 3 years beginning in first grade, although retained students could enroll for a fourth year at age 10. Comprehensive services include reduced class sizes, teacher aides for each class, instructional coordination by the curriculum parent resource teacher, parent involvement activities in the parent resource room, and extra resources for supplies and equipment (see Reynolds, 2000; Reynolds & Temple 1998).

Figure 3.5 shows the pattern of reading achievement for four groups of students before, during, and after students' participation in the CPC school-age intervention. Two major findings are evident. First, although retained students participating in school-age intervention had slightly higher reading scores at age 9 than retained students who did not receive the intervention, reading scores from ages 10 to 15 were equivalent between groups. Second, the reading performance of the low-achieving, promoted students with school-age intervention substantially exceeded that of retained students with CPC intervention from ages 10 to 15. The equivalent performance at age 9 of students receiving retention-plus and students receiving promotion-plus quickly disappeared by age 10.

Turning to high school dropout by age 20, a similar pattern of findings emerged. As shown in Figure 3.6, students in the retention plus CPC intervention group did not experience a lower rate of school dropout than students in the retention-only group (it was somewhat higher). Moreover, the low-achieving, promoted group with CPC intervention) had a lower rate of school dropout than the retention plus CPC intervention group (59% vs. 69%). Irrespective of retention and school-age intervention, the rates of school dropout for all of these urban students is high. Substantially more than retention and school-age intervention is needed to address the learning difficulties of these students.

Thus, our findings based on student participation in the Child-Parent Center school age program suggest that students retained in the first three grades who receive extra educational support for 1 or more years after being retained do not get a boost in their academic performance. Moreover, they are more likely than low-achieving promoted students receiving intervention to drop out of school later. Findings for achievement and school dropout indicate the superior performance of promotion plus remediation over retention plus remediation. These findings have important policy implications given that the CPC follow-on program

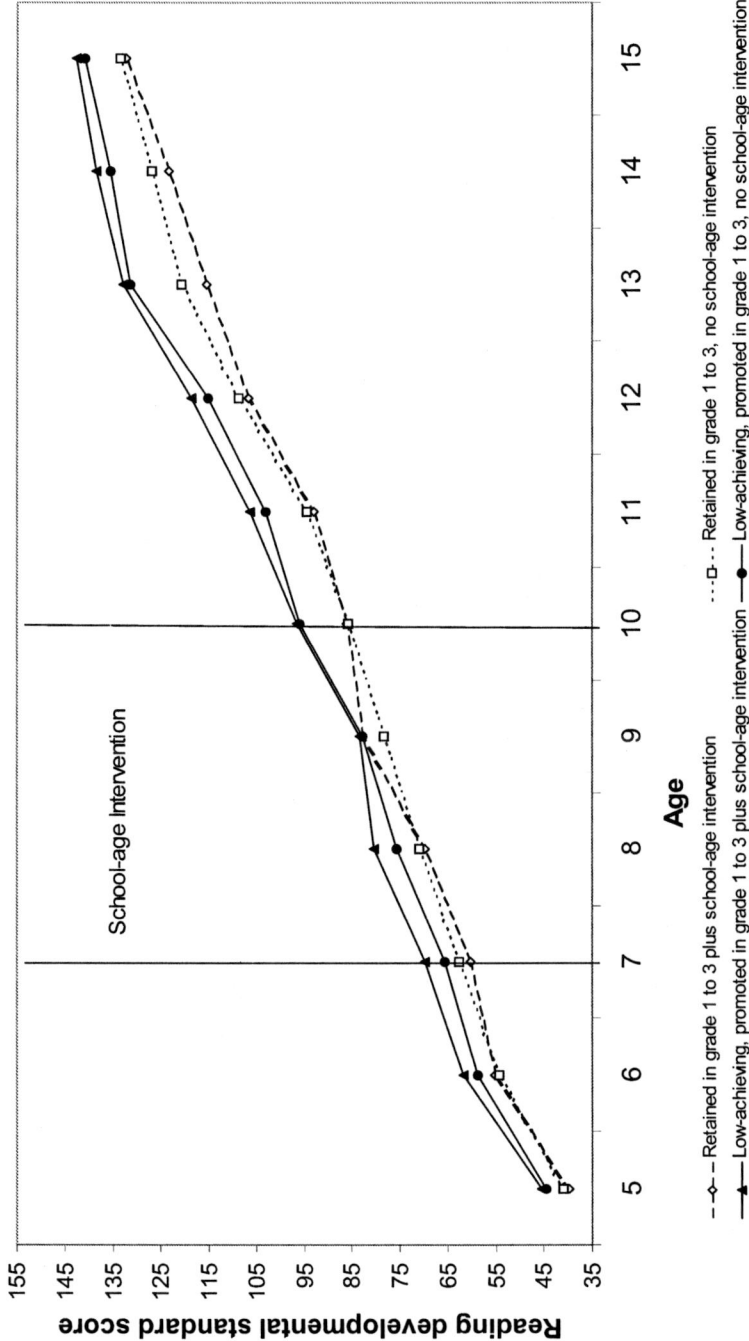

Figure 3.5. Reading performance of retained and promoted students with and without school-age intervention.

59

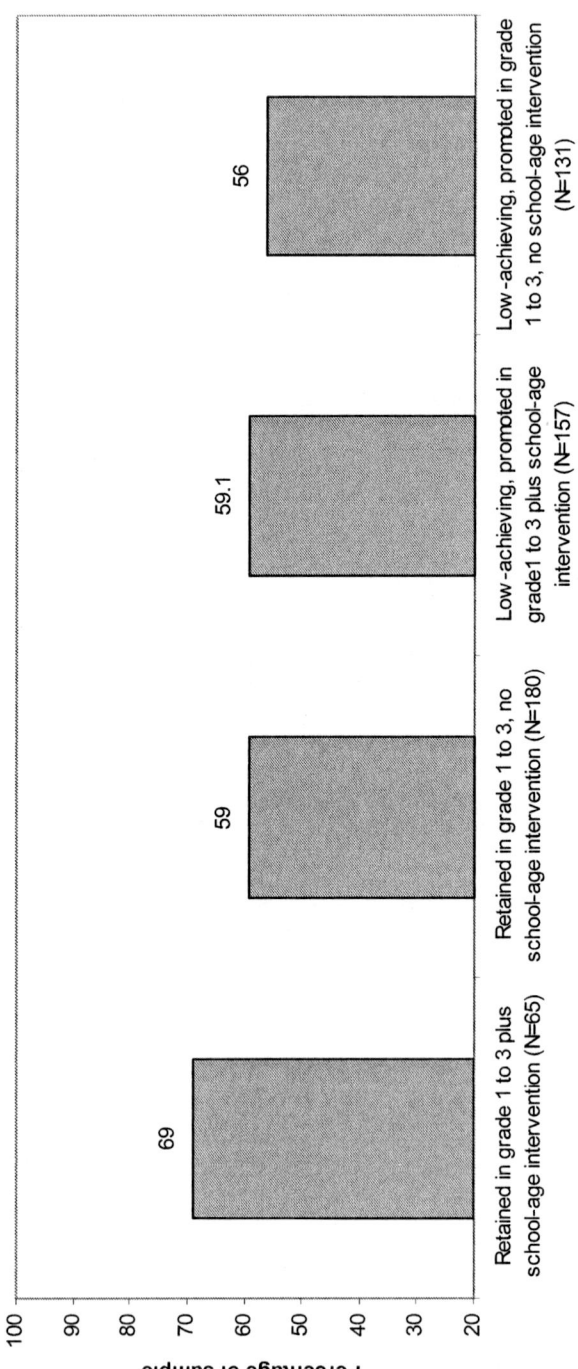

Figure 3.6. School dropout rates for four retained and promoted groups.

is longer in duration and more comprehensive in services than most contemporary remedial help for retained students.

DISCUSSION

Our findings indicate that grade retention—no matter when it occurs—is associated with significantly lower levels of school achievement and higher rates of school dropout. Even before dropping out, the students who were retained fell further and further behind their similarly low-achieving former classmates as early as kindergarten and first grade (see Figure 3.2). By the end of their 8th grade year, retained students were 1 to 2 years behind these former classmates. Retained students had a rate of school dropout that was 25% higher than that of promoted students (controlling for preretention achievement growth and other factors). This finding provides further validation to the demonstrated link between grade retention and school dropout (Alexander, Entwisle, & Dauber, 2003; Alexander, Entwisle, & Kabbani, 2003; Anderson, 1994; Ensminger & Slusrick, 1992; Grissom & Shepard, 1989; Jimerson, 1999).

Does grade retention harm students, or are the large estimated adverse effects of grade retention due—at least in part—to the difficulty in controlling for observed and unobserved differences between retained and promoted students that may be correlated with later educational attainment? The main strength of our study was the inclusion of a variety of preretention control variables such as achievement at different times that take account of such differences. Our results indicated that although there were substantial differences between the unadjusted and adjusted models, both indicated a significant link between grade retention and school dropout as well as lower rates of school completion.

Retention Plus Remediation

Our finding that students who were retained in the first three grades did not benefit academically from 1 to 3 years of participation in the Child-Parent Center program suggests that retention plus remediation strategies may not prevent the typical achievement declines that have been shown for simple grade retention without remediation. Indeed, the CPC follow-on intervention is more comprehensive and longer-lasting than most remedial services that retained students receive under many current retention practices in schools. Moreover, comparable students who were promoted (instead of retained) and then participated in intervention for 1 to 3 years had substantial performance advantages over students who were retained and then participated in intervention (see Figures 3.5 and 3.6).

Findings that the retention-plus strategy of remediating underachievement led to lower levels of achievement and no reductions in the rate of school dropout over either retention-alone and promotion plus intervention are consistent with recent results of a study of the Chicago Public Schools promotion policy. As reported by Roderick et al. (2000), the average growth in reading scores over 3 years (1997–1999) for students retained in third and sixth grade under the new policy of test-based retention with remediation, respectively, was 2.3 and 2.4 grade equivalents. Yet the average growth in reading scores for comparable 3rd and 6th grade students who were socially promoted under the old retention policy was higher at 2.7 grade equivalents. Moreover, the researchers found that the 2-year school dropout rate for students who were retained in eighth grade or who enrolled in transition centers under the new policy was 29% compared to a 14% dropout rate for all eighth graders and a 21% dropout rate for low-achieving eighth graders.

Combined with the existing knowledge base, both these studies raise major questions about the effectiveness of current "get tough" policies ending social promotion, especially given the substantial financial costs needed to operate large-scale retention-plus programs. For example, in the late 1990s, the annual cost of the Chicago Public Schools retention policy, including instructional supports, approached $100 million. Policymakers might want to think about how less intensive retention-plus programs can be expected to yield benefits when retained children who receive comprehensive instructional and family-support intervention from 1 to 3 years gain no performance advantage over children who are retained without remediation or who are social promoted.

The Missing Link: Prevention of Learning Difficulties

Grade retention is a response to serious academic problems. The intervention involves increasing the amount of time needed to meet minimum grade-level standards, often without continuing intervention. Little attempt is made to address the underlying conditions that cause underachievement such as low motivation, poverty, poor nutrition, or inadequate instruction. As explained by Jimerson and Kaufman (2003), it is unlikely that retention as a single intervention could substantially alter children's achievement given the typically great needs of these low-achieving students. As suggested by our Figure 3.2, underachieving children require earlier educational experiences that affect their rates of early learning.

Contrast the reactive approach of retention with a proactive approach of preventing learning difficulties. Instead of waiting until the early signs of academic failure are evident, proactive education support would seek to promote the skills and attitudes needed for mastery of the grade-level curriculum before learning problems are observed. Prevention programs do this by addressing the underlying causes that give rise to underachievement such as building language and literacy skills before formal reading instruction, instilling pride in achievement, enhancing motivation to learn, and promoting family-school partnerships to help reinforce learning at home. Not surprisingly, research has shown that programs that succeed in these areas are associated with higher levels of school achievement and lower rates of grade retention.

The importance of prevention is easily lost in an era of school accountability and high-stakes testing. Given the consistent evidence that retention is not an effective strategy of improving low-achieving children's school success and the growing evidence that retention plus remediation strategies do little to enhance these children's achievement, the alternatives to retention appear to deserve much higher funding priority than they usually receive in school districts across the country. Among these are universal access to high-quality preschool education, full-day kindergarten programs (rather than part-day programs), reduced class sizes in the early grades, family-school partnerships that provide family resource centers in schools, and school restructuring programs.

Investments in preschool education have shown significant positive long-term effects on the school success of children at risk. One of the most consistent findings in the 35 years of research is that participation in preschool programs for low-income, at-risk children reduces the need for grade retention in the elementary grades. For example, in 36 programs reviewed by Barnett (1995), participation in early childhood intervention was associated with a 31% reduction in grade retention in the elementary grades, and a 50% reduction in special education. In four programs reviewed by the same author, early childhood intervention was associated with a 32% reduction in high school dropout. Studies of the Child-Parent Center Program in which children in our study participated (beginning in preschool) are consistent with these findings (Reynolds 2000; Reynolds & Temple, 1998; Reynolds, Temple, Robertson, & Mann, 2001) and show that long-term effects can be demonstrated for large-scale programs. A cost-benefit analysis of the Child-Parent Center Program has recently been completed and the results are reported in Reynolds, Temple, Robertson, and Mann (2002).

Policymakers concerned about the school performance of students at risk of school failure should be aware that early education programs need to be high in quality in order to be effective. Moreover, the presence of environmental supports at home and in school (e.g., parent involvement, teacher expectations) appear crucial for helping to maintain learning gains over time. To the extent that these supports can be improved by prevention programs, a focus on these family-school linkages can help break the cycle of school failure. In contrast, educational interventions that wait until school failure has already occurred may be too late to be effective.

APPENDIX A

Patterns of ITBS reading achievement for retained and promoted students in the CLS

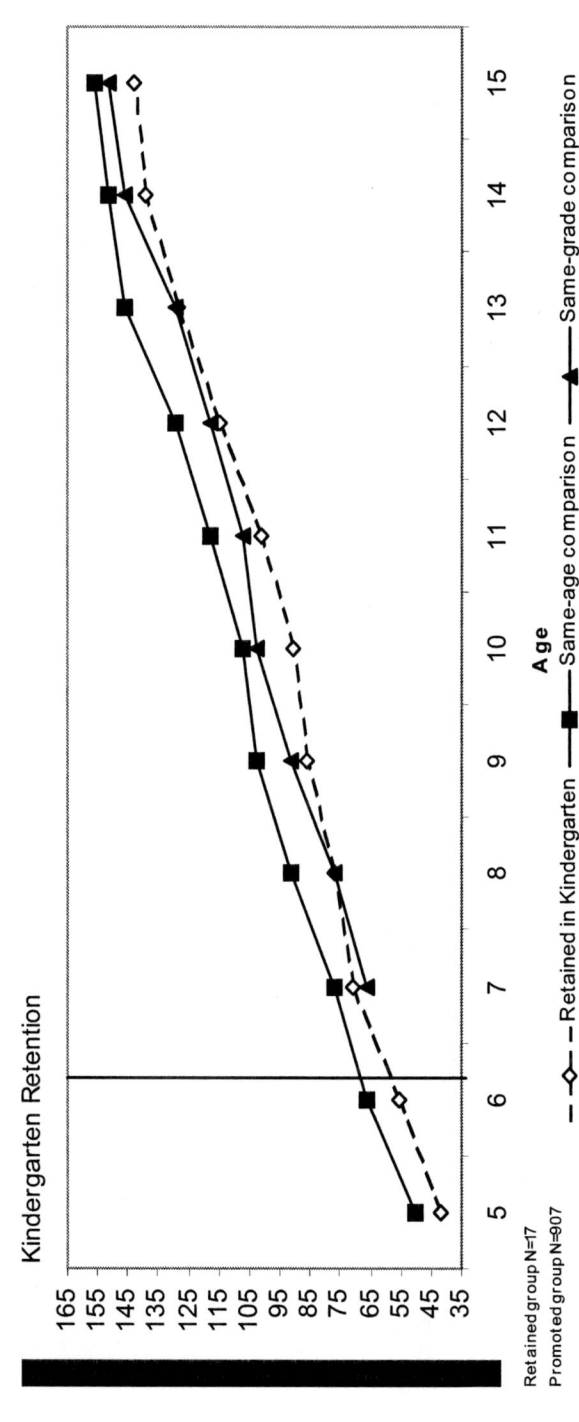

APPENDIX B
Logistic Regression Odds Ratio of Model Predicting Age 20 Dropping Out

Predictors	Model 1	Model 2	Model 3	Model 4
Grade retention (1 = ever retained from kindergarten to grade 8)	2.76***	2.25***	1.92***	1.60**
Sociodemographic Factors				
Sex (1 = boys)		1.56***	1.52***	1.50**
Race (1 = black)		2.12**	2.13**	1.82*
Overage in kindergarten		1.62	1.60	1.43
If parent completed high school (through child's age 12)		.55***	.58***	.60***
Ever reported free lunch		2.45**	2.41**	2.31**
Income level is 60% + poverty for school area		.87	.82	.77
Missing data from parent education or free lunch report		1.20	1.20	.98
Years of CPC intervention		.99	1.01	1.06
Early adjustment Indicators				
Word analysis (Kindergarten)			.99	.99
Math achievement (Kindergarten)			1.00	1.01
Math achievement (grade 1)			.99	.99
Reading achievement (grade 1)			1.00	1.0
Missing data from reading or math achievement or teacher rating (grade 1)			1.15	1.14
Grade in reading (grade 1)			.96	.98
Intervening School-based Factors				
School Mobility (grade 4–8)				1.41***
Parent involvement (grade 1–6)				.83***
Special education placement (grade 1–8)				1.02
–2 log likelihood	1,564.1	1,501.3	1,492.0	1,446.3
χ^2	59.19***	122.0***	131.3***	177.0***
Overall predicted percent correct	60.29	62.34	63.28	66.35
Number of cases	1,171	1,171	1,171	1,171

*$p < .05$. **$p < .01$. ***$p < .001$.

APPENDIX C

Logistic Regression Odds Ratio of Model Predicting Age 20 High School Completion

Predictors	Model 1	Model 2	Model 3	Model 4
Grade retention (1=ever retained from kindergarten to grade 8)	.28***	.35***	.43***	.53***
Sociodemographic Factors				
Sex (1 = boys)		.61***	.63***	.64***
Race (1 = black)		.47**	.46**	.57
Overage in kindergarten		.62	.63	.75
If parent completed high school (through child's age 12)		1.88***	1.78***	1.72***
Ever reported free lunch		.36***	.37***	.38***
Income level is 60% + poverty for school area		1.23	1.31	1.43*
Missing data from parent education or free lunch report		.80	.82	1.02
Years of CPC intervention		1.02	.99	.94
Early Adjustment Indicators				
Word analysis (Kindergarten)			1.01	1.01
Math achievement (Kindergarten)			.99	.99
Math achievement (grade 1)			1.01	1.01
Reading achievement (grade 1)			1.00	.99
Missing data from reading or math achievement or teacher rating (grade 1)			1.07	.95
Grade in reading (grade 1)			1.01	1.04
Intervening School-based Factors				
School Mobility (grade 4–8)				.68***
Parent Involvement (grade 1–6)				1.25***
Special education placement (grade 1–8)				.88
−2 log likelihood	1,492.5	1,420.4	1,407.4	1,351.7
χ^2	83.48***	155.6***	168.6***	224.3***
Overall predicted percent correct	60.39	64.59	67.66	68.89
Number of cases	1,141	1,141	1,141	1,141

*$p < .05$. **$p < .01$. ***$p < .001$.

REFERENCES

Alexander, K. L., Entwisle, D. R., & Dauber, S. L. (2003). *On the success of failure: A reassessment of the effects of retention in the primary grades* (2nd ed.). New York: Cambridge University Press.

Alexander, K. L., Entwisle, D. R., & Kabbani, N. (2003). Grade retention, social promotion, and "Third Way" alternatives. In A. J. Reynolds, M. C. Wang, & H. J. Walberg (Eds.), *Early childhood programs for a new century* (pp. 197–258). Washington, DC: CWLA Press.

Anderson, D. K. (1994). *Paths through secondary education: Race/ethnic and gender differences.* Unpublished doctoral thesis, University of Wisconsin–Madison.

Barnett, W. S. (1995). Long-term effects of early childhood programs on cognitive and school outcomes. *The Future of Children, 5*(3), 25–50.

Byrd, R. S., & Weitzman, M. L. (1994). Predictors of early grade retention among children in the U.S. *Pediatrics, 93,* 481–487.

Cook, W. (1941). *Grouping and promotion in the elementary school.* Minneapolis, MN: University of Minnesota Press.

Easton, J. Q., & Storey, S. (1990, June). *Grade retention in Chicago public elementary schools: 1989.* Chicago Panel on Public School Policy and Finance, Chicago, IL.

Eide, E., & Showalter, M. (2001). The effect of grade retention on educational labor market outcomes. *Economics of Education Review, 20,* 563–576.

Ensminger, M. E., & Slusrick, A. L. (1992). Paths to high school graduation or dropout: A longitudinal study of a first-grade cohort. *Sociology of Education, 45,* 95–113.

Grissom, J. B., & Shepard, L. A. (1989). Repeating and dropping out of school. In L. A. Shepard & M. L. Smith (Eds.), *Flunking grades: Research and policies on retention* (pp. 34–63). London: Falmer Press.

Heubert, J. P., & Hauser, R. M. (Eds.). (1999). *High stakes: Testing for tracking, promotion, and graduation.* Washington, DC: National Academy Press.

Holmes, C. T. (1989). Grade level retention effects: A meta-analysis. In L. A. Shepard & M. L. Smith (Eds.), *Flunking grades: Research and policies on retention* (pp. 16–33). London: Falmer Press.

Jackson, G. B. (1975). The research evidence on the effects of grade retention. *Review of Educational Research, 45,* 613–635.

Jimerson, S. R. (1999). On the failure of failure: Examining the association between early grade retention and education and employment outcomes during late adolescence. *Journal of School Psychology, 37,* 243–272.

Jimerson, S. R., Anderson, G. E., & Whipple, A. D. (2002). Winning the battle and losing the war: Examining the relation between grade retention and dropping out of high school. *Psychology in the Schools, 39,* 441–457.

Jimerson, S. R., & Kaufman, A. M. (2003). Reading, writing, and retention: A primer on grade retention research. *Reading Teacher, 56,* 622–635.

Karweit, N. A. (1992). Retention policy. In M. C. Alkin (Ed.), *Encyclopedia of educational research* (pp. 1114–1118). New York: MacMillan.

McCoy, A. R., & Reynolds, A. J. (1999). Grade retention and school performance: An extended investigation. *Journal of School Psychology, 37,* 273–298.

Meisels, S. J., & Liaw, F. (1993). Failure in grade: Do retained students catch up? *Journal of Educational Research, 87,* 69–77.
Reynolds, A. J. (1992). Grade retention and school adjustment: An explanatory analysis. *Educational Evaluation and Policy Analysis, 14,* 101–121.
Reynolds, A. J. (1994). Effects of a preschool plus follow-on intervention for children at risk. *Developmental Psychology, 30,* 787–804.
Reynolds, A. J. (1999). Educational success in high-risk settings: Contributions of the Chicago Longitudinal Study. *Journal of School Psychology, 37,* 345–354.
Reynolds, A. J. (2000). *Success in early intervention: The Chicago Child-Parent Centers.* Lincoln, NE: University of Nebraska Press.
Reynolds, A. J., & Temple, J. A. (1998). Extended early childhood intervention and school achievement. *Child Development, 69,* 231–246.
Reynolds, A. J., Temple, J. A., Robertson, D. L., & Mann, E. A. (2001). Long-term effects of an early childhood intervention on educational achievement and juvenile arrest: A 15-year follow-up of low-income children in public schools. *Journal of the American Medical Association, 285,* 2339–2346.
Reynolds, A. J., Temple, J. A., Robertson, D. L., & Mann, E. A. (2002). Age 21 cost-benefit analysis of the Title I Child Parent Centers. *Education Evaluation and Policy Analysis, 24,* 267–303.
Roderick, M. (1994). Grade retention and school dropout: Investigating the association. *American Educational Research Journal, 31,* 729–759.
Roderick, M., Bryk, A., Jacob, J., Easton, J. Q., & Allensworth, E. (1999, December). *Ending social promotion I: Results from the first two years.* Chicago, IL: Consortium on Chicago School Research.
Roderick, M., Nagaoka, J., Bacon, J., & Easton, J. Q. (2000, September). *Update: Ending social promotion: Passing, retention, and achievement trends among promoted and retained students 1995–1999.* Chicago, IL: Consortium on Chicago School Research.
Roderick, M., Jacob, B. A., & Bryk, A. S. (2002, Winter). The impact of high-stakes testing in Chicago on student achievement in promotional gate grades. *Educational Evaluation and Policy Analysis, 24,* 333–357.
Rothstein, R. (1998). *The way we were? The myths and realities of America's student achievement.* New York: Century Foundation Press.
Temple, J. A. (1998). Recent Clinton urban education initiatives and the role of school quality in metropolitan finance. *National Tax Journal, 51,* 517–529.
Temple, J. A., Reynolds, A. J., & Miedel, W. T. (2000) Can early intervention prevent high school dropout? Evidence from the Chicago Child-Parent Centers. *Urban Education, 35,* 31–56.
U. S. Department of Education, National Center for Education Statistics. (1996). *Urban schools: The challenge of location and poverty* (NCES Publication No. 96-184). Washington, DC: Author.

CHAPTER 4

IS GRADE RETENTION EDUCATIONAL MALPRACTICE?

Empirical Evidence from Meta-Analyses Examining the Efficacy of Grade Retention

Shane R. Jimerson

Research indicates, and common sense confirms, that passing students on to the next grade when they are unprepared neither increases student achievement nor properly prepares students for college and future employment. At the same time, research also shows that holding students back to repeat a grade (retention) without changing instructional strategies is ineffective. Much evidence suggests that the achievement of retained students still lags behind that of their peers after repeating a grade, making it an ineffective strategy for enabling students to catch up. Retention in grade also greatly increases the likelihood that a student will drop out of school—and being held back twice makes dropping out a virtual certainty. (U.S. Department of Education, 1999, p. 4)

Current trends appear to be moving toward increased retention rates as "standards" and "accountability" have received increased emphasis in the field of education. Despite conclusions over 30 years ago that retention is "an unjustifiable, discriminatory, and noxious" policy (Abidin, Golladay,

& Howerton, 1971, p. 410), grade retention has increased over the past 25 years (Hauser, Pager, & Simmons, 2000; McCoy & Reynolds, 1999; U.S. Department of Commerce, Bureau of Census, 1966, 1990). Estimates suggest that in the United States, 5 to 10% of students are retained annually—that translates to over 2.4 million children every year that must complete an extra year of schooling (Dawson, 1998a; Shepard & Smith, 1990). Research during the past decade indicates that by ninth grade 30% to 50% of students will be retained at least once (Alexander, Entwisle, & Kabbani, 1999; McCoy & Reynolds, 1999; Shepard & Smith, 1989). This meta-analysis emerges amidst a political zeitgeist characterized by repeated calls for an end to social promotion, and the recent development of educational policies related to legislation (e.g., *No Child Left Behind*) aimed at increasing standards and emphasizing accountability, which may result in more children being retained at grade level (U.S. Department of Education, 1999).

Considering the research and scholarly analysis examining the efficacy of grade retention and alternative educational intervention strategies during the past century, the results beg the question, is grade retention educational malpractice? The concept of educational malpractice emphasizes the responsibility of educational professionals to provide intervention strategies that are either promising or proven (based on empirical evidence) to be effective in facilitating student's academic success. While the methodological considerations limit unequivocal conclusions from any single study, the confluence of results from educational research warrants serious consideration. The following provides a brief synopsis of seminal reviews and meta-analyses of the retention literature, including the most recent systematic summary and meta-analysis of empirical studies published between 1990–1999 examining the efficacy of grade retention (Jimerson, 2001a).

OVERVIEW OF SEMINAL REVIEWS AND META-ANALYSES

Four seminal reviews capture much of the research spanning the first 9 decades of the twentieth century (1900–1999; Holmes, 1989; Holmes & Matthews, 1984; Jackson, 1975; Jimerson, 2001a). Based on a review of research during each of the respective periods, each concluded that the cumulative evidence does not support the use of grade retention as an academic intervention. A brief summary of these major reviews is provided in the following paragraphs. This synthesis includes the results from published meta-analyses of research examining outcomes associated with grade retention (Holmes, 1989; Holmes & Matthews, 1984; Jimerson, 2001a). In brief, meta-analysis is based on the concept of effect size

(*ES*; Cohen, 1988; Cooper & Hedges, 1994; Glass, 1978; Holmes, 1984). Calculation of effect sizes allows researchers to systematically pool results across studies. Thus, results from multiple studies may be included in order to examine the relative benefit of an educational intervention. Meta-analysis statistical procedures provide a measure of the difference between two groups that is expressed in quantitative units that are comparable across studies. Because each effect size is standardized relative to the comparison group standard deviation, it is possible to combine the results from different measures at different grade levels. Analyses resulting in a negative effect size suggest that an intervention (retention, in this case) had a negative or deleterious effect relative to the comparison groups of promoted students. When possible, quotations from these authors are used to convey the original statements without interpretation.

Jackson 1975 Systematic Review

Over 25 years ago, Jackson (1975) provided one of the first systematic reviews of research examining the efficacy of grade retention. This review included 30 studies published between 1911–1973.

> The purpose of this review was to determine, whether students who are doing poor academic work or who manifest emotional or social maladjustment in school are generally likely to benefit more from being retained in a grade than from being promoted to the next one. (Jackson, 1975, p. 615)

Jackson divided the studies into three groups based on their design type (naturalistic, pre-post, and experimental; see Jimerson, 2001a for a discussion of this review). Based on the systematic review, Jackson (1975) concludes:

> One general conclusion about the effects of grade retention relative to grade promotion is clearly warranted by all the results taken as a whole: There is no reliable body of evidence to indicate that grade retention is more beneficial than grade promotion for students with serious academic or adjustment difficulties. This is clearly indicated by the pattern of results from analyses using either of the two designs that investigated this comparison (Design I and III). This conclusion can be drawn by referring to the few results from the most valid analytical design, or by referring to the pattern of statistically and nonstatistically significant results of both designs. Thus, those educators who retain pupils in a grade do so without valid research evidence to indicate that such treatment will provide greater benefits to students with academic or adjustment difficulties than will promotion to the next grade. (p. 627)

Holmes and Matthews 1984 Meta-Analysis

Holmes and Matthews (1984) performed a meta-analysis exploring the effects of retention on elementary and junior high school students, including both achievement and socioemotional outcomes. This 1984 meta-analysis included 44 studies published between 1929 and 1981 (including 4,208 retained students and 6,924 regularly promoted students). Of these 44 studies, 18 included comparison samples matched on various combinations of IQ ($n = 12$), achievement tests ($n = 10$), socioeconomic status (SES; $n = 3$), gender, grades ($n = 1$), and other dimensions ($n = 13$). The Holmes and Matthews 1984 meta-analysis indicated statistically significant differences favoring the promoted students in each area of comparison (e.g., academic achievement, language arts, reading, mathematics, work study skills, social studies, personal adjustment, social adjustment, emotional adjustment, behavior, self-concept, attitude toward school, and attendance). The results of the meta-analysis indicated that overall, the retained students had lower academic achievement, poorer personal adjustment, lower self-concept, and held school in less favor than promoted students. The studies using a comparison group with matched students revealed similar results favoring promoted students. Based on the results of the meta-analysis, Holmes and Matthews (1984) concluded,

> Those who continue to retain pupils at grade level do so despite cumulative evidence showing that the potential for negative effects consistently outweighs positive outcomes. Because this cumulative research evidence consistently points to negative effects of nonpromotion, the burden of proof legitimately falls on proponents of retention plans to show there is compelling logic indicating success of their plans when so many other plans have failed. (p. 232)

Holmes 1989 Meta-Analysis

During the same decade, Holmes (1989) included 19 additional studies and completed another meta-analysis (using a total of 63 studies published between 1925–1989 to compare retained students to promoted students). Of the 63 studies in this review, 25 of these studies included matched participants (e.g., IQ, achievement, SES, gender, grades, and other variables). Holmes reported that 54 studies found overall negative effects associated with grade retention, including socioemotional maladjustment and lower academic achievement. Holmes reported that of the nine studies that yielded positive results, the benefits of retention appeared to diminish over time. For example, in these studies, students often demonstrate gains during the repeated year and sometimes the following year, however, subsequent comparisons across the years usually demonstrated no significant differences and sometimes favored the comparison group. Based on the results of the meta-analysis of 63 studies, Holmes (1989) concluded,

> When only well-matched studies were examined, a greater negative effect was found for retention than in the research literature as a whole. In studies where retained children and promoted controls matched on IQ and prior achievement, repeating a grade had an average negative effect of −.30 standard deviations. The weight of empirical evidence argues against grade retention. (p. 28)

Jimerson 2001 Systematic Review and Meta-Analysis

The most recent systematic review and meta-analysis examining the efficacy of grade retention was published in 2001. Following a systematic literature search, Jimerson (2001a) included 20 articles published between 1990–1999, totaling over 1,100 retained students and over 1,500 regularly promoted students. The studies also included samples from diverse geographic regions across the United States (see Figure 4.1). One of the key criteria for selection in the Jimerson (2001a) meta-analysis was that the study must have included an identifiable comparison group of promoted students. The Jimerson review indicated that comparison groups ranged from those with only one matched variable to those with students who were recommended for retention but were not retained and essentially matched on all variables considered (i.e., IQ, academic achievement, socioemotional adjustment, SES, and gender). Eighteen of the 20 studies included two or more matching variables. Across the 20 studies included, 45% matched on or controlled for IQ, 65% matched on or controlled for academic achievement, 30% matched on or controlled for socioemotional adjustment, 75% matched on or controlled for SES, and 70% matched on or controlled for gender. Most studies included only students retained during kindergarten, first, second, and third grades; however, a few included students retained kindergarten through eighth grade (Alexander, Entwisle, & Dauber, 1994; Gottfredson, Fink, & Graham, 1994; Hagborg, Masella, Palladino, & Shepardson, 1991; McCoy & Reynolds, 1999; Pierson & Connell, 1992). Most of the studies examined outcomes through grade 7, whereas five included outcomes during eighth grade and beyond. Of the 20 studies, the authors of 16 (80%) did not report favorable conclusions regarding the efficacy of grade retention intervention for academic achievement and socioemotional adjustment.

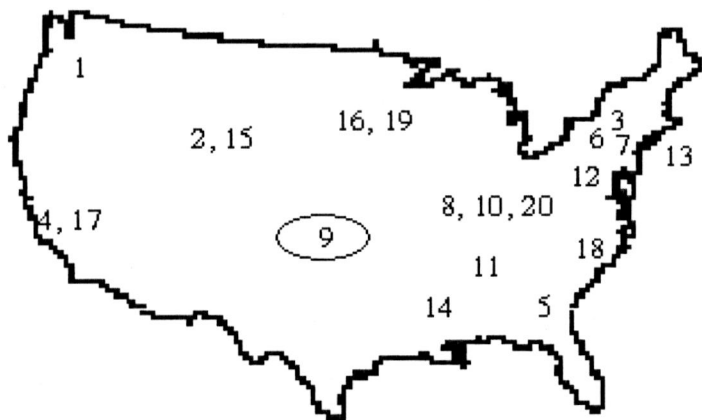

1 Sunnyside, WA (n = 20 & 17) (Johnson, Merrell, & Stover, 1990)
2 Uinita, WY (n = 46 & 20) (Ferguson, 1991)
3 Chatham, NY (n = 38 & 38) (Hagborg et al., 1991)
4 Marin, CA (n = 53 & 53) (Mantzicopoulos & Morrison, 1992)
5 Rural, GA (n = 31 & 31) (McCombs-Thomas et al., 1992)
6 NY (n = 24 & 24) (Phelps, Dowdell, Rizzo, Ehrlich, & Wilczenski, 1992)
7 Upstate, NY (n = 74 & 69) (Pierson & Connell, 1992)
8 Chicago, IL (n = 231 & 200) (Reynolds, 1992)
9 Nationwide, U.S. (n = 3,203 & 13,420) (Meisels & Liaw, 1993)
10 Chicago, IL (n = 1,255) (Reynolds & Bezruczko, 1993)
11 Metropolitan, TN (n = 60 & 60) (Rust & Wallace, 1993)
12 Baltimore, MD (n = 242 & 60) (Alexander, Entwisle, & Dauber, 1994)
13 RI (n = 25 & 17) (Dennebaum & Kulberg, 1994)
14 Southern Inner City (n = 197 & 204) (Gottfredson et al., 1994)
15 Uinita, WY (n = 33 & 14) (Ferguson & Mueller-Strieb, 1996)
16 Minneapolis, MN (n = 32 & 50) (Jimerson et al., 1997)
17 Marin, CA (n = 25 & 15) (Mantzicopoulos, 1997)
18 Charlottesville, VA (n = 49 & 52) (Pianta, Tietbohl, & Bennett, 1997)
19 Minneapolis, MN (n = 20 & 23) (Jimerson, 1999)
20 Chicago, IL (n = 315 & 843) (McCoy & Reynolds, 1999)

Parentheses indicate the number of retained students and matched comparison group students.

Figure 4.1. Distribution of retention samples included in published research 1990-1999 for each study included in the Jimerson 2001 meta-analysis.

Results of the meta-analysis indicated that overall, retained students had lower academic outcomes and more maladjusted socioemotional and behavioral outcomes, relative to the comparison group of promoted students. Based on the results of 20 studies published between 1990–1999, Jimerson concluded,

Studies examining the efficacy of early grade retention on academic achievement and socioemotional adjustment that have been published during the past decade report results that are consistent with the converging evidence and conclusions of research from earlier in the century that fail to demonstrate that grade retention provides greater benefits to students with academic or adjustment difficulties than does promotion to the next grade. (2001a, p. 27)

The discussion below includes effect sizes from the 83 studies published between 1925–1999 included in the three previous meta-analyses (Holmes, 1989; Holmes & Matthews, 1984; Jimerson, 2001a). Results of the meta-analyses and additional empirical research are used to examine the academic achievement, socioemotional adjustment, and high school dropout.

THE EFFECTS OF GRADE RETENTION ON ACADEMIC ACHIEVEMENT

The confluence of research results fails to demonstrate academic achievement advantages for retained students relative to comparison groups of low-achieving promoted peers. Holmes (1989) reported that 54 studies indicated negative achievement effects when retained children went on to the next grade level. Of nine studies that reported positive short-term achievement effects, the benefits were shown to diminish over time and disappear in later grades (Holmes, 1989). The overall effect sizes for academic achievement outcomes in the Holmes and Matthews (1984) and Holmes (1989) meta-analyses were −.44 and −.19 respectively (see Table 4.1). Jimerson (2001a) indicated that of the 175 analyses of academic achievement outcomes, nine resulted in significant statistical differences favoring the retained students and 82 resulted in significant statistical differences favoring the comparison group of low-achieving peers. Of the nine analyses favoring the retained students, six reflect differences during the repeated year (e.g., second year in kindergarten). While there were a few analyses that indicated achievement gains in the years immediately following the retention, these gains were not shown to be maintained at subsequent grade levels. The Jimerson meta-analysis yielded an overall average effect size across academic achievement outcomes of −.39, with a high of −.54 for mathematics and a low of −.18 for grade point average (see Table 4.1). Thus, results indicated that, overall, the retained group scored .39 of a standard deviation unit lower than the comparison promoted group. The results of the meta-analyses of nearly 700 analyses emerging from research during the past 75 years reveal consistent negative effects of grade retention on subsequent academic achievement.

Table 4.1. Summary of Mean Effect Sizes (*ES*) from Three Meta-analyses Examining the Outcomes of Studies Exploring the Efficacy of Grade Retention

	Jimerson (2001a)	Holmes (1989)	Holmes & Matthews (1984)
Overall Effect Size	−.31 [246]	−.15 [861]	−.37 [575]
Academic Achievement	−.39 [169]	−.19 [536]	−.44 [367]
Language Arts	−.36 [11]	−.16 [106]	−.40 [85]
Reading	−.54 [52]	−.08 [144]	−.48 [75]
Mathematics	−.49 [48]	−.11 [137]	−.33 [77]
Total/Composites	−.20 [13]	na	na
GPA	−.18 [45]	−.58 [4]	−.58 [4]
Socioemotional Adjustment	−.22 [77]	−.09 [234]	−.27 [142]
Social	−.08 [12]	−.09 [101]	−.27 [60]
Emotional	−.28 [13]	.03 [33]	−.37 [9]
Behavioral	−.11 [30]	−.13 [24]	−.31 [13]
Self-Concept	−.04 [16]	−.13 [45]	−.19 [34]
Adjustment Composite	−.15 [4]	na	na
Attitude Toward School	na	−.05 [39]	−.16 [26]
Attendance	−.65 [2]	−.18 [7]	−.12 [6]

Note. Negative numbers represent that results of analyses favored the matched comparison group of students relative to the retained students.
na = not available
Numbers in brackets indicate the number of effect sizes used in calculating the mean effect size.
Source. Table adapted from Jimerson (2001b) *The California School Psychologist* journal.

THE EFFECTS OF GRADE RETENTION ON SOCIOEMOTIONAL ADJUSTMENT

Relatively fewer studies have addressed the social and psychological adjustment outcomes of retained students; about 320 analyses are included in the meta-analyses. Considering over 40 studies including 234 analyses of socioemotional outcomes, Holmes (1989) concluded, on average the retained students display poorer social adjustment (−.09), attitudes toward school (−.05), attendance (−.18), and more problem behaviors (−.13) in comparison to matched controls (Table 4.1). Jimerson (2001a) reported that 16 studies yielded 148 analyses of socioemotional adjustment outcomes of retained students relative to a comparison group of students. Of these, eight resulted in statistical significance favoring the retained students and 13 were statistically significant favoring the comparison group. The overall average effect size across studies published between 1990–1999 was −.22. It is noted that those studies focusing on older children generally report poorer adjustment for retained students (Bachman, Green, & Wirtanen, 1971; Finlayson, 1975; Godfrey, 1972; Hubbell, 1981; Jimerson, 1999; Jimerson, Carlson, Rotert, Egeland, & Sroufe, 1997; Plummer & Graziano, 1987; Safer, 1986; White & Howard, 1973). In addition, related research indicates that many retained students have difficulties with their peers (Byrnes, 1989; Shepard & Smith, 1990). The author knows of no published research evidence of beneficial effects of grade retention on social and personal adjustment in junior high or high school.

In this era of emphasizing evidence-based educational intervention strategies, educational professionals should be prepared to present a summary of results from systematic, comprehensive reviews and meta-analyses of research examining the efficacy of grade retention, as this literature provides remarkably consistent results across the past 25 years (Holmes, 1989; Holmes & Matthews, 1984; Jackson, 1975; Jimerson, 2001a).

GRADE RETENTION AND LONG-TERM OUTCOMES

Few studies have examined long-term outcomes associated with grade retention. One such study is a 21-year longitudinal study examining outcomes through age 20 (Jimerson, 1999). The results of this 21-year prospective longitudinal study comparing retained students, low-achieving but promoted students, and a control group, revealed that retained students have a greater probability of poorer educational and employment outcomes during late adolescence. In particular, retained students had lower levels of academic adjustment at the end of 11th grade, were more likely to drop out of high school by age 19, were less likely to receive a diploma by age 20, were less likely to be enrolled in a postsecondary education program, received lower education/employment status ratings, were paid less per hour, and received poorer employment competence ratings at age 20 in comparison to a group of low-achieving students (Jimerson, 1999). In addition, the low-achieving promoted group was comparable to the control group on all employment outcomes at age 20. Results from other longitudinal samples yield similar findings, suggesting poorer long-term outcomes for retained students relative to a comparison group (Alexander, Entwisle, & Dauber, 2000; Sandoval & Fitzgerald, 1985; Temple, Reynolds, & Ou, 2000). The association of grade retention and subsequent dropout has received much attention in the past decade.

In their book reviewing research on grade retention, Shepard and Smith (1990) concluded, "Although grade retention is widely practiced, it does not help children to 'catch up.' Retained children may appear to do better in the short term, but they are at much greater risk for future failure than their equally achieving, nonretained peers" (p. 84). Studies examining the association of grade retention and dropping out of high school consistently have demonstrated that students who are retained are more likely to drop out of school prior to graduation than students who are not retained (Jimerson, Anderson, & Whipple, 2002). The striking association of grade retention and dropping out of high school recently led to the statement "we've won the battle but lost the war," in reference to the long-term outcomes of grade retention (Dawson, 1998b, p. 21). Moreover, dropping out is associated with numerous deleterious outcomes including fewer employment opportunities, substance abuse, and arrests (Cairns & Cairns, 1994; Catterall, 1987; Center for the Study of Social Policy, 1994; McDill, Natriello, & Pallas, 1986; Steinberg, Blinde, & Chan, 1984). School psychologists and others reviewing the efficacy of grade retention on academic success would benefit from awareness of the literature addressing the association between grade retention and dropping out.

Jimerson et al. (2002) provide a comprehensive review of dropout research that examines grade retention as a predictor variable. A systematic review of 17 studies examining dropping out of high school prior to graduation suggests that grade retention is one of the most powerful predictors of dropout status. In fact, all 17 found grade retention to be associated with subsequent dropout. Educational professionals, researchers, parents, and policymakers considering the efficacy of grade retention are encouraged to consider the implications of these findings. The research demonstrates that children retained during elementary school are at an increased risk of dropping out of high school (Jimerson et al., 2002). Tuck (1989) reported that up to 78% of dropouts were retained at least once, while other studies suggest that grade retention increases the risk of dropping out between 20% and 50% (Bachman, Green, & Wirtanen, 1971; Jimerson, 1999). Research suggests that retained students are 2 to 11 times more likely to drop out (Alexander, Entwisle, & Kabbani, 1999; Bachman et al., 1971; Cairns, Cairns, & Neckerman, 1989; Ensminger & Slusarick, 1992; Fine, 1989, 1991; Grissom & Shepard, 1989; Lloyd, 1978; McDill et al., 1986; Pallas, 1986; Roderick, 1994, 1995; Rumberger, 1987, 1995; Shepard & Smith, 1989, 1990; Stroup & Robins, 1972; Tuck, 1989). Grade retention has been identified as the single most powerful predictor of dropping out (Rumberger, 1995). Jimerson et al. (2002) provide a summary of each of the above studies. The empirical evidence indicates that repeating a grade provides few remedial benefits and is associated with a higher risk of dropping out of school (Jimerson, 1999, 2001b; Jimerson et al., 1997, 2002; Roderick, 1995). Educational professionals, researchers, and politicians reviewing the efficacy of grade retention on academic success would benefit from awareness of the literature addressing the association between grade retention and dropping out.

EMPIRICAL EVIDENCE AND RECENT LITERATURE REVIEWS

During the past decade, several authors have offered reports and perspectives addressing the efficacy of early grade retention (Biegler & Green, 1993; Dawson, 1998a; Foster, 1993; Karweit, 1992; Nason, 1991, Roderick, 1995; Shepard & Smith, 1990; Sherwood, 1993; Tanner & Combs, 1993; Tanner & Galis, 1997; Walters & Borgers, 1995). These recent reports do not attempt to examine all studies during a certain period, but rather it is typical that each includes highlights and conclusions from systematic reviews such as Jackson (1975) and Holmes (1989). Often these reports focus selectively on the results of only a handful of studies and discuss these results informally, thus, resulting in a limited summary of selected literature.

With the above caveat, it is noted that these reports consistently conclude that the practice of grade retention is ill advised as an educational intervention to facilitate academic success. Karweit (1992) reports there is consensus among recent extensive reviews of grade retention that grade retention does not positively affect academic achievement or student personal adjustment. Tanner and Combs (1993) discuss the disparity between the research and practice of grade retention, suggesting that many educational professionals are unaware of the results of research or choose to disregard studies in favor of their own beliefs regarding the efficacy of grade retention. Biegler and Green (1993) summarize selected retention literature and conclude that the evidence indicates retention provides little advantage for students and these studies clearly suggest that students exhibit greater academic progress when promoted with peers, and encourage educational professionals to find effective strategies to assist students. Foster (1993) presents much evidence against the practice of retaining children in grade and posits that failing children increases the likelihood that they will perform poorly in school, develop poor self-concepts, and eventually drop out of school.

Sherwood (1993) cautions against the practice of grade retention, concluding that research during the 1970s and 1980s indicates that grade-level retention produces little improvement in student achievement and discusses potential deleterious outcomes associated with retention (e.g., self-esteem, adjustment). Walters and Borgers (1995) present literature on elementary grade retention and report that most research indicated grade level retention did not increase academic achievement among low-achieving students, and suggest that policymakers and educators consider the cumulative research evidence.

Dawson (1998a) reported that

> No researcher has found long-term, substantial benefits to the practice of grade retention. No study has shown that students who are retained do better in high school or after high school than students who are not retained on any measure, even when controlling for important factors such as school achievement, ability, demographic variables, etc. (p. 29)

Alexander and colleagues (1999) conclude:

> Grade retention, especially plain vanilla grade repetition without supplemental services, should be a last recourse, not a first recourse. It is expensive (the cost of a year's pupil expenditures), it costs children a year of their lives, and it separates children from their age-mates, which under present organizational arrangements apparently creates problems for them later. (p.32)

Thus, the results yielded from recent reviews and meta-analyses provide converging *prima facia* evidence suggesting that a strong case could be made for grade retention as "educational malpractice" given that research has failed to demonstrate the effectiveness of grade retention as an academic intervention.

BEYOND GRADE RETENTION AND SOCIAL PROMOTION

Most educational professionals and researchers recognize that neither repeating a grade nor merely moving on to the next grade provides the necessary scaffolding to improve academic and social skills for students at risk of academic failure. Instead, it is necessary to implement and examine specific remedial strategies that can facilitate academic success. During the past decade, various publications have included reviews of current intervention strategies and specific suggestions to optimize student achievement trajectories (Forness, Kavale, Blum, & Lloyd, 1997). Thus, both scientists and practitioners are encouraged to consider the following information in developing and implementing empirically validated early intervention programs to assist children at risk of school failure. Although delineating all possible alternative intervention strategies and discussing assorted merits and limitations are beyond the scope of this chapter, examples of strategies supported in previous meta-analyses are presented below.

Emphasizing the importance of the cumulative evidence regarding various intervention strategies, educational professionals are encouraged to consider the results of recent meta-analyses examining the effectiveness of interventions in special education and related services that reveal several effective educational intervention strategies (Forness et al., 1997). Intervention strategies producing the most powerful effect sizes include: (a) mnemonic strategies (Mastropieri & Scruggs, 1989); (b) enhancing reading comprehension (Talbott, Lloyd, & Tankersley, 1994); (c) behavior modification (Skiba & Casey, 1985) and cognitive behavior modification (Robinson, Smith, Miller, & Brownell, 1999);) (d) direct instruction (White, 1988); (e) formative evaluation (Fuchs & Fuchs, 1986); (f) early intervention (Casto & Mastropieri, 1986); and (g) parental involvement (Fan & Chen, 2001). When demonstrating the effectiveness of an intervention, generally effect sizes (ES) of .40 and higher are considered significant.

Mnemonic Strategies

Results of meta-analyses indicate a very large positive effect for using mnemonic strategies (ES = 1.63; Mastropieri & Scruggs, 1989). Mnemonic strategies generally aim to enhance memory and have been found to improve students' organization of knowledge (clustering) and higher-order thinking (e.g., knowledge application involving inference making) with learned information (Dretzke & Levin, 1996). Such interventions are commonly used for learning vocabulary and processing text (Jones, Levin, Levin, & Beitzel, 2000) as well as for enhancing memory in other subject areas including science and history (Dretzke & Levin, 1996). Mnemonic strategies appear valuable for increasing both short-term and long-term recall. It is also reported that students have increased confidence in their knowledge of information that was learned using mnemonic strategies (Jones et al., 2000; Mastropieri & Scruggs, 1998).

Enhancing Reading Comprehension

Reading is an important skill for all subsequent knowledge acquisition and early reading programs have been found to contribute to higher student success (Slavin, Karweit, & Wasik, 1994; Slavin & Madden, 2001). Results of meta-analyses indicate that enhancing reading comprehension is another powerful intervention strategy to facilitate academic achievement (ES = 1.13; Talbott et al., 1994). Assisting students in the process of decoding and providing opportunities to practice reading are also valuable strategies and these results are supported in an additional meta-analysis that provides converging evidence (Mastropieri, Scruggs, Bakkeu, & Whedon, 1996).

Behavior Modification and Cognitive Behavior Modification

The use of behavior modification strategies has also been demonstrated as an effective intervention strategy with students whose behavior is interfering with their learning ($ES = .61$ and 1.57, behavior and academic outcomes, respectively; Skiba & Casey, 1985). Teaching self-evaluation and self-management of behaviors can be useful because it gives the student a sense of greater control over his or her behavior and the consequences thereof (Rathvon, 1999). While behavior modification focuses mostly on the overt behaviors, cognitive behavioral modification also addresses the underlying cognitions influencing the behaviors. Cognitive behavioral modification involves combining behavior approaches such as modeling, feedback, and reinforcement with cognitive approaches such as "cognitive think alouds" to teach strategies like anger control and self-coping. A recent meta-analysis reported that cognitive behavioral modification provided lasting effects in reducing hyperactivity-impulsivity and aggression ($ES = .71$; Robinson et al., 1999).

Direct Instruction

Meta-analysis of direct instruction strategies have also demonstrated positive effects on achievement ($ES = .84$; White, 1988). Traditional direct instruction includes seven basic principles: scripted presentations, small-group instruction, unison responding (during small group instruction), signals (to help pace students through lesson), pacing (fast-paced), corrections (rehearsal of corrected strategies), and praise (Engelmann & Carnine, 1982). Research with children who have mild handicaps has consistently supported the efficacy of this approach for increasing academic engaged time in reading and math (White, 1988).

Formative Evaluation

Meta-analytic review has also indicated that formative evaluation is associated with positive effects on achievement ($ES = .70$; Fuchs & Fuchs, 1986). Moreover, studies in this meta-analysis that included positive reinforcement and systematic ongoing assessment yielded robust effect sizes ($ES = 1.12$; Fuchs & Fuchs, 1986). The formative evaluation process involves the systematic ongoing evaluation and modification of teaching programs. While much of the research on formative evaluation has been conducted with special education students, formative evaluation may be used with regular education students as well. Formative evaluation allows for both teacher and student feedback so that the program can be modified if unsuccessful, or continued if successful.

Early Intervention

Meta-analysis of early intervention programs have been found to be associated with positive effects ($ES = .68$; Casto & Mastropieri, 1986). Many preschool intervention programs are aimed at assisting at-risk students in developing cognitive and social skills that will provide a foundation for learning in the early grades. Head Start and the Chicago Child-Parent Centers (CPC) are two such programs that provide early literacy instruction, as well as a range of individualized services in the areas of health, nutrition, and parent involvement that are designed to foster healthy development in low-income children. Results of evaluations vary; however, studies of the CPC indicate that participants experience a reduction in grade retention, a reduction in the rate of special education placement, and reduction in time spent receiving special education services through age 15. Based on the results of research evaluating early interventions starting in the preschool years, Zigler and Styfco (2000) emphasize the importance of (1) having clear standards for evaluation and (2) continuing to serve students throughout the primary grades.

Parental Involvement

Results of a recent meta-analysis also demonstrate the benefits of parental involvement ($ES = .25$; Fan & Chen, 2001). Parent involvement in school has consistently been found to lead to greater success among students (Christenson, 1995; Harrison, 1999; Swap, 1993). Weekly routine, structure and use of time out of school, homework practices, and family attitude toward the child's education are all factors that can affect a child's school performance (Sheridan & Kratochwill, 1992). Parent education can facilitate meaningful involvement to facilitate student's educational success.

Additional meta-analyses indicate less robust but positive effect sizes for computer assisted instruction ($ES = .52$; Schmidt, Weinsten, Niemic, & Walberg, 1986) and peer tutoring ($ES = .46$; Cook, Scruggs, Mastropieri, & Casto, 1986). Results of such educational research warrant further attention by educational professionals attempting to facilitate developmental and achievement trajectories of children. Although a detailed description of research-based interventions is beyond the scope of this chapter, the above suggestions offer an example of interventions that are supported by empirical evidence. Most studies of these intervention strategies have been among children receiving special services or low-achieving students, thus, there are direct implications for incorporating such strategies with students who may otherwise be retained at grade level.

Meta-analytic research has also provided evidence regarding intervention strategies that are not effective. For instance the Feingold diet (in which foods containing certain synthetic additives are restricted in an attempt to reduce hyperactivity) has been demonstrated as an intervention that does not work ($ES = .12$; Kavele & Forness, 1983). While clearly below the $ES = .40$ criteria, it is notable that the Feingold diet—which is dismissed by most educational professionals—and the available empirical evidence, has an average effect size of .12, in contrast to the $-.31$ overall effect size associated with grade retention in the most recent meta-analysis. As discussed above, meta-analysis of the reading outcomes of retained students indicate a $-.54$ effect size. Despite the empirical evidence regarding deleterious outcomes associated with grade retention, many educational professionals continue to retain students at grade level.

POLITICS, POLICIES, AND PROGRESS

During the past decade, political rhetoric and legislation continue to emphasize increased standards and accountability in the field of education. The ongoing emphasis on standards and accountability may provide an opportunity for educational professionals to secure resources to implement necessary strategies to promote achievement of at-risk students. Resources are necessary to assist children at risk of academic failure and it seems the current sociopolitical zeitgeist may provide leverage to yield such additional resources. In particular, as "academic excellence" emerges as a prominent national issue, it is important to accept the *responsibility* of facilitating the progress of students who do not meet district/school/state standards. Children in kindergarten, first, second, and third grade do not fail; their lack of academic success reflects the failure of adults to provide appropriate support and scaffolding to facilitate their early developmental and academic trajectories. Acknowledging basic principles of child development and early education, it is preposterous to imagine that children are failing to meet standards. Rather, advocating on behalf of children, it should be recognized that we as educational professionals, politicians, and parents have failed to adequately prepare these students to meet the standards. In short, when a student fails, adults have failed these children; thus, student failures are our failures. Simultaneously embracing a melioristic and realistic orientation, all educational professionals, families, and students must collaborate to insure that everything is done to facilitate student progress toward educational standards. Rather than focusing on whether or not to retain a child, educational professionals are encouraged to implement intervention strategies to facilitate student achievement.

The U.S. Department of Education (1999) published a guide for educators and state and federal leaders titled "Taking Responsibility for Ending Social Promotion." As reflected in the quote at the beginning of this chapter, and emphasized by Sandra Feldman of the American Federation of Teachers, "Neither social promotion nor holding kids back without help is a successful strategy for improving learning" (U.S. Department of Education, 1999, p. 4). The former United States Secretary of Education, Richard Riley, indicates that, "Taking responsibility for ending social promotion means ensuring that students have the opportunity and assistance they need to meet challenging standards" (U.S. Department of Education, 1999). This recent rhetoric underscores the importance of appropriate remedial strategies and emphasizes the responsibility of all educational professionals and families in facilitating achievement trajectories of these students.

In reviewing recent literature addressing social promotion, it has been striking that often "grade retention" could be substituted for "social promotion" and conclusions would remain the same. For instance, consider the quote above from the Secretary of Education, taking responsibility for ending *grade retention* also means ensuring that students have the opportunity and assistance they need to meet challenging standards. In addition, the content of former President Clinton's Memorandum (February 23, 1998, included in U.S. Department of Education, 1999) for the Secretary of Education addressing the subject of "Helping Schools End Social Promotions" is consistent with the basis for helping schools end *grade retention*. For example,

> In our efforts to promote higher standards and to lead to increased student achievement, the standards must count. Students must be required to meet them and schools must adequately prepare each student to do so.... Neither promoting students when they are unprepared nor simply retaining them in the same grade is the right response to low student achievement.... Ending social promotions by simply holding more students back is the wrong choice. Students who are required to repeat a year are more likely than other students to eventually drop out, and few catch up academically with their peers. The right approach is to ensure that more students are pre-

pared to meet challenging academic standards in the first place.... Schools must implement those proven strategies that will prepare students to meet rigorous standards the first time. (U.S. Department of Education, 1999, p. 1-2)

Too often educational professionals debate the merits and limitations of "social promotion" versus "grade retention." A more constructive discussion would focus on specific educational interventions to facilitate the education of children at risk of academic failure. Given the cumulative nature of development and considering the results of research in the fields of education, child development, and psychology, specific academic and socioemotional early education programs warrant further emphasis.

CONCLUSION

This chapter provides a review of all published meta-analyses that include research examining the academic and socioemotional outcomes associated with early grade retention. Results of the meta-analysis of studies published between 1990 and 1999 (Jimerson, 2001a) are consistent with meta-analyses of research published during the preceding 90 years (Holmes, 1989; Holmes & Matthews, 1985). The research fails to demonstrate that grade retention provides greater benefits to students with academic or adjustment difficulties than does promotion to the next grade. As we educate children in the new millennium, we must move beyond the question "to retain or not to retain?" Instead, researchers, educators, administrators, and legislators should commit to implement and investigate specific remedial intervention strategies designed to facilitate socioemotional adjustment and educational achievement of our nation's youth. It is time to move beyond the rhetoric regarding retention and social promotion, we are informed by nearly a century of research and we should embrace this knowledge to effectively educate children.

Given the research examining the effectiveness of grade retention and alternative educational intervention strategies during the past century, the results appear to beg the question, "Is grade retention educational malpractice?" Invoking the concept of "educational malpractice" emphasizes a standard of care in educating children and the responsibility of educational professionals to provide intervention strategies that are determined to be generally effective (or at least promising) in facilitating students' academic success. The use of grade retention as an academic intervention is particularly disconcerting given that (a) meta-analyses of grade retention consistently yield negative overall effects for both academic and social/emotional/behavioral outcomes (and meta-analyses of many alternative intervention strategies yield positive effects) and (b) students of ethnic minority and low socioeconomic (SES) backgrounds are retained at higher rates (Hauser et al., 2000).

Research indicates that those children from the most disadvantaged backgrounds are the most likely to be retained as an intervention to address academic, social, or behavioral problems. Research also reveals that students experiencing the most deleterious outcomes following grade retention are those with the lowest achievement and poorest social skills prior to retention (Ferguson, Jimerson, & Dalton, 2001). Thus, it could be said that those children who are in greatest need, suffer the most when experiencing grade retention. Essentially, in the absence of specific interventions designed to address the individual needs of the student, academic success and positive adjustment are unlikely. Whereas 30 years ago educational researchers declared grade retention to be "an unjustifiable, discriminatory, and noxious" intervention (Abidin, Golladay, & Howerton, 1971, p. 410), considering the results of research failing to support grade retention as an academic intervention, and the evidence indicating positive effects of other educational interventions, in addition to the disproportionate use of grade retention among children of ethnic minority and low SES backgrounds, one could argue that the continued use of grade retention is educational malpractice.

REFERENCES

Abidin, R. R., Golladay, W. M., & Howerton, A. L. (1971). Elementary school retention: An unjustifiable, discriminatory, and noxious policy. *Journal of School Psychology, 9,* 410–414.

Alexander, K., Entwisle, D., & Dauber, S. (1994). *On the success of failure: A reassessment of the effects of retention in the primary grades.* New York: Cambridge University Press.

Alexander, K., Entwisle, D., & Dauber, S. (2000, October). *Dropout in relation to grade retention: An accounting from the beginning school study.* Paper presented at the National Invitational Conference hosted by the Laboratory for Student Success at Temple University Center for Research in Human Development and Education, Alexandria, VA.

Alexander, K., Entwisle, D., & Kabbani, N. (1999, November). *Grade retention, social promotion, and "third way" alternatives.* Paper presented at the National Invitational Conference hosted by the Laboratory for Student Success at Temple University for Center for Research in Human Development and Education, Alexandria, VA.

Bachman, J., Green, S., & Wirtanen, I. (1971). *Dropping out: Problem or symptom?* Ann Arbor, MI: Institute for Social Research.

Biegler, C. D., & Green, V. P. (1993). Grade retention: A current issue. *Early Child Development & Care, 84,* 117–122.

Byrnes, D. (1989). Attitudes of students, parents, and educators toward repeating a grade. In L. A. Shepard & M. L. Smith (Eds.), *Flunking grades: Research and policies on retention* (pp. 16–33). London: Falmer Press.

Cairns, R., & Cairns, B. (1994). *Lifelines and risks: Pathways of youth in our time.* Cambridge, England: Cambridge University Press.

Cairns, R., Cairns, B., & Neckerman, H. (1989). Early school dropout: Configurations and determinants. *Child Development, 60,* 1437–1452.

Casto, G., & Mastropieri, M. A. (1986). The efficacy of early intervention programs: A meta-analysis. *Exceptional Children, 52,* 417–424.

Catterall, J. (1987). On the social costs of dropping out of school. *High School Journal, 71,* 19–30.

Center for the Study of Social Policy. (1994). *Kids count data: State profiles of child well-being.* Washington, DC: U.S. Government Printing Office.

Christenson, S. L. (1995). Supporting home-school collaboration. In A. Thomas & J. Grimes (Eds.), *Best practices in school psychology III* (pp. 253–268). Washington, DC: National Association of School Psychologists.

Cohen, J. (1988). *Statistical power analysis for the behavioral sciences* (2nd ed.). Hillsdale, NJ: Erlbaum.

Cook, S. B., Scruggs, T. E., Mastropieri, M. A., & Casto, G. C. (1986). Handicapped students as tutors. *Journal of Special Education, 19,* 486–492.

Cooper, H., & Hedges, L. V. (1994). *The handbook of research synthesis.* New York: Sage.

Dawson, P. (1998a). A primer on student grade retention: What the research says. *Communique', 26*(8), 28–30.

Dawson, P. (1998b). A review of the book *On the success of failure: A reassessment of the effects of retention in the primary grades. Communique', 26*(8), 20–21.

Dennebaum, J. M., & Kuhlberg, J. M. (1994). Kindergarten retention and transition classrooms: Their relationship to achievement. *Psychology in the Schools, 31,* 5–12.

Dretzke, B. J., & Levin, J. R. (1996). Assessing students' application and transfer of a mnemonic strategy: The struggle for independence. *Contemporary Educational Psychology, 21,* 83–93.

Engelmann, S., & Carnine, D. (1982). *Theory of instruction: Principles and applications.* New York: Irvington.

Ensminger, M., & Slusarick, A. (1992). Paths to high school graduation or dropout: A longitudinal study or a first grade cohort. *Sociology of Education, 65,* 95–113.

Fan, X., & Chen, M. (2000). Parental involvement and students' academic achievement: A meta-analysis. *Educational Psychology Review, 13,* 1–22.

Ferguson, P. (1991). Longitudinal outcome differences among promoted and transitional at-risk kindergarten students. *Psychology in the Schools, 28,* 139–146.

Ferguson, P., Jimerson, S. R., & Dalton, M. (2001). Sorting out successful failures: Exploratory analyses of factors associated with academic and behavioral outcomes of retained students. *Psychology in the Schools, 38,* 327–342

Ferguson, P., & Mueller-Streib, M. (1996). Longitudinal outcome effects of non-at-risk and at-risk transition first-grade samples: A follow-up study and further analysis. *Psychology in the Schools, 33,* 38–45.

Fine, M. (1989). Why urban adolescents drop out of public high school. *Teachers College Record, 87,* 393–409.

Fine, M. (1991). *Framing dropouts: Notes on the politics of an urban public high school.* Albany, NY: State University of New York Press.

Finlayson, H. J. (1975). *The effect of non-promotion upon the self concept of pupils in primary grades.* Unpublished doctoral dissertation, Temple University.

Forness, S. R., Kavale, K. A., Blum, I. M., & Lloyd, J. W. (1997, July/August). Mega-analysis of meta-analyses: What works in special education and related services. *Teaching Exceptional Children, 29,* 4–9.

Foster, J. (1993). Reviews of research: Retaining children in grade. *Childhood Education, 70,* 38–43.

Fuchs, L. A., & Fuchs, D. (1986). Effects of systematic formative evaluation: A meta-analysis. *Exceptional Children, 53,* 199–208.

Glass, G. (1978). Integrating findings: The meta-analysis of research. *Review of Research in Education, 5,* 351–379.

Godfrey, E. (1972). The tragedy of failure: Results of a North Carolina survey. *Education Digest, 37,* 34–35.

Gottfredson, D. C., Fink, C. M., & Graham, N. (1994). Grade retention and problem behavior. *American Educational Research Journal, 31,* 761–784.

Grissom, J., & Shepard, L. (1989). Repeating and dropping out of school. In L. A. Shepard & M. L. Smith (Eds.), *Flunking grades: Research and policies on retention* (pp. 16–33). London: Falmer Press.

Hagborg, W. J., Masella, G., Palladino, P., & Shepardson, J. (1991). A follow-up study of high school students with a history of grade retention. *Psychology in the Schools, 28,* 310–317.

Harrison, P. (Ed.). (1999). Beginning school ready to learn: Parental involvement and effective educational programs [Special issue]. *School Psychology Review, 28.*

Hauser, R., Pager, D., & Simmons, S. (2000, October). *Dropout in relation to grade retention: An accounting from the beginning school study.* Paper presented at the National Invitational Conference hosted by the Laboratory for Student Success at Temple University Center for Research in Human Development and Education, Alexandria, VA.

Holmes, C. T. (1984). Effect size estimation in meta-analysis. *Journal of Experimental Education, 52,* 106–109.

Holmes, C. T. (1989). Grade-level retention effects: A meta-analysis of research studies. In L. A. Shepard & M. L. Smith (Eds.), *Flunking grades: Research and policies on retention* (pp. 16–33). London: Falmer Press.

Holmes, C. T., & Matthews, K. M. (1984). The effects of nonpromotion on elementary and junior high school pupils: A meta-analysis. *Reviews of Educational Research, 54,* 225–236.

Hubbell, B. A. (1981). Grade retention policies at the elementary school level. *Dissertation Abstracts International, 41,* 2932A. (UMI No. 81-02736)

Jackson, G. (1975). The research evidence on the effects of grade retention. *Review of Educational Research, 45,* 613–635.

Jimerson, S. (1999). On the failure of failure: Examining the association of early grade retention and late adolescent education and employment outcomes. *Journal of School Psychology, 37*, 243–272.

Jimerson, S. R. (2001a). Meta-analysis of grade retention research: Implications for practice in the 21st century. *School Psychology Review, 30*, 420–437.

Jimerson, S. R. (2001b). A synthesis of grade retention research: Looking backward and moving forward. *The California School Psychologist, 6*, 46–59.

Jimerson, S. R., Anderson, G. E., & Whipple, A. D. (2002). Winning the battle and losing the war: Examining the relation between grade retention and dropping out of high school. *Psychology in the Schools, 39*, 441–457.

Jimerson, S., Carlson, E., Rotert, M., Egeland, B., & Sroufe, L. A. (1997). A prospective, longitudinal study of the correlates and consequences of early grade retention. *Journal of School Psychology, 35*, 3–25.

Johnson, E. R., Merrell, K. W., & Stover, L. (1990). The effects of early grade retention on the academic achievement of fourth-grade students. *Psychology in the Schools, 27*, 333–338.

Jones, M. S., Levin, M. E., Levin, J. R., & Beitzel, B. D. (2000). Can vocabulary-learning strategies and pair-learning formats be profitably combined? *Journal of Educational Psychology, 92*, 256–262.

Karweit, N. (1992). Retention Policy. In M. Alkin (Ed.), *Encyclopedia of educational research* (pp. 1114–1118). New York: Macmillan.

Kavale, K. A., & Forness, S. R. (1983). Hyperactivity and diet treatment: A meta-analysis of the Feingold hypothesis. *Journal of Learning Disabilities, 16*, 324–330.

Lloyd, D. (1978). Prediction of school failure from third-grade data. *Educational and Psychological Measurement, 38*, 1193–1200.

Mantzicopoulos, P. (1997). Do certain groups of children profit from early grade retention? *Psychology in the Schools, 34*, 115–127.

Mantzicopoulos, P., & Morrison, D. (1992). Kindergarten retention: Academic and behavioral outcomes through the end of the second grade. *American Educational Research Journal, 29*, 182–198.

Mastropieri, M. A., & Scruggs, T. E. (1989). Constructing more meaningful relations: Mnemonic instruction for special populations. *Educational Psychology Review, 1*(2), 83–111.

Mastropieri, M. A., & Scruggs, T. E. (1998). Constructing more meaningful relationships in the classroom: Mnemonic research into practice. *Learning Disabilities Research & Practice, 13*, 138–145.

Mastropieri, M. A., Scruggs, T. E., Bakkeu, J. P., & Whedon, C. (1998). Reading comprehension: A synthesis of research in learning disabilities. In T. Scruggs & M. Mastropieri (Eds.), *Advances in learning and behavioral disabilities* (Vol. 10, pp. 277–303). Greenwich, CT: JAI Press.

McCombs-Thomas, A., Armistead, L., Kempton, T., Lynch, S., Forehand, R., Nousianen, S., Neighbors, B., & Tannenbaum, L. (1992). Early retention: Are there long term beneficial effects? *Psychology in the Schools, 29*, 342–347.

McCoy, A. R., & Reynolds, A. J. (1999). Grade retention and school performance: An extended investigation. *Journal of School Psychology, 37*(3), 273–298.

McDill, E., Natriello, G., & Pallas, A. (1986). A population at risk: Potential consequences of tougher school standards for student dropouts. *American Journal of Education, 94,* 135–181.

Meisels, S. J., & Liaw, F. R. (1993). Failure in grade: Do retained students catch up? *Journal of Educational Research, 87,* 69–77.

Nason, B. (1991). Retaining children: Is it the right decision? *Childhood Education, 67,* 300–304.

Pallas, A. (1986). School dropouts in the United States. In J. Stern & M. Williams (Eds.), *The condition of education: Statistical report from the Center for Educational Statistics* (pp. 158–174). Washington, DC: U.S. Government Printing Office.

Pianta, R. C., Tietbohl, P. J., & Bennett, E. M. (1997). Differences in social adjustment and classroom behavior between children retained in kindergarten and groups of age and grade matched peers. *Early Education and Development, 8,* 137–152.

Pierson, L., & Connell, J. (1992). Effect of grade retention on self-system processes, school engagement and academic performance. *Journal of Educational Psychology, 84,* 300–307.

Phelps, L., Dowdell, N., Rizzo, F. G., Ehrlich, P., & Wilczenski, F. (1992). Five to ten years after placement: The long-term efficacy of retention and pre-grade transition. *Journal of Psychoeducational Assessment, 10,* 116–123.

Plummer, D. L., & Graziano, W. G. (1987). Impact of grade retention on the social development of elementary school children. *Developmental Psychology, 23,* 267–275.

Rathvon, N. (1999). *Effective school interventions: Strategies for enhancing academic achievement and social competence.* New York: Guilford.

Reynolds, A. J. (1992). Grade retention and school adjustment: An exploratory analysis. *Educational Evaluation and Policy Analysis, 14,* 101–121.

Reynolds, A. J., & Bezruczko, N. (1993). School adjustment of children at risk through fourth grade. *Merrill Palmer Quarterly, 39,* 457–480.

Robinson, T. R., Smith, S. W., Miller, M. D., & Brownell, M. T. (1999). Cognitive behavior modification of hyperactivity-impulsivity and aggression: A meta-analysis of school-based studies. *Journal of Educational Psychology, 91,* 195–203.

Roderick, M. (1994). Grade retention and school dropout: Investigating the association. *American Educational Research Journal, 31,* 729–759.

Roderick, M. (1995). Grade retention and school dropout: Policy debate and research questions. *The Research Bulletin, 15,* 88–92.

Rumberger, R. (1987). High school dropouts: A review of issues and development. *Review of Educational Research, 57,* 101–121.

Rumberger, R. (1995). Dropping out of middle school: A multilevel analysis of students and schools. *American Educational Research Journal, 32,* 583–625.

Rust, J., & Wallace, K. (1993). Effects of grade level retention for four years. *Journal of Instructional Psychology, 20*(2), 162–166.

Safer, D. J. (1986). Nonpromotion correlates and outcomes at different grade levels. *Journal of Learning Disabilities, 19*(8), 500–503.

Sandoval, J., & Fitzgerald, P. (1985). A high school follow-up of children who were promoted or attended a junior first grade. *Psychology in the Schools, 22,* 164–170.

Schmidt, M., Weinstein, T., Niemic, R., & Walberg, H. J. (1985–1986). Computer-assisted instruction with exceptional children. *Journal of Special Education, 19,* 497–509.

Shepard, L. S., & Smith, M. L. (1989). *Flunking grades: Research and policies on retention.* London: Falmer Press.

Shepard, L. S., & Smith, M. L. (1990). Synthesis of research on grade retention. *Educational Leadership, 47*(8), 84–88.

Sheridan, S. M., & Kratochwill, T. R. (1992). Behavioral parent-teacher consultation: Conceptual and research considerations. *Journal of School Psychology, 30,* 117–139.

Sherwood, C. (1993). *Retention in grade: Lethal lessons.* Available: www.edrs.com (ERIC Document Reproduction Service No. ED361122)

Skiba, R., & Casey, A. (1985). Interventions for behaviorally disordered students: A quantitative review and methodological critique. *Behavioral Disorders, 10,* 239–252.

Slavin, R. E., Karweit, N. L., & Wasik, B. A. (1994). *Preventing early school failure: Research, policy, and practice.* Boston: Allyn & Bacon.

Slavin, R. E., & Madden, N. A. (2001). *One million children: Success for all.* Thousand Oaks, CA: Corwin Press.

Steinberg, L., Blinde, P., & Chan, K. (1984). Dropping out among language minority youth. *Review of Educational Research, 54,* 113–132.

Stroup, A., & Robins, L. (1972). Elementary school predictors of high school dropout among black males. *Sociology of Education, 45,* 212–222.

Swap, S. M. (1993). *Developing home-school partnerships: From concepts to practice.* New York: Teachers College Press.

Talbott, E., Lloyd, J. W., & Tankersley, M. (1994). Effects of reading comprehension interventions for students with learning disabilities. *Learning Disability Quarterly, 17,* 223–232.

Tanner, C. K., & Combs, F. E. (1993). Student retention policy: The gap between research and practice. *Journal of Research in Childhood Education, 8,* 69–77.

Tanner, C. K., & Galis, S. A. (1997). Student retention: Why is there a gap between the majority of research findings and school practice? *Psychology in the Schools, 34,* 107–114.

Temple, J., Reynolds, A., & Ou, S. (2000, October). *Grade retention and school dropout: Another look at the evidence.* Paper presented at the National Invitational Conference hosted by the Laboratory for Student Success at Temple University Center for Research in Human Development and Education, Alexandria, VA.

Tuck, K. (1989, April). *A study of students who left: DC public school dropouts.* Paper presented at the meeting of the American Educational Research Association, San Francisco, CA.

U.S. Department of Commerce, Bureau of the Census. (1966). *Current population reports. School enrollment: Social and economic characteristics of students.* Washington, DC: U.S. Government Printing Office.

U.S. Department of Commerce, Bureau of the Census. (1990). *Current population reports. School enrollment: Social and economic characteristics of students.* Washington, DC: U.S. Government Printing Office.

U.S. Department of Education. (1999). *Taking responsibility for ending social promotion: A guide for educators and state and local leaders*. Washington, DC: U.S. Government Printing Office.
Walters, D. M., & Borgers, S. B. (1995). Student retention: Is it effective? *School Counselor, 42,* 300–310.
White, W. A. T. (1988). A meta-analysis of effects of direct instruction in special education. *Education and Treatment of Children, 11,* 364–374.
White, K., & Howard, J. (1973). Failure to be promoted and self-concept among elementary school children. *Elementary School Guidance and Counseling, 7,* 182–187.
Zigler, E., & Styfco, S. J. (2000). Pioneering steps (and fumbles) in developing a federal preschool intervention. *Topics in Early Childhood Education, 20*(2), 67–70, 78.

CHAPTER 5

RACE-ETHNICITY, SOCIAL BACKGROUND, AND GRADE RETENTION[1]

Robert M. Hauser, Devah I. Pager, and Solon J. Simmons

Despite the visible popularity of policies "to end social promotion," little is known about the prevalence of grade retention in American schools or about the effects of race-ethnicity and other social and economic background characteristics on retention. Age-grade retardation has been common and growing in American schools from the 1970s through the 1990s. Our analysis focuses on the period from 1972 to 1998 and on grade retardation across ages 6, 9, 12, 15, and 17. By age 9, the odds of grade-retardation among African American and Hispanic youth are 50% larger than among White youth, but these differentials are almost entirely explained by social and economic deprivation among minority youth, along with unfavorable geographic location. Because rates of age-grade retardation have increased at the same time that social background characteristics of students have become more favorable to rapid progress through school, the observed trend toward more age-grade retardation substantially understates growth in the tendency to hold students back in school. While there is presently little evidence of direct race-ethnic discrimination in progress through the elementary and secondary grades, the recent movement toward high-stakes testing for promotion could magnify race-ethnic differentials in retention.

Recent proposals for test-based grade promotion and retention are based on politically attractive, but scientifically unsupported claims about the benefits of retention, and minority students are more likely to be subject to them. Sound bites about "ending social promotion" are appealing to politicians and to the general public. Sound data about rates, trends, and differentials in grade retention are scarce (Hauser, 2001), and current retention rates are much higher than is generally believed.

AGE-GRADE RETARDATION AND GRADE RETENTION

Age-grade retardation refers to enrollment below the modal grade level for a child's age (and no broader meaning is either intended or implied); from national data on *age-grade retardation*, it is possible to draw inferences about *grade retention* practices. The best current source of information on national levels, trends, and differentials in age-grade retardation is the Current Population Survey (CPS) of the U.S. Bureau of the Census—the same large monthly household survey that provides estimates of the unemployment rate. Using the annual October School Enrollment Supplement of the CPS, it is possible to track the distribution of school enrollment by age and grade each year for groups defined by sex and race/ethnicity. These data have the advantage of comparable national coverage from year to year, but they say nothing directly about educational transitions. We can only infer the minimum rate of grade retention by observing changes in the enrollment of children below the modal grade level for their age in successive cross-sectional surveys. Suppose, for example, that 10% of 6-year-old children were enrolled below the first grade in October of 1994. If 15% of 7-year-old children were enrolled below the second grade in October of 1995, we would infer that at least 5% of children had been held back in the first grade between 1994 and 1995.

At least 15% of pupils are retained between ages 6 to 8 and ages 15 to 17, and a large share of retention occurs either before or after those ages (Hauser, 2001; National Research Council, Committee on Appropriate Test Use, 1999). The recent history of age-grade retardation is summarized in Figure 5.1. It shows age-grade retardation at ages 6 to 8, 9 to 11, 12 to 14, and 15 to 17 among children who reached ages 6 to 8 between 1962 and 1996. We have organized the data by year of birth (birth cohort), rather than by calendar year, so it is possible to see the evolution of age-grade retardation throughout the schooling of a birth cohort, as well as changes in age-grade retardation rates from year to year.[2] The horizontal axis shows the year in which an age group reached ages 6 to 8, so vertical comparisons among the trend lines at a given year show how age-grade retardation cumulated as a birth cohort grew older.

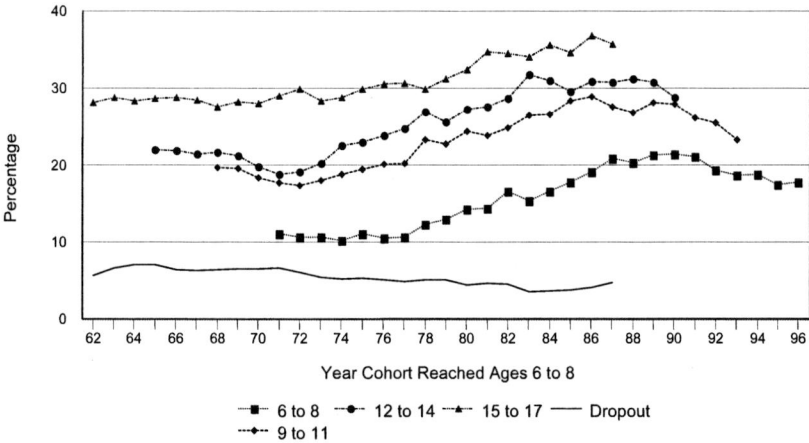

Figure 5.1. Percentage of children enrolled below modal grade for age by age group and year in which cohort was 6 to 8 years old.

For example, consider children who were 6 to 8 years old in 1987—the most recent cohort whose history can be traced all the way from ages 6 to 8 up through ages 15 to 17. At ages 6 to 8, 20.9% were enrolled below the modal grade for their age. By 1990, when this cohort reached ages 9 to 11, age-grade retardation grew to 27.6%, and it was 30.8% in 1995, when the cohort reached ages 12 to 14. By 1996, when the cohort reached ages 15 to 17, 35.8% were either below the modal grade level or had left school. Almost all of the growth in retardation after ages 12 to 14, however, was due to dropout (4.8%), rather than grade retention among the enrolled.

One could think of the rate of enrollment below the modal grade at ages 6 to 8 as a baseline measure, that is, as if it did not necessarily indicate that grade retention had taken place. Relative to that baseline, increases in enrollment below the modal grade at older ages clearly show the net effects of retention in grade. This reading of the data would suggest that, in most birth cohorts, retention occurs mainly between ages 6 to 8 and 9 to 11 or between ages 12 to 14 and 15 to 17.[3] This way of looking at the data surely understates the prevalence of grade retention, for it often takes place at or below ages 6 to 8 (Hauser, 2001, 2004.

The series for ages 15 to 17 includes early school dropout, which is also shown as a separate series along the bottom of the figure. Dropout, rather than retention, evidently accounts for a substantial share of the increase in age-grade retardation between ages 12 to 14 and ages 15 to 17.

The *trend* in age-grade retardation at ages 6 to 8, 9 to 11, 12 to 14, and 15 to 17 can be read across Figure 5.1 from left to right. Age-grade retardation increased in every age group from cohorts of the early 1970s through those of the middle to late 1980s. Age-grade retardation increased at ages 15 to 17 after the mid-1970s despite a slow decline in its early school dropout component throughout the period. That is, grade retention increased while dropout decreased. Among cohorts entering school after 1970, the percentage enrolled below the modal grade level was never less than 10% at ages 6 to 8, and it exceeded 20% for cohorts of the late 1980s. The trend-lines suggest that age-grade retardation has declined slightly for cohorts entering school after the mid-1980s, but rates have not approached the much lower levels of the early 1970s. Overall, a large share of each birth cohort now experiences grade retention during elementary school. Among children aged 6 to 8 from 1982 to 1992, age-grade retardation reached 25 to 30% by ages 9 to 11.

SOCIAL DIFFERENTIALS IN AGE-GRADE RETARDATION

While there are similarities in the age pattern of grade retardation among major population groups—boys and girls and majority and minority groups—there are also substantial differences among them, many of which develop well after school entry. The gender differential gradually increases with age from five percentage points at ages 6 to 8 to 10 percentage points at ages 15 to 17 (Hauser, 2001). As shown in Figure 5.2, the odds that a boy is below grade level are 40% greater than for a girl at age 6, 50% greater at age 9, and 70% greater by age 17. That is, boys are initially more likely than girls to be placed below the modal grade for their age, and they fall further behind girls as they pass through childhood and adolescence.

The differentiation of age-grade relationships by race and ethnicity is even more striking than that by gender. Figure 5.3 shows the development of age-grade retardation by race/ethnicity from age 6 to age 17. Here, unlike the case of gender differentiation, the rates of age-grade retardation are not exceptionally different among Whites, Blacks, and Hispanics at age 6. In fact, Blacks are *less* likely than Whites to be enrolled below the first grade at age 6. However, by age 9 the odds of enrollment below the modal grade level are almost 50% higher among Blacks or Hispanics than among Whites. The differentials continue to grow with age, and at ages 15 to 17, rates of grade retardation range from 40 to 50% among Blacks and Hispanics, while they have gradually drifted up from 25 to 35% among Whites. By age 17, the odds of age-grade retardation are about 150% higher among Blacks or Hispanics than among Whites.

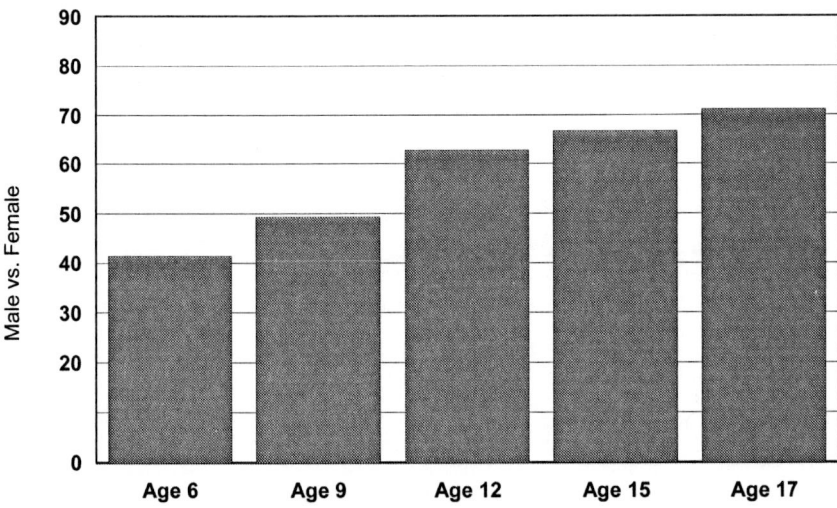

Figure 5.2. Gender differences in odds of age-grade retardation, 1972–1998.

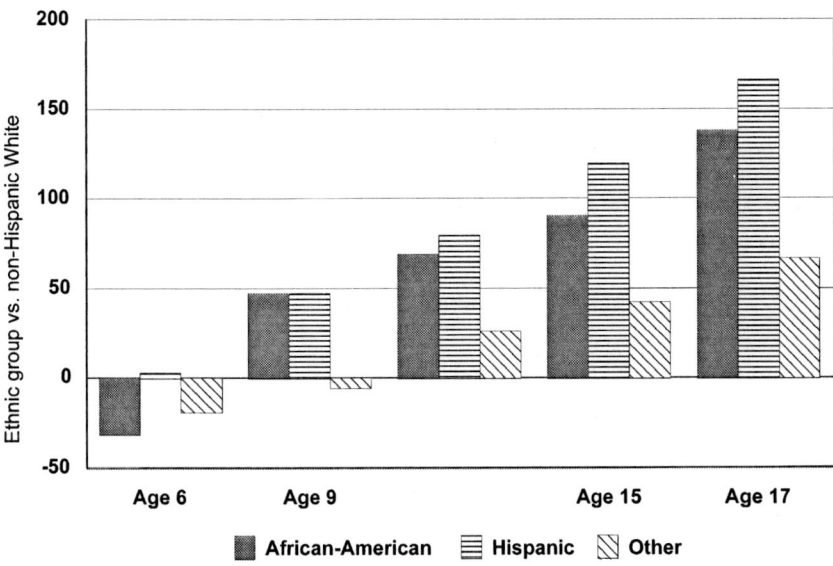

Figure 5.3. Race-ethnic differences in odds of age-grade retardation, 1972–1998.

At older ages, the differential in age-grade between Hispanics and Blacks, favoring the latter, is probably explained by high rates of early school dropout among Hispanics. There is almost no difference in the dropout rates of Whites and Blacks,[4] but Hispanics are much more likely to leave school at an early age. Thus, early high school dropout contributes very little to the observed difference in age-grade retardation between Blacks and Whites.

Gender and race-ethnic differentials in age-grade retardation, as early as age 9, are a consequence of school experience and not primarily of differentials in age at school entry. Social differentials in age-grade relationships are vague at school entry, but a hierarchy is clearly established by age 9, and it persists and grows through the end of secondary schooling. This growth can only be explained by grade-retention. By age 9, there are sharp social differentials in age-grade retardation, favoring Whites and girls relative to Blacks or Hispanics and boys. By ages 15 to 17, close to 50% of Black males have fallen behind in school—30% more than at ages 6 to 8—but age-grade retardation has never exceeded 30% among White girls of the same age. If these rates and differentials in age-grade retardation are characteristic of a schooling regime in which social promotion is perceived to be the norm, it is cautionary to imagine what we might observe when that norm has been eliminated.

SOCIAL BACKGROUND AND AGE-GRADE RETARDATION

While the disproportionate rates of grade retention among minorities are both large and of long standing (Hauser, 2001; National Research Council, Committee on Appropriate Test Use, 1999; U.S. Bureau of the Census, 1979), relatively little research has focused on the role that socioeconomic and family differences between population groups play in accounting for those differences. At the national level, one can look back only to a few simple tabulations from the 1976 Survey of Income and Education (U.S. Bureau of the Census, 1979) and to an exploratory—but exemplary—analysis of family background and age-grade retardation in the October Current Population Survey of 1979 (Bianchi, 1984). Both of these analyses suggest that social and economic background, rather than minority status per se, accounts for a large share of group differences in retention.

Using data from 27 October Current Population Surveys in 1972 to 1998, we report analyses of race-ethnic and socioeconomic differentials in age-grade retardation among 6-, 9-, 12-, 15-, and 17-year-olds. These ages span the period between normative entry to graded school and the later years of high school, but do not extend to ages where a substantial minority of youth no longer live in parental or quasi-parental households.[5] At these ages, the modal October grade levels are 1, 4, 7, 10, and 12. By looking at several ages, we observe typical developmental patterns of retention and of differentials in retention. From 1972 to 1998, the October CPS data files include between 57,500 and 63,500 cases at each age (Hauser & Hauser, 1993; Hauser, Jordan, & Dixon, 1993). For each youth in the sample, we know sex, race-ethnicity, enrollment status, grade level, region of residence, and metropolitan location.[6] Also, we have linked several relevant social and economic characteristics of the household and householders to each child or youth's record: family income, number of children in the household, single-parent household, education of household head and of spouse of head, head or spouse without an occupation, occupation of household head and of spouse of head, and home ownership.

SOCIAL BACKGROUND, RESIDENTIAL LOCATION, AND AGE-GRADE RETARDATION

In order to analyze differentials and trends in age-grade retardation in more detail, we have carried out logistic regression analyses of enrollment below modal grade level versus enrollment at or above modal grade level. We omit the details of these analyses and report only six major findings: effects of maternal education, single-parent household, family income, home tenure, metropolitan status, and regional location.

Maternal Educational Attainment

Figure 5.4 shows the effect of each year of a mother's primary and secondary schooling, that is, between kindergarten and high school graduation, on the odds of her child's age-grade retardation.[7] At each age, the left-hand panel shows the overall relationships between a one-year change in maternal education and age-grade retardation, while the right-hand panel shows the effect of maternal education when all of the other family and socioeconomic background characteristics (listed above) are controlled statistically. While a one-year change in maternal schooling has almost no effect on age-grade retardation of six year-olds, its association with age-grade retardation rises sharply and regularly with the age of the child, especially between ages 6 and 9. At age 9, a one year increase in maternal schooling is associated with an 11% reduction in the odds of age-grade retardation, and by age 17, it is associated with an 18% reduction in the odds. Just about half of that association is explained by the correlation of maternal educational attainment with other family and socioeconomic background variables, but the effects remain impressive. The influence of maternal education increases with age of child, and at age 17, a one-year increase in maternal schooling is associated with an 8% reduction in the odds of age-grade retardation.

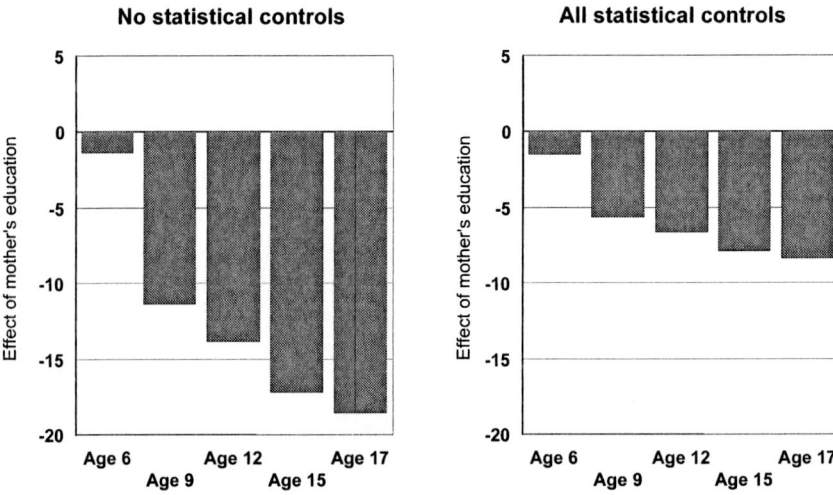

Figure 5.4. Maternal K–12 education and odds of age-grade retardation, 1972–1998.

Single-Parent Household

At age 6, there is essentially no relationship between living in a single-parent household and grade retention. As shown in Figure 5.5, when other variables are controlled, such children are at a slight advantage relative to 6-year-old children from two-parent households. By age 9 there is a sharp differential in age-grade retardation, favoring children from two-parent households, whose odds of age-grade retardation are 38% less than those of children from single-parent households. The differential remains strong and increases with age. At age 17, even when all other background variables are controlled, a child living in a single-parent household faces odds of age-grade retardation that are almost 27% larger than those of a child from a two-parent household.

Family Income

Figure 5.6 shows the effects on age-grade retardation of family income, with and without controls for other background variables. Family income has been transformed to a logarithmic scale, so the effects shown reflect proportional changes of income, not dollar changes. As with the other background variables, the overall association between family income and age-grade retardation is weak among 6-year-olds, but by age 9 it is very strong. A one-unit increase in the log of family income is associated with a 33% decline in the odds of enrollment below the first grade. About half

Race-Ethnicity, Social Background, and Grade Retention 105

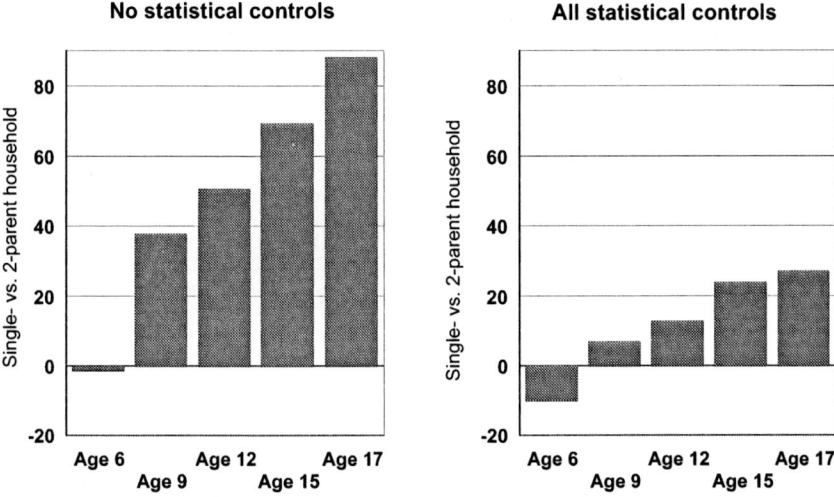

Figure 5.5. Single parent household and odds of age-grade retardation, 1972–1998.

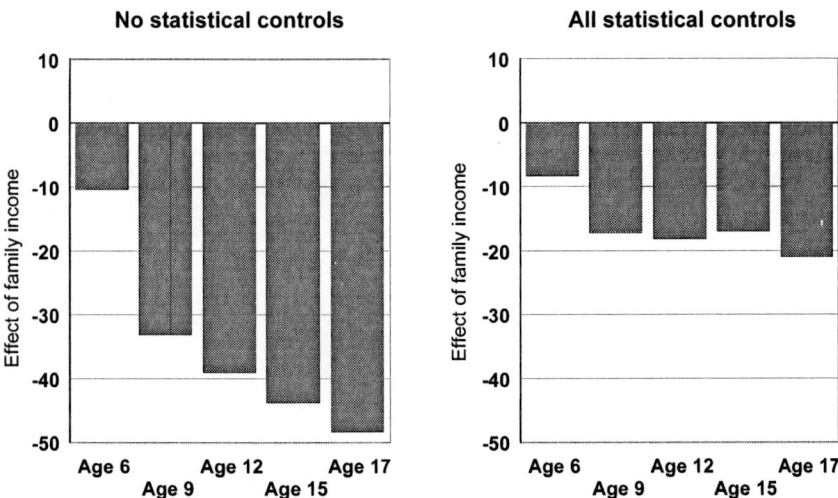

Figure 5.6. Family income (log) and odds of age-grade retardation, 1972–1998.

this association is explained by the correlation of family income with other background variables. When the other variables are controlled, a one-unit increase in family income leads to a 17% decline in the odds of age-grade retardation. That effect of family income is essentially the same among older children.

Home Ownership

Home ownership versus renting is also strongly associated with age-grade retention (see Figure 5.7). The reasons for this are not clear. Home ownership may be an indicator of family wealth, or it may indicate greater stability in residential location and family arrangements than is typical among renters. Figure 5.7 shows that home ownership is weakly related to age-grade retardation at age 6. However, by age 9 it is associated with more than a 35% reduction in the odds of age-grade retardation, and at age 17 it is associated with a 60% reduction in the odds of age-grade retardation. Again, about half of this association is explained by the correlation of home ownership with other background variables, but the effect of home ownership remains large. At age 17, home ownership reduces the odds of falling behind in school or dropping out by almost 37%.

Metropolitan Location

Residential location is also associated with patterns of age-grade retardation, and in somewhat surprising ways. Across time, the October CPS data permit consistent distinctions among six types of locations: central cities of the 17 largest metropolitan areas, suburbs of those metropolitan areas, central cities of smaller metropolitan areas, suburbs of the smaller areas, nonmetropolitan areas, and a residual category of other areas. At each age, Figure 5.8 compares the odds of age grade retardation in the

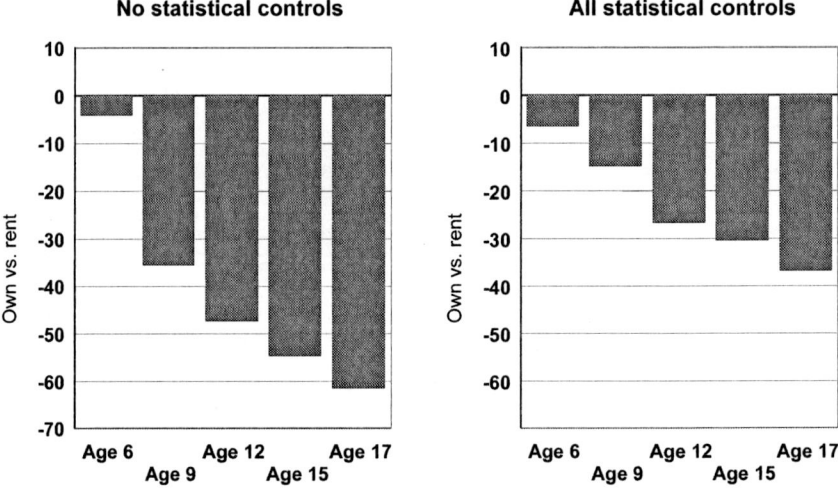

Figure 5.7. Home tenure (own vs. rent) and odds of age-grade retardation, 1972–1998.

central cities of the largest metropolitan areas with the odds in each other type of area. The most striking relationship in these data, whether or not family and socioeconomic background characteristics are controlled, is that on-time entry to the first grade is much more likely in the largest central cities than in any other type of area. This relationship gradually changes as children age, and the age variation is somewhat clearer in the right-hand display, that is, after other social and economic background characteristics have been controlled. While students in large central cities are much less likely to be behind their same-age peers from other areas at age 6, by age 17, the students in central cities are somewhat more likely to have fallen behind. The norms for age at school entry are followed more closely in the largest central cities, but grade retention after school entry is consistently more likely to occur in the largest central cities than in any other areas.

Regional Location

Figure 5.9 contrasts the odds of age-grade retardation in the East with those in the Midwest, South, and West. Children in the Midwest are much more likely to have entered regular school late than children in any other region, and this effect holds up whether or not social and economic background have been controlled. However, that effect also declines rapidly with age, and by age 17 there are very modest differences in age-grade retardation among the East, Midwest, and West. The South is different; above age 9, the odds of age-grade retardation are consistently more than

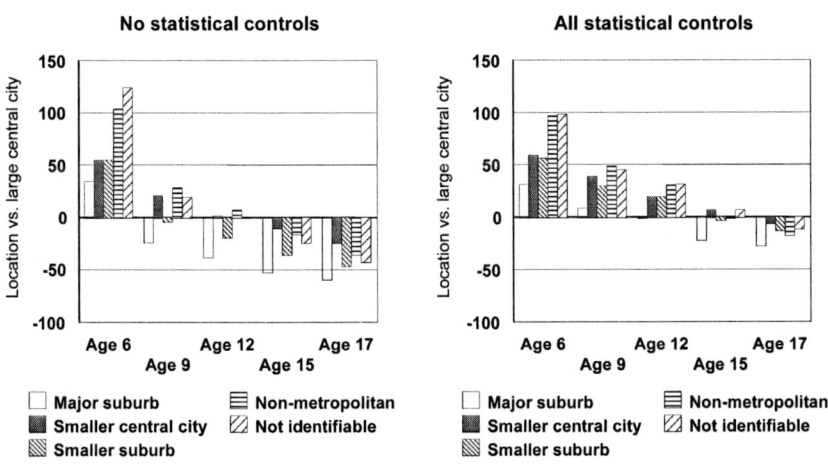

Figure 5.8. Metropolitan status and odds of age-grade retardation, 1972–1998.

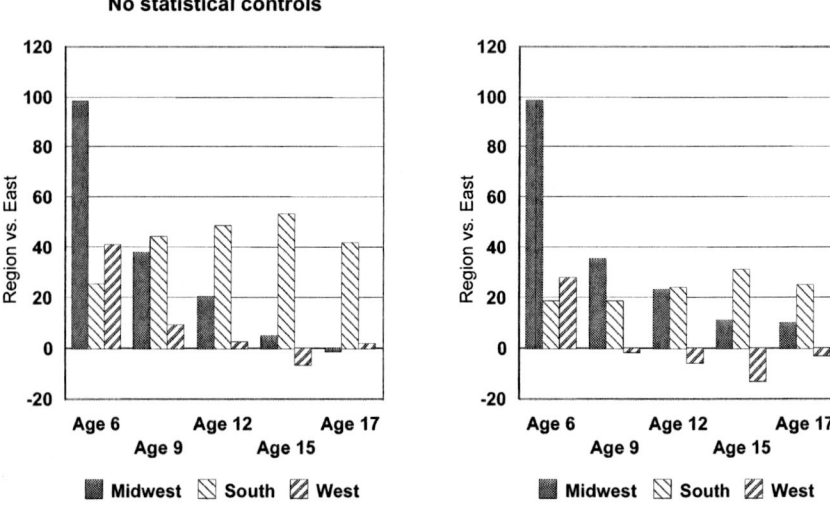

Figure 5.9. Region and odds of age-grade retardation, 1972–1998.

40% greater in the South than in the East. Also, differences between the South and the other three regions tend to increase with age. After social and economic background variables have been controlled, the odds of age-grade retardation are 19 to 31% greater in the South than in the East at ages 9 and above.

EXPLAINING RACE-ETHNIC DIFFERENTIALS

Recall the large differentials in age-grade retardation between Whites and minorities—Black, Hispanic, and other—which were displayed in Figure 5.3. Are these direct and possibly discriminatory effects of minority status, per se, or do they simply reflect differences in the residential location or social and economic statuses of majority and minority populations? Figure 5.10 shows the independent effects of race-ethnicity, comparing each minority group to Whites, after all of the other social and economic background characteristics have been controlled. To make our findings clear, we have used exactly the same vertical scale in Figure 5.10 as in Figure 5.3. In a nutshell, the race-ethnic differentials in age-grade retardation almost disappear when the other social and economic background variables have been controlled. Only at age 17 are there consistent and nontrivial effects of minority status on the odds of age-grade retardation, each of which is slightly larger than 10%. These compare with observed differentials of 138% among African Americans and

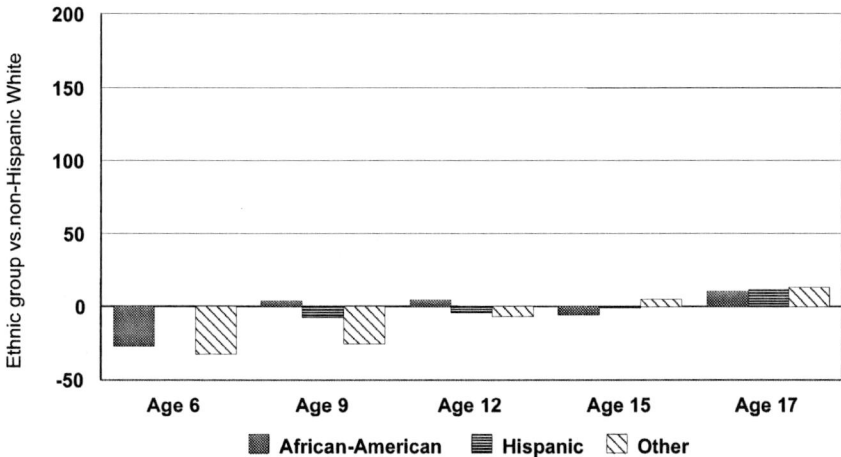

Figure 5.10. Effects of race-ethnicity on odds of age-grade retardation, 1972–1998.

166% among Hispanics. As American schools have functioned across the past 30 years, Blacks, Hispanics, and other minorities have fallen behind their same-age peers because of their social background and residential location, and not directly because of the color of their skin.

We have examined one variation of our finding: the idea that region and metropolitan location, and not socioeconomic background and family structure explain the race-ethnic differentials in age-grade retardation. The data are not at all consistent with this hypothesis. At each age, race-ethnic differentials in age-grade retardation are virtually the same, whether or not region and metropolitan location have been controlled. Race-ethnic differentials in age-grade retardation are almost entirely due to group differences in socioeconomic and family background. It would be overly simple to say that class, rather than race was the dominant factor affecting rates of progress through elementary and early secondary school. It would be better to say that a broader set of social and economic background variables, not including race-ethnicity per se, were responsible for most observable race-ethnic differentials in age-grade retardation.

EXPLAINING TRENDS IN AGE-GRADE RETARDATION

Just as population groups differ in social and economic background, so have the social background characteristics of children changed over the past 30 years. There is insufficient space for us to describe those changes in detail, but the most important changes are increasing numbers of single-parent households, decreasing numbers of children per family, and increasing levels of parental educational attainment. On balance, the last two changes have reduced the chances of age-grade retardation. That is, parental schooling and number of siblings both have powerful effects on age-grade retardation, and parental schooling has increased a great deal, while numbers of children have declined sharply.

While controls for social and economic background reduce or eliminate group differences in age-grade retardation, similar statistical controls increase rates of age-grade retardation across time. For example, Figure 5.11 shows two versions of the trend in age-grade retardation among 17-year-olds. In the first version, the solid line shows the odds of age-grade retardation relative to their level in 1972. There was a period of relative stability from 1972 to 1988, after which the odds of age-grade retardation increased by about 40% between 1988 and 1992. The second version of the trend series, the dashed line, differs only in that social and economic background have been controlled. Here, the increase in age-grade retardation appears earlier, after 1982, and it continues throughout the 1990s. Furthermore, in every year after 1972, the adjustment for changes in social and economic background increases the odds of age-grade retardation. In the observed data, the increase in the odds of age grade retardation is about 50%, but the rate has doubled by 1998 among children with similar social and economic background.

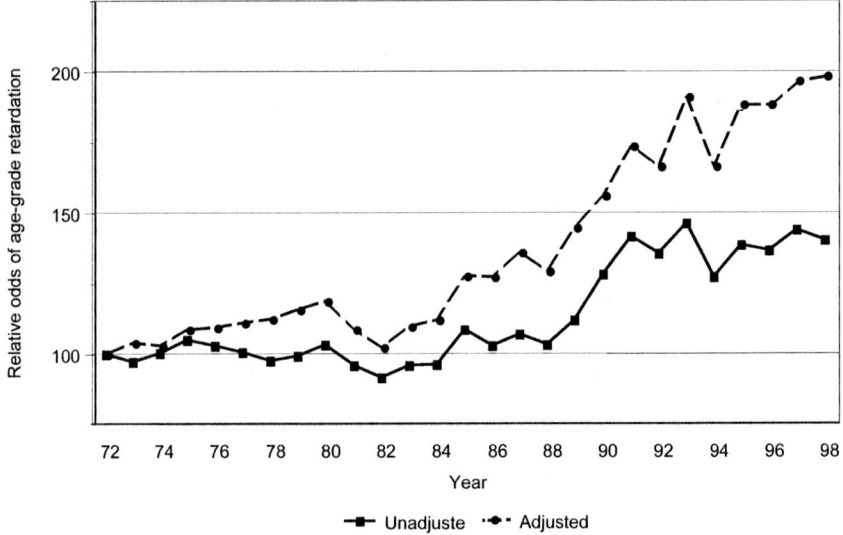

Figure 5.11. Enrollment below modal grade.

EFFECTS OF GRADE RETENTION

The preceding findings would be of little importance if age-grade retardation had little or no effect on the life chances of children and youth. The scientific evidence about the effects of retention in grade is strong and clear: The academic benefits of retention typically are both ephemeral and costly (Hauser, 2001; Holmes, 1989). When previous academic performance and relevant social characteristics are controlled, past grade retention accelerates current school dropout (Rumberger & Larson, 1998). There is no evidence for claims that new retention policies will be coupled with effective remediation of learning deficits that would be worth their cost or would offset the well-established long-term negative effects of retention (Hauser, 2001; Moore, 1999; Roderick, Bryk, Jacob, Easton, & Allensworth, 1999).

The typical organization of American schools into grades by the ages of their students is challenged by large variations in achievement within ages and grades. The resulting tension is reduced somewhat by overlap in the curriculum from one grade to the next. It is also reduced by strategies for grouping students by observed levels of aptitude or mastery: These include special education placement, academic tracking, extended kindergarten, and grade retention. The age at entry into grade school has gradually crept upward since the early 1970s, reversing one of the major historic trends contributing to the growth of schooling in the United States. Data on early school transitions and on the possible reasons for change in those transitions are grossly inadequate, but it would appear that retention in prekindergarten and kindergarten has played some role in the rise of age at entry into the first grade. Excepting the ubiquitous tendency for girls to enter (and complete) primary and secondary school at earlier ages than boys, there is little sign of social differentiation in age at school entry.

Socially differentiated patterns of grade retention develop rapidly after entry into graded school, and they persist through secondary school. White girls progress through school most rapidly, while African American boys are most often held back in grade. By ages 15 to 17, about 30% of White girls, but close to half of African American boys are below the modal grade for all students of their age—or have left school. Rates of grade retardation at those ages have remained high, even though school dropout has declined.

Given the high rates of retention created by current evaluation practices—and their disparate impact on minority youth—the possibility of substantially increased, test-based retention creates a number of concerns. For example, the costs of grade repetition are large—both to those retained and those who must pay for repeated schooling. The presence of older students creates serious management problems for schools. Most important, the available evidence shows that retention has no lasting educational benefits, that it typically leads to lower achievement (than promotion) and to higher rates of school dropout.

It is possible to imagine an educational system in which test-based promotion standards are combined with effective diagnosis and remediation of learning problems, yet past experience suggests that American school systems may not have either the will or the means to enact such fair and effective practices. Such a system would include well-designed and carefully aligned curricular standards, performance standards, and assessments. Teachers would be well trained to meet high standards in their classrooms, and students would have ample notice of what they are expected to know and be able to do. Students with learning difficulties would be identified years in advance of high-stakes deadlines, and they and their parents and teachers would have ample opportunities to catch up before deadlines occur. Accountability for student performance would not rest solely or even primarily on individual students, but also, collectively, on educators and parents. There is no positive example of such a system in the United States, past or present, whose success is documented by credible research.

NOTES

1. This paper is based, in part, on material in Chapter 6 of National Research Council (1999). Samuel Messick, Marguerite Clarke, Jay P. Heubert, and Taissa S. Hauser contributed substantially to that chapter of the NRC report. Original research reported herein was supported by the William Vilas Estate Trust and by the Graduate School of the University of Wisconsin-Madison. Computation was carried out using facilities of the Center for Demography and Ecology at the University of Wisconsin-Madison, which are supported by a P30 Center Grant from the National Institute of Child Health and Human Development. We thank Linda Jordan for advice and assistance in the preparation of data from October Current Population Surveys. The opinions expressed herein are those of the authors. Address correspondence to Robert M. Hauser, Center for Demography and Ecology, University of Wisconsin-Madison, 1180 Observatory Drive, Madison, Wisconsin 53706 or e-mail to Hauser@ ssc.wisc.edu.
2. These data have been assembled from Historical Statistics, Table A-3, "The Population 6 to 17 Years Old Enrolled Below Modal Grade: 1971 to 1998," which is available from the U.S. Bureau of the Census at http://www.census.gov/population/socdemo/school/taba-3.txt.
3. We ignore the logical possibility that age-retardation at younger ages could be counter-balanced by double-promotion at older ages.
4. Dropout by ages 15 to 17 does not indicate ultimate rates of failure to complete high school because large numbers of youth complete regular school-

ing through age 19 or, alternatively, pass the GED exam through their late 20s (Hauser, 1997).
5. Our analyses are limited to dependent children and youth living in parental or quasi-parental households.
6. Except at age 17, a very small fraction of the sample is not enrolled in school. Regardless of age, those individuals are classified as below the modal grade level for their age. That is, school dropout is treated here as a form of age-grade retardation.
7. The effects in Figure 5.4 are similar to those of postsecondary education of mothers and to the pre- and postsecondary educational attainments of fathers.

REFERENCES

Bianchi, S. M. (1984). Children's progress through school: A research note. *Sociology of Education, 57*, 184–192.

Hauser, R. M. (1997). Indicators of high school completion and dropout. In R. M. Hauser, B. V. Brown, & W. R. Prosser (Eds.), *Indicators of children's well-being* (pp. 152–184). New York: Russell Sage Foundation.

Hauser, R. M. (2001). Should we end social promotion? Truth and consequences. In G. Orfield & M. L. Kornhaber (Eds.), *Raising standards or raising barriers? Inequality and high-stakes testing in public education* (pp. 151–178). New York: Century Foundation Press.

Hauser, R. M. (2004). Progress in schooling: A review. In K. Neckerman (Ed.), *Social dimensions of inequality*. New York: Russell Sage Foundation.

Hauser, R. M., & Hauser, T. S. (1993). *Current population survey, October person-household files, 1968–90: Cumulative codebook.* Madison, WI: University of Wisconsin-Madison, Center for Demography and Ecology, Department of Sociology.

Hauser, R. M., Jordan, L., & Dixon, J. A. (1993). *Current population survey, October person-household files, 1968–90.* Madison, WI: University of Wisconsin-Madison, Center for Demography and Ecology, Department of Sociology.

Holmes, C. T. (1989). Grade level retention effects: A meta-analysis of research studies. In L. A. Shepard & M. L. Smith (Eds.), *Flunking grades: Research and policies on retention* (pp. 16–33). London: Falmer Press.

Moore, D. R. (1999). *Comment on "Ending social promotion: Results from the first two years."* Chicago: Designs for Change.

National Research Council, Committee on Appropriate Test Use. (1999). *High stakes: Testing for tracking, promotion, and graduation.* Washington, DC: National Academy Press.

Roderick, M., Bryk, A. S., Jacob, B. A., Easton, J. Q., & Allensworth, E. (1999). *Ending social promotion: Results from the first two years.* Chicago: Consortium for Chicago School Research.

Rumberger, R. W., & Larson, K. A. (1998). Student mobility and the increased risk of high school dropout. *American Journal of Education, 107*, 1–35.

U.S. Bureau of the Census. (1979). *Relative progress of children in school: 1976* (Report No. Series P-20, No. 337). Washington, DC: U.S. Government Printing Office.

CHAPTER 6

RACE EFFECTS ON ABILITY GROUP OUTCOMES

Maureen T. Hallinan

Assigning students to ability groups for instruction is a common practice in most middle and secondary schools in the United States. Ability grouping is seen as an efficient and effective method to instruct a large population of students. The efficiency of ability grouping stems from the fact that it provides a fairly straightforward basis on which to assign students to classes. Its effectiveness results from allowing teachers to gear instruction to the ability level of their students and to utilize pedagogical techniques appropriate to the students' level of understanding. For these reasons, many, if not most, teachers prefer instructing students in ability-grouped classes rather than in heterogeneously grouped classes.

Despite its pedagogical advantages, ability grouping has many critics. The major criticism is based on the belief that students learn less in low-ability groups than in higher ability groups. Critics claim that ability grouping provides unequal learning opportunities to students. Empirical research lends support to this belief by showing that students assigned to higher ability groups make greater gains in achievement than those assigned to lower ability groups, controlling for student ability.

Critics further argue that the practice of ability grouping discriminates against minority students. They point to empirical data demonstrating that minority students are disproportionately assigned to lower ability groups. Relative to the demographic characteristics of a school, a number of studies show that a greater proportion of minority students are assigned to low-ability classes than are White students. Since students are believed to have fewer learning opportunities in low-ability groups than in higher groups, critics insist that the practice of ability grouping disadvantages Black students.

To determine whether racial or ethnic biases affect the assignment of students to ability groups, several empirical studies have examined the assignment process (Alexander, Cook, & McDill, 1978; Kubitschek & Hallinan, 1996; Oakes, 1985; Rehberg & Rosenthal, 1978). These studies identify a number of factors that influence ability group placement, including standardized test scores, grades, previous course history, teacher and counselor recommendations, parental choice, and student choice. In addition, organizational factors, such as the availability of teachers, the size of classrooms, the master schedule, and school resources affect placement decisions. These studies find that controlling for student characteristics and organizational factors, neither race nor ethnicity affects ability group placement. Indeed, some studies find a bias favoring the assignment of minority students to higher ability groups. For example, Hallinan and Sorensen (1985) show that at the elementary- and middle-school levels, principals and teachers tend to expand the size of higher ability groups to insure racial and ethnic diversity in these groups.

Despite the failure of critics to find evidence of racial or ethnic bias in the assignment of students to ability groups, concern about the use of ability grouping for student instruction is still widespread. Even if race or ethnicity does not influence the level of the ability group to which a student is assigned, many minority students are still placed in lower ability groups—a practice that may disadvantage them by limiting their opportunities to learn. Hence, the concern is whether the practice of ability grouping is equitable.

The approach this investigation takes to the ability grouping debate differs from current empirical research examining the practice. In an effort to shed new light on the effects of ability grouping on the achievement gains of Black and White students, the research examines whether race would affect the amount of change in a student's achievement if the student were moved to a higher ability group. If achievement gains associated with assignment to a higher ability group differed by race, then educators and researchers would have evidence that the instructional process that characterizes higher level ability groups possesses some characteristics that disadvantage students by race. This finding would call for studies that examine and identify factors that may dampen the learning of some students while facilitating the progress of others.

RACE DIFFERENCES IN ACHIEVEMENT GAINS IN HIGHER ABILITY GROUPS

In a recent study (Hallinan, 2003), I examined the impact of ability group level on student achievement by analyzing whether students would benefit academically by being assigned to a higher ability group. Enrollment in a higher ability group provides advantages in terms of a more challenging curriculum and a strong academic climate. Would these advantages affect all students equally, regardless of their ability and background, or do the advantages of higher placement accrue only to students with specific characteristics? Due to data limitations, the possible effects of student discouragement resulting from difficulty in learning the material in higher groups could not be taken into account in this study. With that caveat, the research shows that virtually all students, regardless of race, ability, or academic background, would benefit from assignment to a higher ability group.

This empirical finding raises new questions about how ability grouping might disadvantage Black students. Even if all students benefit from placement in a higher ability group, they may not benefit to the same extent. In particular, students of one race may make greater academic gains than students of another race when assigned to a higher ability group.

Race differences in the academic advantages of higher group placement could result from a number of factors. First, differences may occur in the way Black and White students learn, with the learning conditions that characterize higher ability groups being more supportive of the learning style of one race than another. Recent learning theory has pointed to a number of different learning styles, including visual, auditory, and kinetic (Gardner, 1993). As yet, it is unclear whether these learning differences are associated with background characteristics, with socialization processes, or both. Studies have found evidence that girls have weaker spatial relations skills than boys, Hispanic students learn better in a cooperative setting than non-Hispanic students, and Asian students prefer a quieter environment when studying than non-Asian students.

Research is needed to examine whether Black students have a different learning style than White students and whether learning style interacts with ability group level to affect achievement. It may be, for example, that Blacks prefer a cooperative learning environment, while Whites are more comfortable in a competitive setting. If ability groups vary in the emphasis they place on cooperation and competition, then an ability group might have a differential impact on Black and White students' achievement.

Second, teacher expectations and peer pressures may differ across ability groups by race. Teacher expectations influence the academic demand teachers place on students and the nature and content of teacher-student interactions. If teachers hold lower expectations for the performance of Black students, or communicate less confidence in their potential, then the achievement of Black students is likely to suffer. Moreover, Black and White students may develop different norms for academic behavior, creating variation in motivation and effort. Finally, the pressure peers exert on classmates to strive for academic success or to become involved in nonacademic activities may differ by race, creating different achievement outcomes.

A third factor that might predict racial differences in achievement growth in higher ability groups is student ability. Components of student ability include prior knowledge, prior opportunities to learn, and readiness to learn. Ideally, ability groups are designed to be homogeneous, with a small range. In practice, however, ability groups often show considerable variation in ability within a group (Hallinan, 2003). The students at the lower end of the ability distribution tend to be less prepared for the more challenging academic work that characterizes higher ability groups than those at the higher end of the distribution.

If Black students tend to cluster at the lower end of the ability distribution within an ability group, they are likely to find the academic demands of a high-ability group more difficult than students who have a stronger academic background. As a result, Blacks are likely to attain less growth in achievement than their higher ability peers. However, it could well be that ability, not race, is accounting for the differential achievement gains. The lower end of the ability distribution in any ability group, regardless of race or other student characteristics, might show less growth in achievement than students at the upper end of the distribution. If ability explains differential growth in achievement on movement to a higher ability group, then both low-ability Black and White students would be expected to show less achievement growth than higher ability Black or White students when moved to a higher ability group. The aim of this paper is to determine whether the academic gains made by students who are placed in a higher level ability group differ by race.

RESEARCH APPROACHES

Previous research examining race differences in ability-group effects on learning investigated two aspects of the practice: the assignment of students to ability groups and achievement differences in student achievement across ability groups. A number of studies focus on the assignment process and examine whether students who have the same ability but differ by race have equal opportunity for placement in higher ability groups (Hallinan, 1991; Oakes, Gamoran, & Page, 1992). Generally, the research finds no effect of race on assignment to upper level ability groups. While several studies note that Black students are disproportionately assigned to lower ability groups, the race effect on assignment tends to disappear when ability is controlled. In other words, the race effect on ability group assignment is a proxy for an ability effect. The research generally supports the conclusion that race by itself does not affect ability group placement.

Other studies examine whether race affects the impact of ability group level on student achievement. Both cross-sectional and longitudinal analyses show that Blacks typically attain lower test scores than Whites when assigned to the same ability group. When ability is controlled, a race effect is rarely statistically significant (Gamoran, 1992; Hallinan & Kubitschek, 1999). These studies suggest that race and ability are highly related, but that ability is the major determinant of student achievement. However, other factors related to race may create achievement differences. For example, teacher expectations may differ for Black and White students, affecting student motivation and self-confidence and resulting in racial differences in achievement.

The approach to the study of race and ability grouping taken in this paper differs from these previous strategies. Based on Hallinan's (2003) finding that virtually all students make achievement gains when moved to a higher ability group, the analysis examines whether Black and White students make equivalent gains in a higher group. If Black and White students were moved from their assigned Regular ability group to the Honors group, would they make commensurate achievement gains? The analysis will determine whether Black and White students respond in a similar manner to a more demanding academic environment. If the results reveal race differences in achievement gains in higher ability groups, then the factors that affect these differences will be investigated.

METHODOLOGY

Sample

The empirical analysis is conducted on survey data obtained from students in five secondary schools in an urban school district in the Midwest. Two cohorts of students were followed from ninth through 11th grade. Background information on these students, as well as their previous test scores, grades, and ability group assignments from eighth grade were obtained.

The schools were desegregated to insure that the racial composition of the schools reflected that of the community. Since Asian, Hispanic, Native American and other non-White, non-Black students comprised less than 5% of the sample, these non-Black students are classified as White for the analysis. Twenty-seven percent of the sample was Black and 23% qualified for free lunch, a measure of low socioeconomic status.

Special education students, those for whom English was a second language, and students who were not taking English or mathematics in ninth grade, were excluded from the sample. Only the ninthth grade analyses are presented here, since the 10th and 11th grade results are essentially the same as the ninth grade outcomes. The data for both ninth grade cohorts are combined, with a dummy variable for cohort included in the models.

Variables

The dependent variable for the analysis is a student's percentage score on a standardized test in English and mathematics. The test was administered annually, on a statewide basis, to 3rd, 6th, 8th, 9th, and 11th grade students in the school district. A national sample was employed as the reference group. The students in the sample took the test in the spring of eighth and ninth grades.

Independent variables for these analyses include measures of student background: gender, race, age (minus an appropriate integer for that year), number of days absent first semester, and free lunch status. Control variables for cohort and school are added. The exogenous variables included eighth grade ability group, eighth grade grades and eighth grade standardized test scores in English and mathematics.

The middle schools in the district had three ability group levels in eighth grade English: Basic, Regular and Honors, and four levels in eighth grade mathematics: Basic, Regular, Honors, and Advanced. In ninth grade, an Advanced English group and a Very Basic mathematics group were added. (The terms Basic and Very Basic were not used by the schools, but are judged to be appropriate descriptions of the level of the curriculum). Ability group membership for eighth and ninth grades were obtained from school records. Student percentage test scores in eighth grade in English and mathematics also were obtained from school records, as were student grades in these subjects. Grades were converted into the usual four-point scale with A = 4.0, B = 3.0, C = 2.0, D = 1.0, F = 0.0.

Statistical Model

A reasonable analytical model for analysis of student achievement across ability groups would be an ordinary least squares regression (OLS) model. However, in this analysis, the dependent variable—student percentage score on a standardized test—is censored at both ends of the distribution. Students can score neither higher than 99% nor lower than 1%. These ceiling and floor effects bias the coefficient estimates in an OLS model. A preferable model, yielding more consistent parameter estimates, is a two-limit tobit model (Maddala, 1983). In a tobit model, the unobservable, uncensored error distribution is estimated. The observed dependent variable is transformed into this uncensored distribution, and coefficients based on the transformed dependent variable are obtained. The statistical program LIMDEP performs these operations and also yields the standard deviation of the estimated uncensored error distribution, σ.

When the proportion of censored cases in the distribution of a dependent variable is small, as is the case in this analysis, most of the transformed values of the dependent variable are very similar to the observed values of the dependent variable. At the ends of the distribution, the transformed and observed values of the dependent variables may be slightly different. For example, if a student were to score in the 99th percentile on the standardized test, the transformed value might be higher than 100. Similarly, if a student were to score in the 1st percentile, the transformed value might be less than zero. Consequently, predictions based on the tobit transformations, which is what will be used in the following analyses, will be exaggerated at the upper end of the distribution and underestimated at the lower end. However, this characteristic of the tobit model has little substantive effect on the analysis presented here.

In this analysis, the predicted achievement of any student in any designated ability group is obtained by entering the student's characteristics into the tobit model predicting achievement for that ability group. Since the tobit coefficients for a specific ability group are based on the characteristics of the students in that ability group, they become less accurate the more an individual student differs in characteristics from those in the designated group. For example, if students have characteristics that are typical of those in the Basic English group, they would differ somewhat from the students in the Regular group, and even more from those in the Honors and Advanced group. The predicted achievement for the Basic student if placed in the Regular group would be more accurate than the predictions for that student if assigned to the Honors group and least accurate for the Advanced group.

However, even predictions two or more groups away from a student's actual group are still sufficiently accurate to be quite informative. The ability groups overlap considerably in terms of measured student characteristics, especially in terms of prior demonstrated achievement. Thus, one can assume that the ability groups overlap in terms of unmeasured characteristics, such as achievement motivation and effort expended on learning, as well. Moreover, the analysis includes stringent controls for prior achievement, which has been demonstrated to minimize the effects of unmeasured characteristics affecting learning. The chief limitation of predictions is that they are somewhat idealized in that they include no negative effects due to student discouragement or confusion as students are placed in more challenging ability groups.

RESULTS

Table 6.1 shows the means and standard deviations for the variables in the analysis for the full sample and broken down by race for English and mathematics. The data show substantial differences between Blacks and Whites on the dependent variables. Blacks attain an average ninth grade test score of 40% in both English and mathematics, compared to an average White score of about 60% in both subjects.

Similar race differences are seen in the means of the achievement-related independent variables. The standardized test scores of eighth grade White students in English was about 20 percentage points higher than for Blacks. The same difference is found for mathematics. In eighth grade, Whites received an average English grade of 2.4, or about C+, compared to a Black average of 1.8, or about a C−. In mathematics, the White mean in eighth grade was 2.1, or C, while the Black mean was 1.5, between a D+ and a C−.

Black and White students were distributed differently across ability groups in the eighth grade. In English, Blacks were three times as likely as Whites to be enrolled in the Basic group, while Whites were almost three times as likely as Blacks to be assigned to the Honors group. In mathematics, Blacks were more than twice as likely as Whites to be assigned to the Basic group and somewhat more likely to be in the Regular group. Whites were more than three times as likely as Blacks to be assigned to the Honors group and more than four times more likely than Blacks to be in the Advanced-ability group.

Blacks typically missed about 7 days of school during the first semester of ninth grade, compared to about 6 days for Whites. Blacks were about a month and a half older than Whites, and were five times more likely than

Table 6.1. Descriptive Statistics

	English Analyses						Mathematics Analyses					
	Total (N = 2,040)		White (N = 1,482)		(N = 558)		Total (N = 2,032)		White (N = 1,477)		Black (N = 555)	
Variable	mean	s.d.	mean	s.d.	mean	s.d.	mean	s.d.	mean	s.d.	mean	s.d.
9th grade English test score	54.05	24.99	59.47	24.09	39.65	21.40						
9th grade math test score							55.19	26.29	60.86	25.63	40.09	21.67
8th grade English test score	57.96	24.60	63.50	23.08	43.27	22.38	58.12	24.58	63.58	23.10	43.58	22.40
8th grade math test score	59.43	26.42	64.96	25.10	44.71	24.10	59.54	26.37	64.99	25.13	45.02	24.03
8th grade English grade	2.22	1.12	2.38	1.10	1.79	1.07	2.22	1.12	2.38	1.10	1.81	1.08
8th grade math grade	1.95	1.15	2.13	1.12	1.46	1.10	1.95	1.15	2.13	1.12	1.47	1.10
Days absent 1st semester	6.30	6.86	6.05	6.70	6.98	7.22	6.26	6.79	6.08	6.81	6.74	6.70
Cohort 2 = 1	0.51	0.50	0.51	0.50	0.52	0.50	0.51	0.50	0.51	0.50	0.52	0.50
Age in years	-0.03	0.53	-0.07	0.50	0.06	0.60	-0.04	0.53	-0.07	0.50	0.04	0.59
Female = 1	0.50	0.50	0.50	0.50	0.51	0.50	0.50	0.50	0.50	0.50	0.50	0.50
Black = 1	0.27	0.45	—	—	—	—	0.27	0.45	—	—	—	—
Free Lunch = 1	0.23	0.42	0.11	0.31	0.56	0.50	0.23	0.42	0.11	0.31	0.56	0.50
School 1.1 = 1	0.19	0.39	0.20	0.40	0.16	0.36	0.19	0.39	0.20	0.40	0.15	0.36
School 1.2 = 1	0.19	0.39	0.20	0.40	0.17	0.37	0.19	0.39	0.20	0.40	0.17	0.38
School 1.3 = 1	0.24	0.43	0.26	0.44	0.18	0.39	0.24	0.43	0.27	0.44	0.19	0.39
School 1.4 = 1	0.16	0.37	0.15	0.35	0.20	0.40	0.16	0.37	0.15	0.35	0.21	0.41
School 1.5 = 1	0.22	0.42	0.20	0.40	0.29	0.46	0.22	0.41	0.19	0.39	0.28	0.45
8th grade ability group Basic = 1	0.09	0.29	0.06	0.23	0.18	0.39	0.10	0.31	0.07	0.26	0.19	0.39
8th grade ability group Regular = 1	0.58	0.49	0.55	0.50	0.66	0.48	0.60	0.49	0.56	0.50	0.71	0.46
8th grade ability group Honors = 1	0.26	0.44	0.32	0.47	0.12	0.32	0.17	0.38	0.21	0.41	0.06	0.24
8th grade ability group Advanced = 1	—	—	—	—	—	—	0.10	0.30	0.13	0.33	0.03	0.17
8th grade ability group Spec Prog = 1	0.01	0.11	0.01	0.11	0.01	0.10	0.01	0.09	0.01	0.08	0.01	0.09
8th grade not ability grouped = 1	0.01	0.10	0.01	0.12	0.00	0.00	0.01	0.11	0.02	0.13	—	—
8th grade ability group missing = 1	0.05	0.22	0.06	0.23	0.04	0.19	0.01	0.09	0.01	0.09	0.01	0.08

Table 6.2. Means and Standard Deviations of 8th Grade Test Scores by Ability Group and Race

9th Grade Ability Group	8th Grade Test Score—English								
	Full sample			Whites			Blacks		
	mean	s.d.	N	mean	s.d.	N	mean	s.d.	N
Basic	24.71	14.79	251	28.42	16.41	125	21.04	11.94	126
Regular	52.53	19.05	1,129	56.08	18.50	781	44.56	17.82	348
Honors	77.99	14.77	556	79.26	14.09	482	69.71	16.46	74
Advanced	90.16	8.14	104	90.96	7.49	94	82.70	10.48	10
Total	57.96	24.60	2,040	63.50	23.08	1,482	43.27	22.38	558

9th Grade Ability Group	8th Grade Test Score—Mathematics								
	Full sample			Whites			Blacks		
	mean	s.d.	N	mean	s.d.	N	mean	s.d.	N
Very Basic	28.51	18.23	396	31.68	19.47	218	24.62	15.80	178
Basic	48.54	19.04	463	51.70	19.60	292	43.13	16.75	171
Regular	65.99	18.03	722	67.76	17.45	560	59.90	18.71	162
Honors	85.49	11.21	299	86.48	10.62	266	77.52	12.74	33
Advanced	92.16	8.79	152	92.48	8.77	141	88.09	8.46	11
Total	59.54	26.37	2,032	64.99	25.13	1,477	45.02	24.03	555

Whites to qualify for a free lunch. The gender distribution was the same for Blacks and Whites.

Prior achievement is known to be a key factor in track assignments. Table 6.2 presents the means and standard deviations of students' eighth grade achievement scores by race and ability group for English and mathematics. The table shows that for each ability group and for both subjects, the mean test scores for Blacks are lower than those for Whites. That is, within each ability group, Black students in this sample consistently score several percentage points lower than Whites on the state-mandated standardized achievement tests in English and mathematics.

The standard deviations of the means in Table 6.2 are informative. They reveal considerable overlap across ability groups in test scores. In the full sample, for every ability group in both English and mathematics, students one standard deviation above the mean for their ability group have a test score higher than students in the next higher level ability group who have a test score one standard deviation below the mean for their group. For example, a student in Basic English with a test score of 39.5, which is one standard deviation above the mean of 24.7, has a higher score than a student in Regular English with a test score of 33.5, one standard deviation below the group mean of 52.5. In every ability group level, a number of students at the high end of the ability distribution for that group have higher scores than students at the low end of the distribution in the next level ability group.

This result is generally true across race as well. In all ability groups, Blacks who score 1.2 standard deviations above the Black mean in a particular ability group have higher test scores than Whites in the next level ability group who have test scores 1.2 standard deviations below the White mean for that group. In general, a number of Blacks at the high end of the distribution in every ability group in English and mathematics have higher test scores than a number of Whites who score at the bottom end of the distribution in the next level group. The reverse is true as well. A number of Whites in one ability group have higher test scores than Blacks in the next level group.

These results show that ability groups are less homogeneous that usually believed, and that both Black and White students, especially those at the high end of the distribution in their actual ability groups, could likely function as well as or better than some of their peers in the next level ability group. This finding motivates the subsequent analysis examining whether students obtain higher test scores when placed in higher level ability groups and, if they do, whether Blacks and Whites show equal gains.

Inferential Analysis

Tables 6.3a and 6.3b present the coefficients of tobit models predicting student achievement in English and mathematics by ability group. These tables present the coefficients for a model in which race is treated only as a main effect. Also estimated, but with results not shown here, are models in which race is allowed to interact with all the other exogenous variables. The values of the log-likelihood for the models with race as a main effect and the fully interactive models are presented at the bottom of the tables. Also reported is the statistical significance of the difference between the two models for each ability group.

The difference between the model with race as a main effect only and the fully interactive model for English is statistically significant for the Regular and Advanced groups, but not for the Basic and Honors groups. The results for the Advanced group are not particularly meaningful, given that only 10 Blacks are enrolled in this group in the five high schools combined. While the findings indicate that race significantly affects the learning process in the Regular group, there is no clear substantive effect. Only one coefficient is statistically significant at the .05 level, and that coefficient affects less than 5% of Blacks. With only this difference distinguishing the determinants of Black and White learning pro-

Table 6.3a. Tobit Models Predicting 9th Grade English Achievement

	Students in Basic (N = 251) b	Students in Regular (N = 1,129) b	Students in Honors (N = 556) b	Students in Advanced (N = 104) b
8th grade English test score	0.57***	0.79***	0.83***	0.83***
8th grade math test score	0.14	0.43*	0.91**	0.14
8th grade English grade	-0.60	0.92*	0.90	0.21
8th grade math grade	0.30	0.44	-0.90	-0.20
Days absent 1st semester	0.41	-0.24	0.96	0.26
Cohort 2 = 1	1.02	1.50*	1.73*	0.66
Age in years	-2.97***	-2.41***	-1.84	-3.25*
Female = 1	0.59	0.52	0.15	1.62
Free Lunch = 1	0.39	0.31	0.47	0.11
School 1.2 = 1	-2.15	2.68**	-1.12	-3.42
School 1.3 = 1	-1.34	1.86*	-1.29	1.11
School 1.4 = 1	-0.50	0.27	-2.39	-4.95**
School 1.5 = 1	-2.45	2.34**	-0.70	
8th grade ability group Basic = 1	0.18	-3.37**		
8th grade ability group Honors = 1		2.37	2.67**	
8th grade ability group Advanced = 1				2.00
8th grade ability group Spec Program = 1	-0.46	-0.38	0.36	2.92
8th grade not ability grouped = 1		4.40	7.11**	5.02
8th grade ability group missing = 1	-0.56	-2.92*	-0.83	0.46
Black = 1	-1.41	-0.66	-0.22	-5.68**
Constant	11.17***	-0.93	-1.87	-2.17
σ	7.55***	9.43***	7.98***	5.22***
Log-likelihood	-863.43	-4,135.16	-1,933.22	-307.08
Log-likelihood of full interactive race model	-859.15	-4,120.84	-1,924.50	-296.70
Difference in df	16	17	16	9
p	0.93	0.04	0.36	0.01

*p < .05. **p < 0.01. ***p < .001.

Table 6.3b. Tobit Models Predicting 9th Grade Mathematics Achievement

	Students in Very Basic (N = 396) b	Students in Basic (N = 463) b	Students in Regular (N = 722) b	Students in Honors (N = 299) b	Students in Advanced (N = 152) b
8th grade mathematics test score	0.57***	0.46***	0.55***	0.48***	0.65***
8th grade English test score	0.04	0.23***	0.14***	0.08*	-0.00
8th grade mathematics grade	2.45**	1.73*	2.70***	2.59***	2.10*
8th grade English grade	-0.51	-1.32	-1.15	-0.00	0.25
Days absent 1st semester	-0.21**	-0.16	0.04	0.11	0.26
Cohort 2 = 1	2.25	-0.03	2.86**	-0.49	-1.51
Age in years	-2.22*	-1.58	-2.02*	-0.87	1.46
Female = 1	1.24	-2.55*	-1.38	-1.81	-2.45
Free Lunch = 1	0.36	1.55	-0.11	0.41	0.48
School 1.2 = 1	1.64	2.33	-0.57	-1.22	-1.48
School 1.3 = 1	0.85	6.79***	1.45	3.27**	-2.79
School 1.4 = 1	-4.13*	-0.81	-0.83	-8.82***	-3.67
School 1.5 = 1	-0.36	2.33	-5.11***	-5.44***	-2.05
8th grade ability group Basic = 1	-4.23***		4.93		
8th grade ability group Honors = 1			7.76***	8.06***	
8th grade ability group Advanced = 1		10.00*	20.71	11.84***	1.48
8th grade ability group Spec Prog = 1	-4.79	4.76	8.26	-8.73	
8th grade not ability grouped = 1	-3.92	-1.36	1.78	13.05**	
8th grade ability group missing = 1	-2.47	-3.82	-2.36	-11.88	
Black = 1	-1.13	-1.19	-2.84*	-1.68	-3.29
Constant	12.11***	7.93*	9.57***	23.77***	28.97***
σ	10.48***	12.12***	11.54***	7.89***	6.00***
Log-likelihood	-1,489.53	-1,811.93	-2,782.05	-999.25***	-388.76
Log-likelihood of full interactive race model	-1,477.26	-1,803.52	-2,776.29	-993.27	-385.63
Difference in df	16	16	17	15	9
p	0.08	0.40	0.83	0.68	0.71

*$p < .05$. **$p < 0.01$. ***$p < .001$.

cesses within ability groups, it is appropriate to rely on the noninteractive models.

Table 6.3a shows that eighth grade English test scores have a statistically significant positive effect on ninth grade achievement at every ability group level. Eighth grade mathematics test scores have a positive effect on English achievement in every group and reach statistical significance in the Regular and Honors groups. Eighth graders' grades typically have a positive effect on ninth grade achievement, but the effect is weak—likely due to a positive correlation between test scores and grades. The results also show that older students attain significantly lower achievement than younger students. Compared to assignment to the Regular English group in eighth grade, being in the Basic English group has a negative effect on achievement for students in the Regular ninth grade group. Assignment to the Honors group in eighth grade has a positive effect on achievement for students in the ninth grade Honors group. Spending eighth grade in an ungrouped school has a positive effect on achievement for students in ninth grade Regular, Honors, and Advanced groups, though statistical significance is attained only in the Honors group.

Of greatest interest here is the effect of race on student achievement. The race coefficient has a weak negative effect on ninth grade English achievement in every group, but attains statistical significance only in the Advanced group. The small number of Blacks in this group makes this finding difficult to interpret. In general, the results show virtually no main effect of race on level of English achievement in any of the ability groups.

Table 6.3b shows the coefficient estimates for the model containing race as a main effect. It also reports the difference between the log-likelihood value for that model and a fully interactive race model for mathematics. The difference between the two models is not statistically significant at the $p < .05$ level in any of the ability groups. The lowest probability of a nonrandom difference is found in the Very Basic model, where $p < .08$. These results indicate that these factors influence the learning of Black and White students in every mathematics ability group in the same way.

The coefficients of the models in Table 6.3b show that eighth grade mathematics test score has a positive effect on ninth grade mathematics achievement in every ability group, as does eighth grade English test score in the Basic, Regular, and Honors mathematics ability groups. Grade in eighth grade mathematics also has a positive effect on ninth grade mathematics achievement. Being older has negative effect on achievement in the Very Basic and Regular groups. Relative to enrollment in the Regular mathematics group in eighth grade, being in the Basic mathematics group has a negative effect on achievement in the Very Basic group in ninth grade. Being in the Honors mathematics group in eighth grade has a positive effect on ninth grade mathematics achievement in the Regular and Honors group and being in the Advanced group in eighth grade also has a positive effect on achievement in the ninth grade Honors group.

The effects of race on ninth grade mathematics achievement are small. While being Black has a weak negative effect on achievement in all the ability groups, the coefficient is statistically significant only in the large Regular group. Here, being Black is associated with lower achievement.

Tables 6.4a and 6.4b contain three sets of analyses. First, in the first column of results, they show the mean and standard deviation of ninth grade observed test scores by ability group and race. The statistics for each ability group are calculated over those students actually assigned to that group.

The next set of columns (four for English, five for mathematics) show the mean and standard deviation of predicted test scores by ability group and race. These predictions, based on the tobit models, are calculated for students in each ability group, had they been assigned to the different ability groups. For example, White students assigned to the Basic English group have an observed mean test score of 25.6. If the typical student in the Basic group were placed in the Regular group instead, that student's predicted test score would be 24.1. If the student were assigned to the Honors group, the expected score would be 25.5 and an Advanced assignment should yield a score of 27.2. As another example, the mean test score of Black students assigned to the Regular mathematics group is 51.5. If moved to a different group, that student could expect to receive a score of 52.3 in the Very Basic group, 49.3 in the Basic group, 58.0 in the Honors group, and 66.6 in the Advanced group. Caution should be exercised in interpreting the predicted test scores as students are moved increasingly further from the student's actual ability group assignment.

The third set of analyses in Tables 6.4a and 6.4b show the difference between the actual and predicted mean test scores by ability group and race. These results show a pattern of improved test scores with assignment to a higher ability group and worsened test scores with placement in a lower ability group. For example, the achievement of a White student in the Regular English group would fall by 7.5 percentage points if the student were moved to the Basic group, and increase by 1.8 percentage points if moved to the Honors group and 4.4 percentage points if reassigned to the Advanced group. There are exceptions to this pattern, of course, but Basic English is the only ability group that regularly violates it.

A comparison of the magnitude of the change in achievement when a student is moved to a higher or lower ability group for Blacks and Whites reveals a strong race difference. White students show greater gains in

Table 6.4a. Predicted 9th Grade English Achievement by Ability Group

Whites

Actual Ability Group		Actual Test Score	Predicted test score if students were assigned to:				Differences in actual test scores and predicted test score if students were assigned to:			
			Basic	Regular	Honors	Advanced	Basic	Regular	Honors	Advanced
Basic ($N = 125$)	Mean	25.6	25.6	24.1	25.5	27.2	–0.0	–1.5	–0.1	1.7
	s.d.	13.5	10.2	14.2	15.1	16.5				
Regular ($N = 781$)	Mean	50.7	43.2	50.7	52.5	55.1	–7.5	–0.0	1.8	4.4
	s.d.	19.0	11.1	16.0	17.3	18.3				
Honors ($N = 482$)	Mean	76.5	56.8	73.7	76.5	79.1	–19.7	–2.8	0.0	2.5
	s.d.	15.5	8.1	12.4	13.3	14.0				
Advanced ($N = 94$)	Mean	90.1	64.2	84.1	88.2	90.4	–26.0	–6.0	–2.0	0.3
	s.d.	8.6	4.4	6.7	7.3	8.0				

Blacks

Actual Ability Group		Actual Test Score	Predicted test score if students were assigned to:				Differences in actual test scores and predicted test score if students were assigned to:			
			Basic	Regular	Honors	Advanced	Basic	Regular	Honors	Advanced
Basic ($N = 126$)	Mean	20.2	20.2	17.4	19.0	14.7	0.0	–2.9	–1.3	–5.5
	s.d.	9.5	7.4	10.3	10.9	12.1				
Regular ($N = 348$)	Mean	39.8	35.1	39.8	41.3	37.6	–4.8	0.0	1.5	–2.2
	s.d.	17.2	10.8	15.6	16.7	17.7				
Honors ($N = 74$)	Mean	67.0	50.3	64.6	67.0	63.0	–16.7	–2.5	–0.0	–4.1
	s.d.	17.6	9.4	14.6	15.7	15.9				
Advanced ($N = 10$)	Mean	75.1	57.5	75.8	79.0	75.0	–17.5	0.8	4.0	0.0
	s.d.	16.9	5.6	9.3	10.2	12.3				

Note. The mean of the observed test scores for students in an ability group does not exactly equal the predicted mean for students with those characteristics if they were in that ability group because of the nonlinearities of the tobit model.

Table 6.4b. Predicted 9th Grade Mathematics Achievement by Ability Group

Whites

Actual Ability Group		Actual Test Score	Predicted test score if students were assigned to:					Differences in actual test scores and predicated test score if students were assigned to:				
			Very Basic	Basic	Regular	Honors	Advanced	Very Basic	Basic	Regular	Honors	Advanced
Very Basic (N = 218)	Mean	30.2	30.2	30.3	34.2	41.7	50.9	–0.0	0.0	4.0	11.5	20.7
	s.d.	17.3	13.4	12.8	13.3	12.5	13.5					
Basic (N = 292)	Mean	44.8	46.1	44.8	48.2	55.3	64.4	1.3	–0.0	3.4	10.5	19.6
	s.d.	18.5	12.8	13.1	13.5	12.6	13.9					
Regular (N = 560)	Mean	61.6	58.9	56.9	61.6	67.7	75.9	–2.7	–4.7	0.0	6.1	14.3
	s.d.	11.8	13.7	13.4	12.8	12.6	12.6					
Honors (N = 266)	Mean	85.0	71.0	74.8	82.4	85.3	89.2	–14.0	–10.2	–2.6	0.3	4.2
	s.d.	11.4	8.3	9.4	9.8	8.8	7.8					
Advanced (N = 141)	Mean	93.1	75.9	72.9	98.4	92.5	94.5	–17.2	–20.3	5.3	–0.6	1.4
	s.d.	8.0	7.4	7.4	8.0	8.5	7.2					

Blacks

Actual Ability Group		Actual Test Score	Predicted test score if students were assigned to:					Differences in actual test scores and predicated test score if students were assigned to:				
			Very Basic	Basic	Regular	Honors	Advanced	Very Basic	Basic	Regular	Honors	Advanced
Very Basic (N = 178)	Mean	24.6	24.6	24.6	26.1	35.6	42.7	0.0	0.0	1.5	11.0	18.1
	s.d.	14.4	10.4	10.0	10.2	9.9	11.1					
Basic (N = 171)	Mean	35.8	38.8	35.8	37.5	46.0	55.0	3.0	0.0	1.7	10.2	19.2
	s.d.	15.7	11.7	11.7	11.4	10.9	11.5					
Regular (N = 162)	Mean	51.5	52.3	49.3	51.5	58.0	66.6	0.8	–2.2	0.0	6.5	15.1
	s.d.	16.6	12.9	12.6	13.6	12.5	13.2					
Honors (N = 33)	Mean	75.1	63.4	66.3	71.9	75.1	79.8	–11.7	–8.8	–3.2	–0.0	4.7
	s.d.	14.0	9.3	12.2	12.8	12.2	8.6					
Advanced (N = 11)	Mean	85.0	69.9	65.4	89.5	83.2	85.4	–15.1	–19.6	4.5	–1.8	0.4
	s.d.	7.1	6.6	8.6	9.7	9.6	7.2					

Note. The mean of the observed test scores for students in an ability group does not exactly equal the predicted mean for students with those characteristics if they were in that ability group because of the nonlinearities of the tobit model.

achievement when moved to a higher group and greater losses in achievement when moved to a lower group than do Black students. This pattern can be illustrated by comparing Black and White predicted achievement for students in the Regular English group. If White students are moved from the Regular group to the Honors group, they gain 1.8 percentage points, whereas the gain for Black students is only 1.5 percentage points. If Whites move from the Regular group to the Basic group, they lose 7.5 percentage points, compared to only 4.8 for Blacks. Thus, Black students are gaining less than White students when moved to a higher ability group but losing less than Whites when moved to a lower ability group. This pattern holds for most comparisons.

These results suggest that Blacks do not benefit as much as Whites when they are placed in a more challenging learning environment. Three possible causes for race differences in achievement have been suggested: learning differences, differences in teacher expectations and peer influences, and ability differences. The tobit analyses presented in Tables 6.3a and 6.3b address the question of learning differences. The analyses showed no significant race differences in how Black and White students learn when assigned to the same ability group.

The second explanation cannot be tested directly with these data, since teacher expectations and peer influences were not explicitly included in the tobit models. However, these contextual variables influence student motivation, which in turn, is likely correlated with eighth grade test scores and grades. Since both of these prior measures of achievement are controlled for in the analysis, they provide a partial control for teacher expectations and peer influences. The lack of significant differences in the effects of the previous achievement factors suggests that teacher and peer influences do not explain race differences in ninth grade predicted achievement gains.

The third explanation is that it is not race per se that accounts for the differential effect of movement to a higher or lower ability group, but rather ability. As can be seen in Table 6.2, although there is a considerable overlap of Black and White test scores within each ability group, Blacks typically have lower test scores than Whites. It may be ability that explains the differences in achievement gains and losses.

To examine this possibility, the students in each ability group were divided into the top 75% and bottom 25%, based on eighth grade test scores. The predicted achievement for each of these categories was calculated for each ability group. If ability, rather than race, determines the magnitude of achievement gains within an ability group, then the pattern observed for race would be expected to appear for ability as well, although with greater consistency. That is, students in the lower 25% of the ability distribution in each ability group would show smaller gains in achievement when moved to a higher ability group than students in the top 75% of the distribution. Similarly, the achievement of the low 25% of the students should show smaller declines than that of the high 75% when moved to a lower ability group.

Tables 6.5a and 6.5b present the same results as Tables 6.4a and 6.4b, but for the top 75% and bottom 25% of the achievement distribution, instead of by race. Table 6.5a shows that for the highest 75% of students, movement from any English ability group to a higher ability group results in growth in achievement The exception is a slight decline when Basic students are moved to the Regular English group. Movement to a lower ability group results in a considerable drop in achievement.

The typical student in the lowest 25% of the sample shows less improvement when moved to a higher English ability group. The average student in the lowest 25% of the Basic ability group has poorer achievement when moved to any higher ability group. The lowest quartile of students in the Regular and Honors ability groups show almost no change when moved to any higher ability group. For all ability groups, however, the lowest 25% of students show declines in achievement when moved to a lower ability group.

Table 6.5b presents the results for mathematics. Students in the top three quarters of their ability group show strong achievement gains when placed in a higher ability group and significant declines when assigned to a lower group. One exception to this pattern occurs when students from the Very Basic mathematics group move to the Basic group. Such moves have essentially no effect on achievement. It may be that special resources are provided in the Very Basic group, such as smaller class sizes or special tutors, which counterbalance the richer curriculum of the Basic group. This could also account for the improvement when students in the Basic group are moved to the Very Basic group. One other deviation from the pattern is seen in the surprising gains Advanced students would make if reassigned to the Regular group.

Students in the lowest 25% of the mathematics achievement distribution show virtually the same gains and losses as those in the highest 75%. This includes the general pattern of increases when assigned to a higher group and decreases when assigned to a lower group. It also includes most of the exceptions to this pattern.

Comparing Tables 6.4 and 6.5 reveals that the pattern of gains and losses—even the magnitude of gains and losses—that are predicted to accrue from being assigned to higher or lower ability groups is similar whether the students are divided by race or by prior ability and achievement. However, the patterns are somewhat more pronounced and consistent for the ability comparison than for the race comparison. Coupled with the lack of significant differences in the effects of factors contributing

Table 6.5a. Predicted 9th Grade English Achievement by Ability Group

Highest 75% in Group

Actual Ability Group		Actual Test Score	Predicted test score if students were assigned to:				Differences in actual test scores and predicted test score if students were assigned to:			
			Basic	Regular	Honors	Advanced	Basic	Regular	Honors	Advanced
Basic (N = 182)	Mean	26.5	26.3	25.5	27.3	26.6	-0.1	-1.0	0.9	0.1
	s.d.	11.5	8.4	11.7	12.3	14.6				
Regular (N = 842)	Mean	54.4	45.6	54.4	56.6	57.9	-8.7	0.1	2.2	3.5
	s.d.	16.2	8.8	12.5	13.5	15.1				
Honors (N = 417)	Mean	81.7	59.8	78.5	81.7	83.7	-21.8	-3.2	0.0	2.0
	s.d.	11.2	5.0	7.7	8.2	9.4				
Advanced (N = 79)	Mean	91.8	65.5	86.2	90.4	92.4	-26.3	-5.7	-1.4	0.6
	s.d.	7.0	3.1	4.6	5.0	6.2				

Lowest 25% in Group

Actual Ability Group		Actual Test Score	Predicted test score if students were assigned to:				Differences in actual test scores and predicted test score if students were assigned to:			
			Basic	Regular	Honors	Advanced	Basic	Regular	Honors	Advanced
Basic (N = 69)	Mean	13.5	13.8	8.2	8.8	6.1	0.0	-5.6	-5.0	-7.7
	s.d.	7.2	3.3	4.4	4.1	6.1				
Regular (N = 287)	Mean	26.8	26.3	26.6	26.9	25.8	-0.3	0.0	0.3	-0.8
	s.d.	10.0	5.3	7.6	7.8	10.0				
Honors (N = 139)	Mean	55.9	44.3	54.5	56.0	56.5	-11.7	-1.5	0.0	0.5
	s.d.	12.7	5.7	8.6	9.4	10.6				
Advanced (N = 25)	Mean	78.7	57.3	74.4	77.3	77.8	-20.5	-3.4	-0.5	0.0
	s.d.	13.7	4.3	7.3	7.6	9.8				

Note. The mean of the observed test scores for students in an ability group does not exactly equal the predicted mean for students with those characteristics if they were in that ability group because of the nonlinearities of the tobit model.

Table 6.5b. Predicted 9th Grade Mathematics Achievement by Ability Group

Highest 75% in Group

Actual Ability Group		Actual Test Score	Predicted test score if students were assigned to:					Differences in actual test scores and predicated test score if students were assigned to:				
			Very Basic	Basic	Regular	Honors	Advanced	Very Basic	Basic	Regular	Honors	Advanced
Very Basic (N = 294)	Mean	31.9	32.2	31.8	34.7	42.8	51.9	0.3	−0.2	2.8	10.9	19.9
	s.d.	15.8	11.0	10.9	11.7	10.9	11.9					
Basic (N = 343)	Mean	46.4	48.7	46.6	49.6	56.6	66.7	2.3	0.3	3.2	10.3	20.3
	s.d.	17.2	10.1	11.1	11.5	11.0	10.9					
Regular (N = 533)	Mean	65.5	63.0	60.7	65.5	71.0	79.9	−2.5	−4.7	−0.0	5.5	14.4
	s.d.	15.4	8.0	10.8	10.0	10.2	8.6					
Honors (N = 222)	Mean	87.7	73.8	77.4	85.3	88.0	91.8	−13.9	−10.2	−2.3	0.3	4.2
	s.d.	9.3	6.0	7.6	7.3	6.8	5.2					
Advanced (N = 113)	Mean	95.7	78.9	75.6	101.4	95.7	97.5	−16.8	−20.1	5.7	0.0	1.8
	s.d.	4.8	4.0	5.0	4.9	5.8	3.9					

Lowest 25% in Group

Actual Ability Group		Actual Test Score	Predicted test score if students were assigned to:					Differences in actual test scores and predicated test score if students were assigned to:				
			Very Basic	Basic	Regular	Honors	Advanced	Very Basic	Basic	Regular	Honors	Advanced
Very Basic (N = 102)	Mean	15.4	14.5	16.0	18.5	27.9	33.9	0.0	1.5	4.0	13.4	19.3
	s.d.	10.0	4.4	5.3	5.4	5.8	4.8					
Basic (N = 120)	Mean	27.4	28.2	26.6	29.0	38.2	44.5	1.6	0.0	2.3	11.5	17.9
	s.d.	12.1	6.0	6.2	5.8	5.7	5.3					
Regular (N = 189)	Mean	42.0	41.6	39.5	42.1	50.0	56.6	−0.5	−2.6	0.0	7.9	14.5
	s.d.	13.4	7.9	8.1	8.4	8.2	8.1					
Honors (N = 77)	Mean	73.1	59.8	63.6	69.4	73.3	77.5	−13.5	−9.8	−3.9	0.0	4.1
	s.d.	12.9	6.9	9.2	10.1	9.0	6.5					
Advanced (N = 39)	Mean	83.4	65.4	62.8	87.0	80.6	83.4	−18.0	−20.6	3.6	−2.8	0.0
	s.d.	9.0	5.9	6.2	7.3	6.2	5.3					

Note. The mean of the observed test scores for students in an ability group does not exactly equal the predicted mean for students with those characteristics if they were in that ability group because of the nonlinearities of the tobit model.

to achievement by race, this indicates that prior ability, not race, is key in these results.

CONCLUSIONS

A basic concern about grouping students by ability for instruction is whether this practice is equitable. Equity can be determined by examining how students are assigned to ability groups and whether differences in learning opportunities vary across ability group levels. Judging the fairness of the assignment process requires looking at the factors that schools rely on in making ability group placements. Does a school focus solely on indicators of a student's academic ability in deciding the student's ability group level? If so, are these indicators reasonable measures of ability? If grades are used, are the grades of some students inflated or depressed for nonacademic reasons? Are all students given an equal chance to earn high grades? Are high-achieving students advantaged, in terms of grade point average, by taking Honors or Advanced Placement courses? If a high-ability student performs poorly in a particular course, does the teacher assign the earned grade or does the student's reputation as a good student influence the evaluation? If standardized achievement test scores determine ability group assignment, does a cultural bias that may characterize these tests disadvantage minority students in the assignment process?

If factors other than a student's academic ability are taken into account in the assignment process, how do these nonacademic factors affect placement? Many schools consider parental input in making ability group assignments. However, not all parents are equally involved in their children's education, nor do all parents have the same understanding of the impact of ability grouping on educational attainment. Students may be disadvantaged if their parents fail to intervene in placement decisions for their child. A number of schools give students a voice in the assignment process. Yet if a student fails to appreciate the consequences of curriculum decisions for their future educational or career plans, the student may make poor course selections. Another factor influencing ability group assignment is a school's organizational constraints. For example, the structure of the master schedule may force a student to choose between an academic course and, say, band. Constraints on class size also may restrict a student's choice of academic courses.

In most schools, nonacademic factors play a significant role in the process of assigning students to ability groups and explain the academic heterogeneity that characterizes most ability groups. However, research fails to demonstrate that race or ethnicity is among the factors that influence student assignment. Nevertheless, critics of ability grouping continue to point to the disproportionately large number of minority students in the lower ability groups as evidence that the practice is discriminatory. This criticism has been the driving force behind the effort to detrack schools.

To better understand the role of race in the process of assigning students to ability groups, it is necessary examine race differences in student performance. Empirical evidence shows that Black students, on average, lag White students in academic achievement. When ability or prior achievement is taken into account, the effect of being Black on ability group assignment typically disappears. That is, controlling for standardized test scores and grades, Black and White students are equally likely to be assigned to low-ability groups. This finding indicates that academic achievement, not race, is the determining factor in the assignment of students to ability groups. The higher proportion of Black students in lower ability groups is due to the lower academic achievement of Black students compared to White students. Hence, if the assignment process is inequitable, it is not because race is a factor in the placement process.

A second way ability grouping may be inequitable is if unequal learning opportunities are provided to students across ability group levels. Research consistently shows that students in higher ability groups have the advantage of a more challenging curriculum, better instruction, a stronger academic climate, and fewer instructional disruptions than students in lower ability groups. Thus, ability grouping, as typically practiced, advantages students assigned to the higher groups and disadvantages those assigned to the lower groups. Since Black students are more likely to be assigned to low-ability groups, they are more likely to have fewer learning opportunities in school than White students.

Variation in learning opportunities across ability groups is not an essential characteristic of the practice of ability grouping, of course. Educators could create the same opportunities for learning in lower ability groups that exist in the higher groups. By close attention to practices related to ability grouping, such as the assignment of teachers to instructional groups, the quality of the curriculum at each ability group level, and the nature of the reward system in a school, greater equity could be insured in the distribution of learning opportunities across ability groups. However, until the educational opportunities in lower ability groups are improved, students in low-ability groups remain disadvantaged. And since Black students are disproportionately assigned to low groups, they experience the disadvantages of ability grouping to a greater extent than White students.

Even when Black and White students are assigned to the same ability group, they may not receive equal learning opportunities, depending on the nature of the instructional process within the ability group. The instructional techniques that teachers employ and the academic and social climate that characterize ability groups may have a different impact on students who differ by race. The curriculum may be culturally biased in favor of White students, pedagogical techniques may fail to take cultural differences into account, and teacher-student interactions may be more supportive of White students. The achievement gap between Black and White students at every ability group level suggests that this may be the case. However valid the criticism that Black students do not receive the same learning opportunities as White students, it should be aimed at the instructional process in general, rather than at ability grouping.

The analyses presented in this chapter re-examine the question of whether ability grouping disadvantages Black students compared to their White peers. The study builds on recent research showing that nearly all students, regardless of race, benefit from assignment to a higher ability group. The present study investigated whether the advantages of higher group placement benefit Black and White students equally. In the analysis, test scores were predicted for students who were hypothetically advanced one or two ability group levels from the level to which they actually were assigned. The results showed that while all students benefitted from a higher group placement, White students, on average, made greater achievement gains than Black students. Thus Black students appeared to be disadvantaged academically, relative to White students, even in the more demanding learning environment of higher ability groups and even when Black and White students had comparable ability.

This finding could be taken as evidence that ability grouping disadvantages Black students compared to White students, regardless of ability group level. However, an alternative explanation is possible. The results are consistent with the interpretation that academic ability or preparation, not race, accounts for the smaller achievement gains of Black students in ability groups at all levels. In the analysis presented here, the achievement gains of Black and White students at both ends of the ability distribution in each ability group were examined. The analysis showed that students in the lower quartile of the ability distribution at every ability group level had slower growth in achievement than their peers in the top three fourths of the distribution. That is, while all students gained in achievement by placement in a higher ability group, the gains of students at the high end of the achievement distribution in the group were greater than those at the low end of the distribution. This was true regardless of race. These results support the argument that student ability, not race, drives the differential achievement gains of Black and White students assigned to the same ability group.

It must be noted, however, that while the achievement scores of both Black and White students are found at both ends of the achievement distribution in all ability groups, Black students are more likely than Whites to be found in the lower part of the distribution at every ability group level. Thus, Black students are relatively less likely to gain from assignment to a higher ability group than White students, not because of their race, but due to their weaker academic achievement.

In summary, the empirical studies reviewed in this chapter, as well as the new research reported here, show that if Black students are disadvantaged by the practice of ability grouping, the reason is not discrimination, but rather the lower achievement level of Black students relative to that of White students. More Black students are assigned to lower ability groups than White students because Black students tend to have lower achievement scores than their White peers. Black students make slower academic gains in ability groups at any level than do White students because Black students are more likely to be at the lower end of the ability distribution at every ability group level.

These findings suggest two specific policy recommendations for educators and one more general recommendation. The specific recommendations have to do with the practice of ability grouping. The research indicates that students learn more when placed in more challenging academic environments. Since ability groups vary by level in the quantity and quality of instruction provided, students should be assigned to the ability group that provides the most challenging material of which they are capable. Moreover, if a student learns more easily in one subject area than another, they should be placed in a higher ability group in that area. Students are disadvantaged by assignment to an ability group that does not encourage them to work to the best of their ability.

A second policy recommendation is related to the widespread criticism that ability grouping and tracking discriminate against minority students. The research offers no support for this belief. Ability grouping or tracking is an organizational feature of a school designed to make instruction more efficient and effective. The lower quality of instruction associated with lower ability groups is not a necessary component of the practice. With effort, the quality of instruction in lower ability groups or tracks can be improved to equal that found in the higher groups. Consequently, the policy recommendation consistent with the research is to improve instruction in the lower groups through assignment of more skilled teachers, provision of more interesting curricular assignments, creation of a strong academic climate, and use of a reward system to increase the motivation and effort of low-ability students to attain their potential in school.

The more general policy recommendation suggested by this study stems from the finding that Black students are more likely than White students to be assigned to lower ability groups and that even when they are placed in higher groups, Black students make slower achievement gains than their White peers. The study showed that academic ability, rather than race, explains these results. Black students are disproportionately assigned to lower groups not because they are Black, but because they are more likely than Whites to have weaker academic histories. This finding is consistent with the persistence of the achievement gap between Black and White students. It suggests that Black students need compensatory measures to enable them to compete on an equal footing with their White peers. A major national policy providing compensatory education is needed to better prepare minority students for school. To tweak the organizational practice of ability grouping may produce modest improvements in equity, but it does not address the underlying reason for the poor academic performance of many Black students. Providing minority students with a stronger foundation for learning is essential to ensure educational equity.

REFERENCES

Alexander, K. L., Cook, M. A., & McDill, E. L. (1978). Curriculum tracking and educational stratification. *American Sociological Review, 43*, 47–66.

Gamoran, A. (1992). The variable effects of high school tracking. *American Sociological Review, 57*, 812–828.

Gardner, H. (1993). *Multiple intelligences: The theory in practice.* New York: Basic Books.

Hallinan, M. T. (1991). School differences in tracking structures and track assignments. *Journal of Research on Adolescence, 1*, 251–275.

Hallinan, M. T. (2003). Ability grouping and student learning. In D. Ravitch (Ed.), *Brookings papers on educational policy, 2003* (pp. 95–140). Washington, DC: Brookings Institution.

Hallinan, M. T., & Kubitschek, W. N. (1999). Curriculum differentiation and high school achievement. *Journal of Social Psychology of Education, 3*(1), 41–62.

Hallinan, M. T., & Sorensen, A. B. (1985). Class size, ability group size, and student achievement. *American Journal of Education, 22*, 485–499.

Kubitschek, W. N., & Hallinan, M. T. (1996). Race, gender and inequity in track assignments. In A. Pallas (Ed.), *Research in sociology of education and socialization* (Vol. 11, pp. 121–146). Greenwich, CT: JAI Press.

Maddala, G. S. (1983). *Limited-dependent and qualitative variables in econometrics.* New York: Cambridge University Press.

Oakes, J. (1985). *Keeping track: How schools structure inequality.* New Haven, CT: Yale University Press.

Oakes, J., Gamoran, A., & Page, R. (1992). Curriculum differentiation: Opportunities, outcomes and meanings. In P. Jackson (Ed.), *Handbook of research on curriculum* (pp. 570–608). New York: Macmillan.

Rehberg, R. A., & Rosenthal, E. R. (1978). *Class and merit in the American high school.* New York: Longman.

CHAPTER 7

CLASSROOM ORGANIZATION AND INSTRUCTIONAL QUALITY

Adam Gamoran

When teachers divide students into separate classes or groups on the basis of prior performance, they do so because they think students are best served by receiving instruction targeted to their particular levels of accomplishment up to that point. Consider the case of first grade reading: Some children enter school without knowing the alphabet, others are familiar with the letter sounds, and still others are already strong readers. To accommodate these differences, teachers typically divide students into reading groups. For another example, consider ninth grade mathematics: Some students enter high school with eight grade algebra under their belts, others have yet to master arithmetic, and many others are in-between. In response, high schools commonly divide students for ninth grade mathematics into general math, pre-algebra, algebra, and geometry classes. To most teachers, these divisions make sense. They make it possible to think about instruction as organized in a clear sequence, to find each student's place in the sequence using criteria they consider objective, and to provide instruction intended to move each student along the instructional hierarchy. In short, ability grouping seems like a neutral device for matching instruction to students' needs.

Despite this sensible logic, there are three reasons why ability grouping cannot be viewed as neutral. First, it leads to divisions that go beyond academic differences. When teachers divide students on the basis of academic performance, they tend to separate students who differ from one another by race, ethnicity, and social class. These inequalities—that have little to do with school—are perpetuated as students move up the ladder of grade levels (Oakes, Gamoran, & Page, 1992). Students from disadvantaged backgrounds tend to score lower on tests for a host of reasons, many of which are unrelated to schooling, and therefore the division of students on the basis of academic performance results in social as well as academic segregation. Second, when teachers create classes that are relatively homogeneous in student performance, they eliminate much of the diversity that might foster rich and productive conversations in classrooms. Although grouping students by performance level may make it possible to sharpen the delivery of instruction to meet students' levels of skills and knowledge, that sharpening may be double-edged, as it eliminates the very differences that some teachers build on in their instruction. Third, although teachers may intend to provide instruction of equal quality at all levels, in practice, that rarely occurs. Instead, students in lower-ranked classes and groups encounter instruction of lower quality, compared to their peers in higher-ranked classes. Consequently, instead of helping low-achieving students catch up, ability grouping tends to result in wider and wider achievement gaps over time (Gamoran & Berends, 1987; Oakes et al., 1992).

Although we can clearly identify the problems of grouping and tracking, that does not make eliminating these practices an easy solution. On the contrary, detracking is also associated with problems of instructional quality, and successful detracking is rare. Consequently, after we examine the challenges to instruction associated with dividing students by performance level, it will be equally important to consider the instructional challenges associated with mixed-ability grouping.

TRACKING AND INSTRUCTION

James Rosenbaum has studied both tracking and detracking. His case study of a working-class high school in the 1970s was one of the first to show how tracking promoted inequality in schools (Rosenbaum, 1976). Courses in which students enrolled—as early as junior high school—often dictated the opportunities they encountered throughout high school. Tracking was like a "tournament": Students moved down to lower track levels over time, but rarely moved up. Students in high tracks had better academic opportunities than their low-track counterparts, as teachers in high-track classes were more enthusiastic and better prepared for teaching. In the 1980s, Jeannie Oakes (1985) used data from a national study of secondary schools to confirm and extend Rosenbaum's case study findings. She found that teachers in low-track classes spent more time managing students' behavior, whereas high-track teachers could devote relatively more time to instruction. This instructional difference corresponded to differences in student behavior: Rates of off-task behavior were higher in low-track classes, although the magnitude of the difference seems small: 4% compared to 1% off-task in low- and high-track mathematics classes, respectively, and 4% compared to 2% of students off-task in low- and high-track English classes, respectively (p.101).

Oakes also learned, from observations of classes and interviews with teachers and students, that the content of high-track classes was more academically rigorous compared to low-track classes. For example, students were more likely to write essays in high-track than in low-track English classes, and more likely to engage in problem solving in high-track than in low-track mathematics classes. Students in high-track classes had more exposure to high-status content, such as classic and modern literature in English, as opposed to juvenile fiction which was more common in low tracks, and advanced concepts in mathematics as opposed to a focus on facts and computation. When students were asked about the most important thing they learned during the year, a response that typified a high-track science class was, "We have learned the basics of the laws of relativity, and basics in electronics. The teacher applies these lessons to practical situations;" whereas a student in a low-track responded, "I can distinguish one type rock from another" (Oakes, 1985, p. 69, 71).

The Link to Student Achievement

Although the instructional differences are pervasive, they are relatively small, and Oakes (1985) acknowledged that instruction in all classes emphasized teacher lectures and student recitation and seatwork:

> The most significant thing we found is that generally our entire sample of classes turned out to be pretty noninvolving places. As we expected, passive activities—listening to the teacher, writing answers to questions, and taking tests—were dominant at all track levels. And, also not unexpected, the opportunities students had in any group of classes to answer open-ended questions to work in cooperative learning groups, to direct the classroom activity, or to make decisions about what happened in class were extremely limited. In most classes these things just did not happen at all. Any statements that can be made about differences between tracks in this respect must be seen in this context. (p. 129)

If instructional differences are small but persistent, are they large enough to affect student achievement? Research in the 1990s by Gamoran and his colleagues provided quantitative evidence of the connection between unequal instructional opportunities and unequal achievement across tracks. In a study of 25 Midwestern middle and high schools, the authors noted that differences in the quality of instruction in English classes accounted for much of the widening gap in student achievement on a literature test (Gamoran, Nystrand, Berends, & LePore, 1995). Students in low-track classes were more often off-task, less consistent in completing their assignments, and spent less time in class discussion, compared with their high-track counterparts, and these differences accounted for part of the achievement gap. Teachers in high- and low-track classes were about equally likely to ask open-ended questions, but in high-track classes, the open-ended questions focused on the literature students were studying, and this provided an additional advantage on the literature test. In low-track classes, teacher questions about literature generally focused on reporting plot summaries rather than on more interpretive concerns.

Other quantitative studies, ranging from elementary to high school, support the contention that instructional differences across groups and tracks contribute to achievement differences. At the high school level, students in college-preparatory programs enroll in more academic courses, and particularly more advanced mathematics and science courses, and this contributes to their achievement advantages in those subjects (Gamoran, 1987). In elementary school, students in higher-ranked reading groups cover more new words and read more stories over the course of a school year, making the reading gap between high- and low-ranked groups wider at the end of the year than it was at the beginning of the year (Gamoran, 1986; Rowan & Miracle, 1983). Two students who start the school year at similar reading levels, but who are assigned to different reading groups, end up with different reading achievement at the end of the year depending on whether they were assigned to a higher or a lower group. Thus, although providing different instruction to different groups seems like it would help low-achieving students catch up, usually that is not what happens; instead they fall further and further behind.

Can Tracking Help Instead of Harm Low Achievers?

Not all uses of grouping and tracking are as damaging to the prospects of low-achieving students as typically occurs. Catholic high schools, for example, produce less inequality between tracks than do public high schools (Bryk, Lee, & Holland, 1993; Gamoran, 1992). This occurs because Catholic schools place more academic demands on students who are not enrolled in the college-preparatory program, than do public high schools. Case studies also suggests that a school climate of effort and caring common in Catholic schools enhances teacher and student motivation in low-, as well as high-track classes (Camarena, 1990; Valli, 1990). Of course, Catholic schools have the advantage of being able to select their students, and it may be that among low-achieving students, those who attend Catholic schools are more responsive to academic demands than are those who attend public schools.

In the study of English classes in 25 middle and high schools, Gamoran found only two schools in which low-track classes were successful in preventing their students from falling further behind (Gamoran, 1993). Both happened to be Catholic schools; one was a high school and one was a junior high. Gamoran uncovered three commonalities among the two cases of relatively successful low-track classes. First, the schools had no system of assigning weak or inexperienced teachers to low-track classes. This contrasted with other research showing that teachers compete for the privilege of teaching the honors class (Finley, 1984). In these two schools, the same teachers taught high- and low-level classes. Second, the teachers worked hard to conduct oral discourse with students, instead of relying on worksheets to control student behavior as often occurs in low tracks. Third, the teachers exhibited high expectations for student performance, manifested in their refusal to relinquish the academic curriculum. As one teacher exhorted her students, "I know it's not easy, you guys, I know it's not easy, but we're not going to read a *Weekly Reader* in this class. All right. You deserve to have this information. So stick with it" (Gamoran, 1993, p. 15).

A study of highly restructured schools also revealed a case in which high standards helped prevent divisions among students from resulting in instructional inequality (Gamoran & Weinstein, 1998). At Red Lake Middle School, classroom observers found high-quality instruction in both "regular" eighth grade mathematics and in the high-track algebra classes. At both levels, instruction was characterized by rigorous content, higher-order thinking, and serious discussions of academic material. One of the two algebra classes ranked at the highest level on these criteria of any of the 72 mathematics classes that were observed across 24 restructured schools. The other algebra class and the regular class both averaged higher on these criteria than the typical *high-track* class in the study. High-quality instruction at Red Lake was supported by a pervasive ideology of teaching to one's "passions"—teachers were encouraged to develop courses and curricula that energized them, yet the courses were linked to rigorous disciplinary content. Within a differentiated structure, teachers at Red Lake focused on establishing high standards for all students, and by the year after the observations took place, all students were minimally prepared to enroll in algebra when they graduated from Red Lake and entered high school.

In another instance, Andrew Porter and his colleagues examined programs in New York and California designed to improve the quality of high school mathematics instruction for low-achieving, low-income youth (Gamoran, Porter, Smithson, & White, 1997; White, Gamoran, Smithson, & Porter, 1996; White, Porter, Gamoran, & Smithson, 1997). Students were still sorted into separate classes, but teachers attempted to provide instruction that would bridge the gap between elementary and college-preparatory mathematics, so that students could make a transition into college-preparatory courses. The "transition" courses were partially successful in meeting their goals. Students in the transition courses were more likely to complete a college-preparatory sequence than others who initially enrolled in general math (the traditional low-track class). However, students had the best chance of completing the college-preparatory sequence if they skipped the transition course and enrolled immediately in the college-preparatory track. Moreover, student achievement growth in the transition courses fell in between that of general math and that of college-bound courses such as algebra. More rigorous course content accounted for the achievement benefits of the transition courses over the general math classes that they were replacing.

These cases show that, although it is not what usually happens, it may be possible to group students in a way that promotes equity instead of inequity. Maintaining high standards seems a key to success: Providing a rigorous curriculum, communicating expectations, teaching with passion, and avoiding a system in which less experienced teachers are relegated to lower level classes all played important roles in these rare success stories. Evidence from outside the United States also supports the notion that high standards are essential for using grouping more effectively. Hanna Ayalon and Adam Gamoran (2000) compared course work divisions within academic programs in the United States and Israel. In American high schools, the more students differed from one another in their mathematics course taking, the more inequality in achievement among students from different social backgrounds, and the lower achievement overall. In Israel, by contrast, course work differences were associated with no drop in average achievement, and with *less* inequality by social background. The difference between the two systems is that in the United States, where students in low-track classes have little incentive to do more than receive a passing grade, course content tends to be diluted and students exert minimal effort. In Israel, however, students at all levels of academic courses are preparing for important national examinations that occur at the end of high school. Schools that offer different levels of such courses (which correspond to different levels on the examinations) give low-achieving students better chances for success, while maintaining strong incentives for both teachers and students to cover meaningful course material.

DETRACKING AND INSTRUCTION

Even the most successful uses of grouping still encounter the problem of separating students of different social backgrounds. Social and economic inequalities *outside* schools contribute to substantial differences in test scores inside schools, so when educators divide students by achievement level, the result is classes that differ by social background. For this reason, many educators would prefer to avoid the practice altogether rather than trying to use grouping more effectively.

However, detracking offers its own set of challenges to those who wish to provide high-quality instruction. Although tracking often results in poor instruction for low achievers, it also tends to sustain high-quality instruction for high achievers. Thus, efforts to detrack seem to confront the classic tension between excellence and equity. Can this tension be surmounted? Ultimately, it may come down to a question of values: Is it worth sacrificing some opportunities for the highest achievers for the sake of more equitable opportunities for all students? Research can still contribute much to resolving this dilemma by showing what the tradeoffs are and what it might take to provide equitable opportunities *without* sacrificing high standards of excellence. Can we provide the same high-quality instruction in mixed-ability classes that is now typical in high-track classes?

Successful detracking is rare, and Oakes (1992) has explained that three conditions make detracking difficult:

- *Normative barriers*: Widely shared beliefs hold that people differ from one another, and that it is appropriate to create educational structures that correspond to those differences;
- *Political barriers*: Certain individuals and groups have vested interests in maintaining the current tracking system, such as parents of children who would be placed in honors classes, and teachers who seek the opportunity to teach honors classes;
- *Technical barriers*: Few curricula and teaching methods are currently available that have been designed to meet the challenge of teaching students at widely varying levels of academic performance.

Although much of the research literature focuses on the first two barriers, the third barrier is also formidable. Many teachers are reluctant to teach mixed-ability classes, fearing that weak students will not be able to keep up, or that strong students will be held back, or both (Loveless, 1998; White et al., 1996). Indeed, it seems likely that if the technical barriers to detracking could be overcome, the normative and political barriers would begin to weaken.

Resistance to detracking among teachers seems strongest in subjects where they perceive the curriculum as rigidly sequential, so that students must master one topic before they proceed to the next. Mathematics and foreign languages are examples of such subject areas (Gamoran & Weinstein, 1998; Loveless, 1994). It is difficult to know whether these perceptions are inherent in the subject matter, or if they reflect ingrained beliefs that might be successfully challenged if teachers could be shown that high-quality instruction in mixed-ability classes is possible.

Instructional Problems Associated with Detracking

What is the evidence about detracking and instruction? Most studies of detracking are unable to answer this question because they do not look inside classrooms. Instead, they focus on the political battles that embroil detracking reformers (Oakes & Wells, 1998; Oakes, Wells, Yonezawa, & Ray 1997; Wells & Serna, 1996). Indeed, most detracking reforms are not fully implemented, so their implications for classroom activities have been limited.

A small number of cases of fully detracked schools provide evidence about instruction. Rosenbaum's recent study of detracking in a high school social studies department raises important questions about the viability of detracking to create high-quality instructional opportunities for all students (1999). In social studies, one might think that increasing the academic and social diversity of the classroom would increase the richness of instructional activities because teachers could capitalize on differences among students to create varied roles, topics, and activities that would facilitate dialogue and debate. However, high school social studies relies heavily on reading and writing assignments, and the teachers in this school struggled to find the right level of demands. As one teacher explained:

> Piquing the interest of the brighter kids would require extra readings, extra writing assignments, and extra discussions that we would have to schedule outside of class. It's too hard to do all of this. I really don't do enough for them. There's not enough time. (Rosenbaum, 1999, p. 26)

High-achieving students were, perhaps understandably, resistant to the notion of doing more work for no additional reward. At the same time, teachers felt that weaker students were struggling to keep up with the reading and writing assignments.

Because tracking generally is disproportionately harmful to minority students, it is paradoxical that high-achieving minority students are among those who may have most to lose from detracking. In the school Rosenbaum studied, a group of high-achieving Hispanic students was "slowed down and bored, just like the other bright kids," according to one of the teachers, and in the detracked classroom, "the brighter Hispanic students seem to face a lot of peer pressure in the class from other Hispanic kids who aren't doing well in the class" (Rosenbaum, 1999, p. 27). High-achieving minority students are especially vulnerable to changes that reduce academic demands. According to Rosenbaum (1999),

> These minority students come from working- and lower-class families; their parents do not have strong educational backgrounds. If these students do not find academic challenge at school, they may not find it at all. (p. 27)

In the study of highly restructured schools discussed earlier, three high schools were successful in implementing a structure that did not have any tracks or ability groups (Gamoran & Weinstein, 1998). Analysis of these cases revealed that two of them, Wallingford and Marble Canyon, experienced instructional problems similar to the ones Rosenbaum reported. In sharp contrast, the third case, Cibola High, provided evidence of high-quality instruction in mixed-ability classes.

Wallingford High School is located in an eastern city and all of its students come from minority backgrounds. As part of a restructuring program, all divisions of students within grades and subjects were eliminated. Thus, all students were enrolled in the same ninth grade mathematics course. Teachers reported a variety of problems with this approach. According to Gamoran and Weinstein (1998), "two teachers acknowledged that they had lowered their standards for heterogeneous classes, and one said he had given up trying to cover all the intended material. This resulted in students being promoted without being prepared for the next math course" (p. 393). Consistent with these difficulties, observers reported that the quality of instruction was poor:

> Almost none of the observed classes exhibited more than a minimal amount of thoughtfulness and depth. In math, students' tasks consisted mainly of applying algorithms to routine computations. We did not observe students discussing problems with one another; all the lessons used traditional lecture formats. (p. 393)

Similarly, at another urban high school in the east, teachers held low standards for student performance. This school, Marble Canyon, served students who came from a wider range of ethnic backgrounds than Wallingford. Teachers focused on getting students to attend and remain in school, and did not make rigorous academic demands. One teacher explained that, "Because we're aiming at keeping at-risk kids in school, the more motivated kids aren't being stretched enough" (Gamoran & Weinstein, 1998, p. 393).

Detracking and High-Quality Instruction

In contrast to the problems associated with detracking at Wallingford and Marble Canyon High Schools, observers reported extraordinarily high levels of instructional depth, thoughtfulness, and substantive conversation at Cibola High School, the third detracked high school (Gamoran & Weinstein, 1998). Cibola is also located in the east, and it serves an ethnically and economically diverse population: about half its students come from minority backgrounds, and about half are on free or reduced-price lunch (but the minority students are not necessarily the ones on free lunch). Observers rated the quality of instruction at Cibola as the highest of any of the highly restructured schools. How was this accomplished in a context of heterogeneous classes? The finding held in both mathematics and social studies, and it was particularly notable in mathematics where teachers in other schools most strongly resisted detracking. The absence of tracking seemed to enhance learning opportunities in this school, in contrast to other detracked schools in which classes have been observed. What made the difference?

Gamoran and Weinstein (1998) noted several conditions in Cibola High School which supported high-quality instruction in mixed-ability classes. First, the school had a visionary leader who was able to select her staff and, to some degree, her students. Students had to apply to be admitted and those who did not come from the feeder elementary school were interviewed before being admitted. Choosing staff and students made it possible to establish a distinctive school culture that supported instructional innovation. At Cibola, mathematics and science instruction were integrated, and students worked in small, heterogeneous groups on long-term projects that involved mathematical and scientific principles. At the time the researchers observed instruction, students were working on plans for designing an amusement park. Teachers rejected the notion that mathematics had to be taught in a strict sequence. They did not ignore elementary mathematics, but neither they did prevent a student whose arithmetic was weak from working on algebraic problems. One teacher told the students,

If you need work on your basic math skills, I don't slow down for you. You're supposed to be putting in extra time. We have somebody here on Saturdays. You can stay after school.... On Saturday the library is open. There are two teachers and a resource teacher there to tutor. (p. 402)

On the one hand, the teachers' approach of setting forth complex problems and not slowing down meant that all students were challenged. On the other hand, students with academic deficiencies were well supported. Classes were small—limited to 20 students. In addition, the school had won outside grants that supported a Saturday tutoring program. To graduate from Cibola, students had to prepare "portfolios" in 14 subjects and submit 3 of them to be judged by a panel of school insiders and outsiders. Although all students were required to demonstrate competencies through the portfolios, expectations were also somewhat differentiated according to the capacities of the student. Interviews with educators revealed that "grading is highly individualized ... in a context of serious academic content" (p. 403). Thus, the culture of Cibola supported the approach that the teachers Rosenbaum studied were unable to implement: more work for the highest-achieving students, and differential assessment of student performance, though always with a high minimum threshold.

Perhaps the greatest instructional challenge for detracking is teaching secondary school mathematics to students who differ widely in their math skills. Teachers at Cibola were successful in this aim because they rejected the notion that mathematical knowledge has a rigid sequence. Can this approach be adopted more widely? For the past decade, the College Board's Equity 2000 program has attempted to enroll all students in algebra (or a more advanced course) as soon as they enter high school. In their approach, algebraic concepts are introduced throughout the elementary years to increase students' readiness for an algebra course. Working with six pilot sites, the College Board has reported increases not only in the proportion of students enrolling in college-preparatory courses, but increases in rates of passing courses, even when the proportion of the cohort enrolled has increased. For example in 1991, 31% of ninth graders were enrolled in algebra (or higher), and only 25% passed the course. By 1997, 99% were enrolled and 55% passed (College Board, 1999). In one sense that is a remarkable success, but at the same time almost half the ninth graders are not passing their first mathematics class.

An important question about Equity 2000 is whether the rigor of instruction in algebra, and thus the benefits of algebra for student learning, are maintained when detracking occurs. This question has not been addressed by the program, but an analysis of national survey data has indicated that all students benefit from taking algebra, and such benefits are not reduced when the population of algebra-takers in a school is more heterogeneous than when it is more homogeneous (Gamoran & Hannigan, 2000).

One reason teachers at Wallingford and Marble Canyon taught a diluted curriculum to mixed-ability classes is that they did not know what else to offer besides the standard college-preparatory curriculum. This is precisely the technical problem: teachers lack pedagogical strategies and curricula designed for mixed-ability classes—nowhere is this more true than in secondary-school mathematics—and most do not believe such a curriculum is possible. One group of curriculum developers has responded to that challenge by creating the "Interactive Mathematics Program" (IMP), a curriculum that tries to build on the differences among students in the course of problem-oriented, hands-on problems that center on core mathematical issues (Alper, Fendel, Fraser, & Resek, 1997). Small-scale evaluations of IMP are promising, showing that students gained more on average in achievement from IMP than from the traditional course sequence, and high-achieving students gained no less than in traditional classes (Webb, 2003). IMP, along with Equity 2000 and the experience of Cibola High School, suggest that solutions to the technical problems of detracking are possible, even in the most challenging subject areas.

IMPLICATIONS FOR RESEARCH, POLICY AND PRACTICE

Both practitioners and researchers can respond to the research findings about classroom organization and instructional quality. The first reaction from practitioners may be to strengthen their inclinations to reduce reliance on grouping and tracking because these practices are associated with unequal classroom instruction and ultimately with unequal achievement. The research is clear that some forms of tracking should be eliminated because better alternatives are available. For example, the research points towards elimination of general math classes in high school. This course simply repeats the arithmetic curriculum of elementary and junior high school and is a dead end for students, blocking access to college-bound curricula and college enrollment. At the elementary level, the research also indicates that the practice of rigid tracking of students in elementary school for the entire school day on the basis of a sole criterion should cease.

Second, practitioners can consider whether to maintain less extreme versions of tracking, or to eliminate all divisions among students. The research is inconclusive as to which alternative is better, and practitioners must consider their own unique circumstances in deciding which approach best fits their school. One view holds that, as has occurred in some Catholic schools and in a restructured public school, some divisions among students for particular subjects are appropriate, as long as teachers hold students at all levels to high standards of accomplishment. Another view holds that all such divisions should be eliminated. To adopt this approach, it will be necessary to develop curricula and pedagogies that are suited to mixed-ability classes, since the cases of Wallingford and Marble Canyon illustrate the futility of simply following a traditional course with students of widely varying performance levels. In these cases, teachers taught to a lowest common denominator and were concerned that strong students were not challenged. Cibola High School offers a model for successful detracking, but its program was supported by special circumstances including selection of staff and some students, as well as a tutoring program for students who were falling behind.

The lack of conclusive evidence on alternatives to traditional tracking structures also shows where researchers must direct their attention. It is most essential to examine a broader range of schools engaged in responding to the tracking problem so that we can move beyond "existence proofs" to a more generalizable conclusion about the advantages and disadvantages of each policy choice.

REFERENCES

Alper, L., Fendel, D., Fraser, S., & Resek, D. (1997). Designing a high school mathematics curriculum for all students. *American Journal of Education, 106,* 148–179.

Ayalon, H., & Gamoran, A. (2000). Stratification in academic secondary programs and educational inequality: Comparison of Israel and the United States. *Comparative Education Review, 44,* 54–80.

Bryk, A. S., Lee, V. E., & Holland, P. B. (1993). *Catholic schools and the common good.* Cambridge, MA: Harvard University Press.

Camarena, M. (1990). Following the right track: A comparison of tracking practices in public and Catholic secondary schools. In R. Page & L. Valli (Eds.), *Curriculum differentiation: Interpretive studies in U.S. secondary schools* (pp. 159–182). Albany, NY: SUNY Press.

College Board. (1999). *Equity 2000—Impact.* [Electronic version]. New York: Author.

Finley, M. K. (1984). Teachers and tracking in a comprehensive high school. *Sociology of Education, 57,* 233–243.

Gamoran, A. (1986). Instructional and institutional effects of ability grouping. *Sociology of Education, 59,* 185–198.

Gamoran, A. (1987). The stratification of high school learning opportunities. *Sociology of Education, 60,* 135–155.

Gamoran, A. (1992). The variable effects of high school tracking. *American Sociological Review,* 57, 812–828.

Gamoran, A. (1993). Alternative uses of ability grouping in secondary schools: Can we bring high-quality instruction to low-ability classes?" *American Journal of Education,* 101, 1–22.

Gamoran A., & Berends, M. (1987). The effects of stratification in secondary schools: Synthesis of survey and ethnographic research. *Review of Educational Research,* 57, 415–435.

Gamoran A., & Hannigan, E. (2000). Algebra for everyone? Benefits of college-preparatory mathematics for students of diverse abilities in early secondary school. *Educational Evaluation and Policy Analysis,* 22, 241–254.

Gamoran, A., Nystrand, M., Berends, M., & LePore, P. C. (1995). An organizational analysis of the effects of ability grouping. *American Educational Research Journal,* 32, 687–715.

Gamoran, A., Porter, A. C., Smithson, J., & White, P. A. (1997). Upgrading high school mathematics instruction: Improving learning opportunities for low-income, low-achieving youth. *Educational Evaluation and Policy Analysis,* 19, 325–338.

Gamoran, A., & Weinstein, M. (1998). Differentiation and opportunity in restructured schools. *American Journal of Education,* 106, 385–415.

Loveless, T. (1994). The influence of subject areas on middle school tracking policies. *Research in Sociology of Education and Socialization,* 10, 147–175.

Loveless, T. (1998). *The tracking and ability grouping debate.* Washington, DC: Fordham Foundation.

Oakes, J. (1985). *Keeping track.* New Haven, CT: Yale University Press.

Oakes, J. (1992). Can tracking research inform practice? Technical, normative, and political considerations. *Educational Researcher,* 21(4), 12–22.

Oakes, J., Gamoran, A., & Page, R. N. (1992). Curriculum differentiation: Opportunities, outcomes, and meanings. In P. W. Jackson (Ed.), *Handbook of research on curriculum* (pp. 570–608). New York: Macmillan.

Oakes, J., & Wells, A. S. (1998). Detracking for high student achievement. *Educational Leadership,* 55(6), 38–41.

Oakes, J., Wells, A. S., Yonezawa, S., & Ray, K. (1997). Equity lessons from detracking schools. *ASCD Yearbook 1997,* 43–72.

Rosenbaum, J. E. (1976). *Making inequality.* New York: John Wiley and Sons.

Rosenbaum, J. E. (1999). If tracking is bad, is detracking better? *American Educator,* 47, 24–29.

Rowan B., & Miracle, A. J., Jr., (1983). Systems of ability grouping and the stratification of achievement in elementary schools. *Sociology of Education,* 56, 133–144.

Valli, L. (1990). A curriculum of effort: Tracking students in a Catholic high school. In R. Page & L. Valli (Eds.), *Curriculum differentiation: Interpretive studies in U.S. secondary schools* (pp. 45–65). Albany, NY: SUNY Press.

Webb, N. L. (2003). The impact of the interactive mathematics program on student learning. In S. L. Senk & D. R. Thompson (Eds.), *Standards-based school mathematics curricula: What are they? What do students learn?* (pp. 375–398). Mahwah, NJ: Lawrence Erlbaum.

Wells, A. S., & Serna, I. (1996). The politics of culture: Understanding local political resistance to detracking in racially mixed schools. *Harvard Educational Review, 66*, 93–118.

White, P. A., Gamoran, A., Smithson, J., & Porter, A. C. (1996). Upgrading the high school math curriculum: Math course-taking patterns in seven high schools in California and New York. *Educational Evaluation and Policy Analysis, 18*, 285–307.

White, P. A., Porter, A. C., Gamoran, A., & Smithson, J. (1997). Upgrading high school math: A look at three transition courses. *NASSP Bulletin, 81*, 72–83.

CHAPTER 8

GROUPING, TRACKING, AND DE-TRACKING

Conclusions from Experimental, Correlational, and Ethnographic Research

James A. Kulik

The publication of *Nation at Risk* in 1983 ushered in two decades of reforms in America's elementary and secondary schools. The reform reports issued during these decades identified grouping and tracking as major ills in American education, and elimination of these practices became an important item on the reform agenda. Now, evaluators have begun assessing the success of the comprehensive school reforms of the last two decades. The evaluations raise serious questions about the reform view of grouping and tracking.

One of the main conclusions of the reformers was that grouping and tracking are harmful to students. In *The Paideia Proposal*, for example, Adler termed multitrack schools "an abominable discrimination" and called for establishment of schools in which everyone would follow the same course of study and pursue the same goals without regard to ability, temperament, or preference (Adler, 1983). Boyer (1983) also advocated establishment of single-track schools that would provide a general education for all. Goodlad (1984) recommended that schools provide a common core of courses and randomly assign students to the classes.

Oakes elaborated on the reform view of grouping and tracking in her classic volume *Keeping Track* (1985). Grouping and tracking, she wrote, are unfair because they deprive students of their right to a common curriculum. Students in the top tracks gain nothing from homogeneous grouping, Oakes charged, and other children suffer clear and consistent disadvantages from grouping, including loss of academic ground, self-esteem, and ambition. Oakes therefore called for the de-tracking of American schools. De-tracked schools would provide the same curriculum to all, and they would not provide preferential educational opportunities to any on the basis of ability, achievement, or interests.

Recent evaluation reports provide an empirical counterpoint to the reform rhetoric. The reports conclude that evidence of effectiveness is insubstantial for most of the reforms of the past two decades. An important report from the American Institutes for Research, for example, found strong evidence of effectiveness for only 3 of 24 reforms (Herman et al., 1999). Slavin and Fashola (1998) found adequate evidence of effectiveness for only 4 of 16 school reforms. A report by Borman, Hewes, Overman, and Brown (2002) categorized only 3 of 29 comprehensive reform models as "proven" models.

Only two reforms were on the honor rolls of all these evaluators. The successful programs were Direct Instruction and Success for All. Direct Instruction is a teaching approach that separates elementary school children into homogeneous groups according to achievement in a subject and then provides the groups with carefully scripted instruction in the subject (Adams & Engelmann, 1996). Success for All also groups children homogeneously across grades for instruction in reading, writing, and language arts, and then provides instruction tailored to the reading level of each group (Slavin, Madden, Dolan, & Wasik, 1996).

The success of these systems of homogeneous grouping in an era when reformers were roundly condemning grouping and tracking raises troubling and challenging questions. How effective are these two grouping systems? Do other grouping programs also help children? When are grouping and tracking programs effective and ineffective? When and how can grouping harm children?

The purpose of this chapter is to summarize and analyze research findings relevant to these questions. Major approaches to grouping and evidence on the extent of their use in American schools are described. Experimental, correlational, and ethnographic evidence on the effectiveness of grouping and tracking are also described and evaluated. The experimental evidence comes from studies that examined educational outcomes for equivalent students assigned to grouped and nongrouped classes. The correlational evidence comes from studies of performance differences in upper and lower tracks when characteristics of students selecting the tracks are statistically controlled. The ethnographic evidence comes from qualitative observations of upper- and lower-track classrooms.

PROGRAM TYPES AND TERMINOLOGY

Grouping programs are school programs in which teachers use test scores, school records, and student preferences to assign children to classes or groups that differ markedly in predicted learning rate. Schools use grouping for different purposes, and grouping programs come in different shapes and sizes. To make things even more complex, researchers disagree about the names to give various grouping programs. Readers therefore need both a road map and a dictionary to make sense of the area.

Older reviews of grouping research often referred to grouping plans by their place of origin. Otto (1941), for example, described such grouping methods as the Cambridge Plan of 1893, the Santa Barbara Concentric Plan, and additional schemes such as the Pueblo, Portland, Batavia, and North Denver plans. More recent reviews classify grouping methods more systematically and provide more descriptive names:

- Comprehensive grouping programs. Students at a single grade level are divided into groups—often high, middle, and low groups—on the basis of test scores and school records, and the groups receive instruction in separate classrooms for the full day.
- Single-class grouping. Students spend most of the day in heterogeneous classes but receive instruction in subjects such as reading or mathematics in homogeneous classes.
- Cross-grade grouping. Schools assign same-grade children to classes at different grade levels on the basis of their performance in a specific subject rather than on the basis of their age or regular grade placement.
- Within-class grouping. A teacher forms ability groups within a single classroom and provides each group with instruction appropriate to its performance level.
- Advanced and accelerated classes. Gifted or talented students receive above-grade-level instruction that allows them to proceed more rapidly through their schooling or to finish schooling at an earlier age than other students do.
- Enriched classes. Gifted and talented students receive richer, more varied educational experiences than would be available to them in the regular curriculum for their age level.

- High school tracks. High school students select academic, general, and vocational tracks on the basis of their educational goals and past performance in school.

These programs differ from each other in significant ways, but researchers have at one time or other used the terms *grouping* and *tracking* to refer to all of them.

Some researchers use the term *ability grouping* to refer to comprehensive programs alone. This usage is especially common in the older literature, where the term *ability grouping* refers to programs in which children of a given grade level are assigned to separate classes based on their test scores (e.g., Keliher, 1931). Others use the term to refer to within-class programs that separate elementary school students by test scores and performance into separate instructional groups (e.g., Loveless, 1999). Still others use the term to refer to all types of grouping programs except those that involve acceleration and enrichment for the gifted and talented (e.g., Getzels & Dillon, 1973). Yet another group of researchers include all of the above practices under the rubric of grouping (Slavin, 1990b).

Researchers also use the term *tracking* in different ways. Some writers use the term tracking to refer to rigid programs where students are sorted according to scores on intelligence tests and placed in separate classes for fast, medium, and slow learners (Singal, 1991). Others use the term to refer to differentiated curricula of college preparatory, vocational, and general instruction for secondary students. Still other researchers use the terms ability grouping and tracking interchangeably to refer to all of the programs in the above list (Oakes, 1985).

My own preference is to use the term *grouping* to refer to all of the programs listed above. In all of these programs, school personnel use school performance, test scores, and student preferences to assign children to classes or groups that differ markedly in predicted learning rate. I will also use the term *grouping* without the usual modifier *ability* because *ability* suggests innate and unchangeable characteristics. Like Mosteller and his colleagues, I believe these genetic implications are unwarranted in discussions of malleable learning characteristics (Mosteller, Light, & Sachs, 1996). I also prefer to use the term *tracking* in its narrow sense of differentiated academic, vocational, and general curricula for high school students.

EXTENT OF GROUPING

Good national statistics on grouping in American schools are scarce, but the best available evidence suggests that after decades of reform efforts, grouping is still a widespread practice in American schools. Almost all schools in this country use some form of homogeneous grouping for at least some classes, and most children in American schools are grouped homogeneously for at least some of their work. Although grouping occurs at all grades in American schools, grouping practices are different in high schools, middle schools, and elementary schools.

The most widely cited statistics on high school grouping are those from the Office of Educational Research and Improvement's National Educational Longitudinal Survey (NELS) of 1988 (Ingels, Scott, Taylor, Owings, & Quinn, 1998). NELS researchers collected test and survey data from 25,000 students in nearly 1,000 schools in 1988 when the students were eighth graders and then again when they were 10th graders in 1990. NELS researchers also collected information from the teachers of these students. One of the teacher questions asked whether the achievement level of a given student's class was homogeneous (i.e., above average, average, below average) or heterogeneous? Results showed that students were in homogeneous classes most of the time in both eighth and 10th grades. (Rees, Argys, & Brewer, 1996). In the 10th grade, for example, teachers characterized as homogeneous 85% of English classes, 89% of mathematics classes, 88% of science classes, and 82% of social studies classes.

The most widely cited statistics on extent of grouping in middle schools are those from the Johns Hopkins Center for Research on Elementary and Middle Schools. In 1988, the Hopkins researchers asked principals of nearly 1,800 middle schools about their grouping practices (Braddock, 1990; Loveless, 1998). One of the survey questions was: "For which academic subjects are students assigned to homogeneous classes on the basis of similar abilities or achievement levels?" Results showed that middle schools typically group pupils in some subjects, but not all. In the seventh grade, for example, 22% of all students were in homogeneous classes for all subjects; 47% were in homogeneous classes for some subjects; and 31% were in homogeneous classes for no subjects. Distinct levels of curriculum were typical in English and mathematics, but were less common in science and social studies.

The Johns Hopkins Center for Research on Elementary and Middle Schools also collected statistics on the extent of grouping in elementary schools. The Hopkins survey covered elementary schools in the state of Pennsylvania (McPartland, Coldiron, & Braddock, 1987). The researchers found that within-class grouping by ability was used in well over 90% of the schools at the primary level and in 85% to 90% of the schools at the upper elementary level. In addition, many of the schools in the Pennsylvania sample (almost 70%) also grouped children by skill into separate classes in at least one subject.

The best available evidence suggests, therefore, that most students in American schools are grouped homogeneously in high schools, middle schools, and elementary schools. Between-class grouping programs are typical in high schools and middle schools, whereas within-class programs are the norm in elementary schools. The evidence on these points is not definitive, however. Survey data at all educational levels need to be updated, and only regional survey data—not national data—are available from elementary schools.

EXPERIMENTAL STUDIES OF GROUPING

In 1930, two researchers at the University of Minnesota, W. S. Miller and Henry J. Otto, published the first comprehensive review of experimental research on ability grouping. The 20 studies that they reviewed were far from uniform, but Miller and Otto saw enough consistency in the study findings to draw a positive conclusion about grouping effects. When grouping is done properly, Miller and Otto reported, it benefits children. One year later, however, in 1931, a researcher at Columbia University, Alice Keliher, reviewed the same experimental evidence and came to a different conclusion. Grouping, she wrote, is more likely to harm than help students.

The controversy that began went on for five decades. Studies accumulated, reviews piled up, but consensus eluded the reviewers. Writers of narrative reviews were simply unable to find a consistent pattern in the mountains of findings. Finally, during the past two decades, researchers developed quantitative statistical methods for analyzing large bodies of research findings (e.g., Cooper, 1984; Glass, McGaw, & Smith, 1981; J. A. Kulik & Kulik, 1989). When reviewers applied these meta-analytic methods to grouping and tracking research, the patterns in the findings began to come into focus.

Meta-analysis is simply the application of quantitative statistics to the results of a large number of independent studies for the purpose of describing the collected results. The signature statistic of the meta-analyst is the effect size. Meta-analysts associate an effect size with each study result that they locate. The effect size specifies the number of standard deviation units that separate average outcome scores of experimental and control groups. Some researchers include effect-size measures in their reports. When they do not, meta-analysts calculate effect sizes from means and standard deviations reported by researchers. When researchers do not report means and standard deviations for their comparison groups, meta-analysts can often calculate effect sizes from t-tests, F-ratios, chi-square statistics, or exact p values.

Effect sizes are positive when the experimental group outperforms the control group in a study, and negative when the control group comes out on top. To give a sense of effect-size scale, Slavin has pointed out that an effect size of 1.0 would be equivalent to 100 points on the SAT scale, two stanines, 15 points of IQ, or about 21 normal curve equivalents (Slavin & Fashola, 1998). Glass observed that the standard deviation of most achievement tests in elementary schools is 1.0 grade-equivalent units, and the effect size of one year's instruction at the elementary school level is therefore about +1.0 (Glass et al., 1981). Cohen (1977), a pioneer in the use of effect sizes in the social sciences, classified effect sizes of around 0.2 as small, 0.5 as moderate in size, and 0.8 as large. Slavin judges effect sizes above 0.25 to be large enough to be considered educationally and practically significant (Slavin & Fashola, 1998).

The most comprehensive meta-analytic reviews of experimental evidence on grouping and tracking were written by my research group at the University of Michigan (e.g., C.-L. C. Kulik & Kulik, 1982, 1984; J. A. Kulik, 1992; J. A. Kulik & Kulik, 1984, 1987, 1992) and by Robert Slavin at Johns Hopkins University (e.g., Slavin, 1987, 1990b). These meta-analytic reports focus on two major outcome areas: effects on student learning and effects on student self-concept.

Effects on Student Learning

The meta-analytic reviews show that effects on student learning are different for different kinds of grouping programs. Some grouping programs have little or no effect on student learning, other programs have moderate effects, and still other programs have large effects. A key influence on program effects is the amount of curricular adjustment in the grouping program.

Programs without Curricular Adjustment

In 1919, Detroit became the first large city in America to introduce into its schools a formal plan of ability grouping (Courtis, 1925). The Detroit plan called for intelligence testing of all school children at the start of Grade 1 and then placement of children into X, Y, and Z groups on the basis of test results. The top 20% went to the X classes, the middle 60% to Y classes, and the bottom 20% to Z classes. Standard materials and methods were used in all classes, and all classes covered material at the same grade level.

Many school systems followed the Detroit model in subsequent years and instituted their own plans of multilevel grouping. Some developed comprehensive XYZ plans, in which the groups remained separate for the whole day. Other schools used single-subject grouping. Few of the plans relied as much as the Detroit plan on intelligence tests for initial placements, and few separated students at such an early age. Most plans, however, were like the Detroit plan in their basic goal. They were designed to reduce pupil variation in classes, not to provide different curricula for students in XYZ groups.

The meta-analyses from my research group covered 51 studies of XYZ programs (J. Kulik, 1992). Twenty-two of the 51 studies examined comprehensive programs, and 29 studies examined single-subject programs. The meta-analysis showed that grouping has a very small positive effect on students in the high groups and has near-zero effects on students in the middle and low groups. The average effect of XYZ grouping on students in the high groups is an increase in test scores of about 0.1 standard deviations. A student who gains about 1.1 years in the upper classes in an XYZ program would therefore gain only 1.0 years on the scale if taught in a mixed class. Students in the middle and low groups who gain about a year on a grade-equivalent scale in homogeneous classes would also gain about one year on the scale when taught in mixed classes.

Slavin used the term *ability-based class assignment* for what I call XYZ programs, and his analysis covered 49 studies of these programs (Slavin, 1987, 1990b). Of the 49 studies reviewed by Slavin, 30 examined comprehensive programs, and 19 examined single-subject programs. Slavin's findings were similar to mine. Slavin found near-zero effects of grouping on lower, middle, and higher aptitude students. His analysis suggests that students who gain one year on a grade-equivalent scale in a mixed-ability class would also gain one year on the scale if taught in homogeneous classes.

Slavin's results on XYZ grouping differ from my results in only one respect. I found a very small positive effect from XYZ grouping on high groups, whereas Slavin found no effect. I consider this difference in findings to be small and inconsequential. Although statistically reliable, the effect on high groups that I found was too small to be of practical importance. Slavin and I therefore agree that the effects on student learning of XYZ programs—programs without curricular adjustment—are too small to be educationally important.

The developers of XYZ grouping programs had high hopes for these programs when they first implemented them during the 1920s. By the 1930s, however, the limited effects of XYZ grouping were becoming clear to researchers and reviews, and interest in grouping programs began to wane. Looking back at the early history of ability grouping in an article in the *Encyclopedia of Educational Research*, Otto (1950) identified the 1920s and early 1930s as the years of peak interest in grouping. Although XYZ programs were to linger in schools for many years, researchers stopped studying the effects of ability grouping after 1935, Otto reported, and teachers and administrators turned their attention during the 1940s to other educational matters.

Curricular Adjustment for All Students

By the 1950s, alternatives to XYZ grouping began to emerge, and interest in grouping programs revived. The new grouping programs were important innovations because they used grouping not simply for the purpose of achieving homogeneity but rather as a way of providing students with curricula appropriate to their learning rates. Two new approaches that were developed during the 1950s were especially important: cross-grade and within-class grouping programs. With both programs, teachers used test scores and school records to separate children into groups that follow curricula adjusted to their learning rates.

Cross-grade Grouping. The best-known approach to cross-grade grouping is the Joplin plan, which was first used during the 1950s for reading instruction in the Joplin, Missouri, elementary schools. During the hour reserved for reading in the Joplin schools, children in Grades 4, 5, and 6 broke into nine different groups that read at levels between Grade 2 and Grade 9. The children went to their reading classes without regard to their regular grade placement but returned to their age-graded classrooms at the end of the reading period. Almost all formal evaluations of cross-grade grouping involve the Joplin plan for reading instruction in elementary schools.

Both my meta-analysis and Slavin's found that cross-grade programs in elementary and middle schools usually produce positive results (J. Kulik, 1992; Slavin, 1987). My analysis, for example, covered 14 studies of cross-grade grouping. More than 80% of these studies found positive effects from grouping. The average effect size was 0.33 standard deviations. The gain attributable to cross-grade grouping was thus about 3 months on a grade equivalent scale. The typical pupil in a mixed-ability class might gain one year on a grade-equivalent scale in a calendar year, whereas the typical pupil in a cross-grade program would gain 1.3 years. Effects were positive for high, middle, and low groups in cross-grade programs.

Direct Instruction and Success for All are cross-grade grouping programs that use specific, highly scripted teaching materials designed to embody specific instructional principles. Because Direct Instruction and Success for All are complex treatments that include cross-grade grouping and many other program-specific elements, evaluations of these approaches cannot be considered pure evaluations of cross-age grouping. For that reason, neither Slavin nor I examined evidence of effectiveness of Direct Instruction and Success for All when drawing conclusions about the effectiveness of cross-grade grouping. Nonetheless, it is notable that these two acclaimed reforms use cross-grade grouping—among other instructional strategies—to achieve their goal of improving pupil performance.

Unfortunately, the size of learning effects of Direct Instruction and Success for All is still unclear. Meta-analyses by the developers of these systems found large effects for their programs, but an independent meta-analysis found much smaller effect sizes. Specifically, Adams and Engelmann (1996) reported an average effect size of 0.97 in 173 comparisons involving Direct Instruction. Slavin and Madden (2000) found an average effect size of approximately 0.5 in 203 cohorts that received Success for All. Borman and his colleagues, however, found an average effect size of only 0.15 for Direct Instruction in 30 controlled studies, and they found an average effect size of only 0.18 in 41 controlled studies of Success for All (Borman et al., 2002). The developer-reported effect sizes are extraordinarily high; the independently reported effect sizes are too low to be educationally meaningful. I will leave it to future researchers to come to a consensus on the effectiveness of Direct Instruction and Success for All. At this point, it is sufficient to note that the continuing use of Success for All and Direct Instruction in today's schools provides evidence that cross-grade grouping programs are still a viable instructional approach.

Within-class Grouping. Within-class grouping programs also provide differentiated curricula for children at different ability levels. The most popular model for within-class grouping was developed in the 1950s for teaching arithmetic in elementary schools (Petty, 1953). A teacher following the model would use test scores and school records to divide her class into three groups for their arithmetic lessons, and she would use textbook material from several grade levels to instruct the groups. The high group in Grade 6, for example, might use materials from Grades 6, 7, and 8; the middle group might use materials from Grades 5, 6, and 7; and the low group might use materials from Grades 4, 5, and 6. The teacher would present material to one group for approximately 15 minutes before moving on to another group. Other approaches to within-class grouping are possible, but almost all within-class programs evaluated in controlled studies followed this model.

Both my meta-analysis and Slavin's found that within-class programs in elementary and middle schools usually produce positive results (J. A. Kulik, 1992; Slavin, 1987). My analysis, for example, covered 11 studies of within-class grouping. Most of these studies reported clear positive results. Average effect size was 0.25 standard deviations, and the average gain attributable to within-class grouping was thus between 2 and 3 months on a grade equivalent scale. The typical pupil in a mixed-ability class might gain 1.0 years on a grade-equivalent scale in a year, whereas the typical pupil in a within-class program would gain 1.2 to 1.3 years. Effects were similar for high, middle, and low groups.

Linchevski and Kutscher (1998) reported recently that instructional programs that include within-class grouping are still producing dramatic improvements in school performance. Linchevski and Kutscher's study examined effectiveness of a junior-high mathematics program, called TAP. Each student in this program learned math in both a homogeneous within-class group and a heterogeneous group. Control students were taught mathematics in traditional homogeneous classes. At the end of two years of instruction, all students filled out tests of mathematics achievement. Lower and middle aptitude students in TAP classes outscored equivalent control students by at least 20 percentage points, and high-aptitude students performed at about the same level as equivalent controls.

Overall, meta-analytic results, as well as recent research findings, suggest that within-class grouping programs with appropriate curricular differentiation usually have significant positive effects on the performance of students. Findings on within-class programs thus seem to parallel findings on cross-grade grouping. Carefully designed programs that use within-class or cross-grade grouping appear to benefit all students.

Curricular Adjustment for Talented Students

American education has a long tradition of providing special classes for children whose educational needs differ from those of the majority. Special classes have been formed of children who are physically handicapped, emotionally or socially maladjusted, lacking in proficiency in English, and so on. One of the longest traditions is providing special classes for gifted and talented children.

The first classes devised especially for gifted and talented children were accelerated ones (Tannenbaum, 1958). The Cambridge Double Track Plan of 1891 put bright children into special classes that covered the work of six years in four, and the special-progress classes of New York City, originally established in 1900, allowed pupils to complete the work of three years in two. The basic idea behind both these programs of acceleration was to modify the school program so that selected students could complete it at an earlier age or in less time than was usual.

Leta Hollingworth, one of the founders of the field of gifted and talented education, thought that the special-program classes of New York City and similar accelerated classes did not meet the social and emotional needs of gifted youngsters. In 1916 Hollingworth began setting up alternative, enriched classes for unusually gifted youngsters in the New York schools. Gifted children were grouped homogeneously for these enriched classes. Instead of following a telescoped regular curriculum, the children spent about half of their school hours working on the prescribed curriculum, and about half pursuing enriching activities. In Hollingworth's classes for 7- to 9-year-olds, these enrichment activities included conversational French; the study of biography; study of the history of civilization; and a good deal of extra work in science, mathematics, English composition, and music (Gray & Hollingworth, 1931).

My meta-analyses of grouping effects covered 23 studies in which achievement of students in accelerated classes was compared to achievement of equivalent students in nonaccelerated classes (J. A. Kulik, 1992). All of the studies examined moderate acceleration of a whole class of students rather than radical acceleration of individual children. All of the studies found that students in accelerated classes outperformed students in nonaccelerated classes who were equivalent in age and intelligence. In a typical study, the accelerates outperformed the nonaccelerates by approximately one standard deviation on subject-matter tests, or by about one year on a grade-equivalent scale.

My meta-analyses also covered 25 studies of enriched classes for talented students. Twenty-two of the 25 studies found that talented students achieve more when taught in enriched rather than regular mixed-ability classes. In the average study, students in the enriched classes outperformed equivalent students in mixed classes by 0.41 standard deviations, equivalent to about 4 months on a grade-equivalent scale. Thus, children receiving enriched instruction gained about 1.4 years on a grade-equivalent scale in the same period during which equivalent control children gained only 1.0 year.

Overall, the positive effects of accelerated and enriched classes on student learning are probably due to curricular differentiation. Curricular adjustment is at a minimum in XYZ classes; it is moderate in cross-grade and within-class grouping programs; but it is probably at a maximum in accelerated and enriched classes. In accelerated classes, teachers routinely deal with above-grade-level material; in enriched classes, teachers almost invariably introduce some above-grade-level material. The study results show that gifted and talented students rise to the challenge of this advanced and enriched material. The students benefit from advanced and enriched classes, and they suffer academically when held back in classes that work on material better suited to average learners.

Effects on Student Self-esteem

Decades of studies show that good school performance and high self-esteem go together. High-performing students usually get higher scores on self-esteem measures than low-performing students. The size of the correlation between school performance and self-esteem varies somewhat from study to study, but small positive correlations between performance and self-esteem are the general rule (J. M. Coleman & Fults, 1985; Hansford & Hattie, 1982; Marsh, 1987; Wylie, 1979).

Long ago, researchers began investigating grouping contributions to this correlation. Their fundamental question was: Does homogeneous grouping increase the self-esteem gap between good and poor students, or does grouping reduce the gap? One popular hypothesis, the labeling hypothesis, suggests that the gap increases with homogeneous grouping. According to this hypothesis, the self-esteem of poor students drops with homogeneous grouping because of stereotyping. Self-esteem of good students rises with homogeneous grouping for the same reason. The labeling hypothesis simply states that labels become attached to ability groups and that group members come to use the labels to define themselves.

An alternative hypothesis derives from social-comparison theory. This hypothesis states that grouping reduces the self-esteem gap between good and poor students. Advocates of this hypothesis believe that the self-esteem of poor students may actually go up in homogeneous low groups because slower children have an opportunity to participate, to compete, and even to shine in homogeneous classes. In mixed-ability classes, slower children are often overshadowed by quicker classmates. Advocates of social-comparison theory also believe that the self-esteem of top students will drop in homogeneous classes because good students face much stiffer competition in these classes.

Some studies of XYZ grouping examined self-esteem effects. My meta-analyses covered results from 13 such studies and found that average self-esteem scores in XYZ and mixed classes were nearly identical (J. A. Kulik, 1992). Nonetheless, XYZ classes appeared to have a small effect on student self-esteem. On the average, self-esteem scores went up slightly for low-aptitude learners in XYZ programs, and they went down slightly for high-aptitude learners. Thus, brighter children appeared to lose a little of their self-assurance when they were put into classes with equally talented children, whereas slower children gained a little in self-confidence when they were taught in classes with other slower learners.

Coleman and his colleagues have carried out a series of studies of grouping effects on self-esteem, and the results of their studies also support predictions of social comparison theory (e.g., J. M. Coleman & Fults, 1985). Several studies by Coleman's group focused on the self-concepts of slow learners in various instructional settings, including regular classrooms, partially segregated resource rooms, and totally segregated self-contained classes. The researchers repeatedly found that placement in special homogeneous classes can augment the self-concepts of slower learners. Coleman and his colleagues also studied the self-esteem of gifted students in segregated enrichment programs. The researchers found a decline in self-esteem in students who participated in these programs.

Marsh and his colleagues also carried out a series of studies of what Marsh calls the *big-fish little-pond effect* (or BFLPE). The BFLPE occurs when a student's academic self-esteem falls following the student's placement into a high-aptitude group, or rises following the student's placement into a low-aptitude group. Marsh first demonstrated the occurrence of BFLPE in a correlational analysis. With individual ability controlled, the analysis showed that the average ability level in a school affected academic self-concept negatively (Marsh & Parker, 1984). Marsh and his colleagues also showed that students in gifted and talented programs experienced systematic declines over time in academic self-concepts (Marsh, Chessor, Craven, & Roche, 1995). Marsh's findings are consistent with both my meta-analytic findings on XYZ effects and Coleman's findings on self-esteem of slow learners and gifted students. Marsh's unique contribution is to demonstrate that the self-esteem effects of academic grouping are clearer in academic than in nonacademic components of the self-concept.

Overall, research studies of self-esteem have repeatedly shown that a child's self-esteem is affected by the child's academic peer group. Children appear to judge themselves by making comparisons to those they see around them. They judge themselves as inferior when they fail on tasks on which their peers succeed, and they judge themselves as superior when they excel on tasks on which others fail. The results of such comparisons appear to hold more weight for students than do labels. As a result, self-esteem goes up for poorer students when moved to homogeneous academic groups, and self-esteem goes down for stronger students when moved to homogeneous academic groups.

Oakes (1985) claimed that grouping damages the self-esteem of students in lower tracks. It is clear from the evidence, however, that grouping does not ordinarily have this effect. If anything, grouping augments the self-esteem of children in the lower groups. On the other hand, Marsh and his colleagues have expressed concern about the effects of homogeneous grouping on the self-esteem of gifted and talented students (Marsh & Parker, 1984). They suggested that these students may pay too high a price in self-esteem for their membership in special programs and schools. To me, this concern also seems misplaced. Although statistically significant, self-esteem effects of grouping are usually too small to be of practical importance. Most gifted and talented students handle the competition of special programs and upper tracks without a substantial loss of self-esteem. The students usually emerge from these hothouse environments with a little more modesty about their abilities, but they also usually emerge with a healthy sense of their own self-worth.

Conclusions from Experimental Studies

Experimental studies of grouping clearly show that different grouping and tracking programs have different effects on student achievement. Grouping programs that prescribe a common curriculum for children in all groups add little or nothing to student achievement; cross-grade and within-class programs that make moderate curricular adjustments for student groups have moderate effects on student achievement; and programs of accelerated and enriched instruction that make large adjustments for learning rate have strong effects on student achievement. Experimental studies thus suggest that grouping strategies are effective only when grouping arrangements are accompanied by appropriate curricular changes for the groups. Changing a child's associates will not by itself change the amount that a child will learn.

Grouping effects on self-esteem are a different matter. Who a student sits next to may not be crucially important for student learning, but reference groups do affect a child's self-esteem. Students compare themselves to those around them, and their self-esteem may rise or drop depending on the results of their social comparisons.

Some writers have criticized the experimental evidence on grouping on the basis of its age. According to Loveless (1999), for example, the experimental studies reviewed in the Michigan and Hopkins meta-analyses are yesterday's studies, and the meta-analytic conclusions are yesterday's conclusions. Loveless is correct in asserting that many of the studies reviewed in meta-analytic reports are old. The studies included in my comprehensive meta-analysis date from 1928 to 1986, and the studies included in Slavin's analyses are no more recent. But Loveless's criticism ignores the essential fact that experimental findings on grouping have proved to be very robust over a six-decade span. Schools and school cultures changed dramatically during these six decades, but the findings on XYZ grouping, within-class grouping, cross-grade grouping, and accelerated and enriched classes have held constant.

It seems to me that Loveless confuses standards for evaluating experimental research with standards for evaluating survey research. The purpose of surveys is to paint a picture in time of people's behaviors, practices, or preferences. Surveys tell us what people like and dislike at a particular moment, or how they are and are not behaving at some specific time. Experiments, on the other hand, are designed to establish enduring links between experimental treatments and results. With such a link established, we should expect the experimental result to follow whenever the experimental treatment is reproduced.

It is very appropriate to evaluate survey results on the basis of a survey's timeliness. You cannot judge a president's popularity, for example, from last year's polls. But publication date is not an important factor in evaluating experimental results. The key criterion for evaluating experimental research is the quality of the experiment. Was the experimental treatment well-defined? Was the treatment confounded with other factors? Were experimental outcomes measured properly? How good was the analysis of experimental results? Classic research guides discuss at length these and other criteria for evaluating experimental and quasi-experimental studies. But none of these guides mention study date as a criterion for evaluating experimental research. Taking a study's date as the key measure of its value is an error sometimes made in the popular press, but it is an error that researchers and scholars should not perpetuate.

CORRELATIONAL ANALYSES OF TRACKING

Coleman's massive Equality of Educational Opportunity Survey (EEOS) was the stimulus for numerous correlational analyses of tracking (J. S. Coleman et al., 1966). One of the key findings of Coleman's survey was that achievement varies far more within schools than between schools. The finding led sociologically oriented researchers to wonder whether within-school tracking might be the major cause of this within-school variation. To find out, researchers began carrying out correlational analyses of survey data. These analyses examined two main questions: What factors influence students to enroll in different curricular tracks? How much do the tracks influence students?

Jencks (1972) wrote one of the best summaries of results on the first question. He drew four main conclusions about determinants of track placement. First, personal preference is the most important determinant. The Equality of Educational Opportunity Survey, for example, found that 85% of all high school seniors are in the curriculum they want to be in (J. S. Coleman et al., 1966). Second, academic ability is the next most important determinant of curriculum placement. Jencks reported that the correlation between test scores and curriculum assignment is around 0.50. Third, social class does not seem to play an important role in high school curriculum placement, except insofar as it influences test scores. And fourth, race plays an even smaller role in track placement. Blacks have a higher probability of ending up in the college preparatory track than do Whites of equivalent aptitude and socioeconomic status.

The picture has not changed in the years since Jencks wrote his review. Garet and DeLany (1988) drew similar conclusions from their review of the four most influential studies of student placement into curricular tracks (Alexander, Cook, & McDill, 1978; Hauser, Sewell, & Alwin, 1976; Heyns, 1974; Rosenbaum, 1980). Gamoran and Mare (1989) also drew similar conclusions from these studies and from their own analysis of High School and Beyond data.

The second question addressed by correlational studies of tracking is: How much does track membership influence students? Researchers have been less successful in answering this question. Gamoran and Berends (1987) found conflicting answers in 16 national or statewide studies. Some of the studies found that track membership accounted for a significant amount of variation in test scores; others found that it accounted for a nonsignificant amount. The effects of tracking on educational attainment were clearer. All studies found that track membership influences educational attainment after high school. That is, students who are in college preparatory programs are more likely to enroll in college than are equally able students from noncollegiate tracks. Gamoran and Berends did not report any other consistent findings from national surveys of high school students.

My own analysis of the accumulated correlational results showed that the difference in achievement between students in academic and nonacademic tracks is real (J. A. Kulik, 1998). At the end of high school, academic students outperform nonacademic students on standardized achievement tests by about one standard deviation. But only part of the achievement gap is due to curricular-track membership. Most of the gap is due to self-selection. If similar students selected academic and nonacademic programs, the achievement gap at the end of high school would be only 0.2 standard deviations. About half of the difference of 0.2 standard deviations is due to the different number of advanced courses in core subjects taken by academic and nonacademic students. The remaining small difference in achievement of academic and nonacademic groups is due to other curricular and program factors.

Slavin (1990a) concluded that there are severe problems with drawing conclusions from correlational analyses of tracking. First, the statistical controls in these analyses seem to be inadequate. When groups are very different in important respects, correlational controls cannot cancel out the group differences. When comparing high- to low-ability groups, pretest differences of one to two standard deviations are typical. According to Slavin, "No statistician on earth would expect that analysis of covariance or regression could adequately control for such large differences (p. 506). Another problem in correlational analyses is failure to measure all differences between high tracks and low tracks. Many factors determine track placement, and these factors also affect student achievement in both tracked and untracked classes. Researchers cannot control all such factors in their statistical analyses, and these unmeasured and uncontrolled factors can easily produce the outcome differences that are often assumed to be tracking effects.

If Slavin's criticisms are correct, conclusions from correlational analyses are undependable because the analyses are methodologically inadequate. But even if the study methodology is not fatally flawed, the study results are hardly damning to curricular tracking. The studies simply show that most of the variability in achievement observed at the time of high school graduation is the result of differences among students that were apparent at the start of high school. Some variation in achievement, however, is associated with the differentiated curricula that high schools offer. This conclusion is consistent with the experimental evidence on the effects of advanced, accelerated, and enriched classes on students.

ETHNOGRAPHIC STUDIES OF TRACKING

Researchers have also been using ethnographic methods to study effects of grouping. The first generation of ethnographic studies focused on teacher and student behaviors in upper and lower tracks (Oakes, 1985; Page, 1991; Rosenbaum, 1976). A newer generation of studies is now examining the success of recent efforts to de-track American schools (e.g., Gamoran & Weinstein, 1998; Wells & Oakes, 1996).

Of all the first-generation ethnographic studies, the study described by Jeannie Oakes (1985) in her book *Keeping Track* is the best known. Oakes and her coworkers made their observations for a project that John Goodlad described in his 1984 book *A Place Called School*. The observations came from 299 English and math classes (75 high track, 85 average track, 64 low track, and 75 heterogeneous classes) in a national sample of 25 junior and senior high schools. The observations covered course content, quality of instruction, classroom climate, and student attitudes in each of the classes.

To Oakes, instruction seemed to be better in the higher tracks. In English classes, for example, the percentage of time spent on instruction was 81 for the high track and 75 for the low track; in math classes, percentage of time spent on instruction was 81 for the high track and 78 for the low track. In English classes, percentage of time off-task was 2 for the high track and 4 for the low; in math classes, it was 1 for the high track and 4 for the low. In all, more time was spent on instruction and less time was spent off-task in the high tracks. Oakes also reported that there were curricular differences in high- and low-track classes. For example, low-track classes seemed to cover less demanding topics, whereas high-track classes covered more complex material. High-track teachers also seemed to encourage competent and autonomous thinking, whereas low-track teachers stressed low-level skills and conformity to rules and expectations. Oakes did not provide quantitative data to support these observations, however.

Gamoran and Berends (1987) summarized the main results from the first generation of ethnographic studies of tracking. They reported that ethnographers have reached four main conclusions. First, instruction is conceptually simplified and proceeds more slowly in lower tracks. Second, teachers with more experience and those regarded as more successful seem to be disproportionately assigned to the higher tracks. Third, teachers view high-track students positively and low-track students negatively. And fourth, most of a student's friends are found in the same track. Gamoran and Berends also noted that most of these track differences, when quantified, are tiny. The difference of 2% or 3% in time on instruction, for example, is not large. It amounts to a difference of less than 10 minutes per day in time on instruction for low- and high-track classes. Thus, tracks appear to be much more alike than they are different.

Critics have also noted that the first-generation ethnographers may have misinterpreted their observations. Slavin (1990a) suggested, for example, that high- and low-aptitude students might differ as much in ungrouped situations as they do in grouped ones. Noting that time on task is reportedly lower in low-track classes, he asks: "Might it be that low-achieving students are more likely to be off-task no matter where they are?" (p. 505). Ethnographers usually do not provide data from untracked control classes, and without such control data it is impossible to disentangle effects of educational treatments and student characteristics. Slavin also questions the value of some of the indicators of low-quality teaching used by the ethnographers. For example, ethnographers usually interpret reduced content coverage to be an indicator of low-quality teaching. Slavin points out that reduced content coverage does not necessarily indicate poor quality teaching in the lower track classes. Reduced content coverage could simply indicate that students in lower track classes need a slower instructional pace.

A new generation of ethnographic studies is focusing on progress that school reformers have made in de-tracking American schools. Gamoran and his colleagues (Gamoran & Weinstein, 1995) and Oakes and her colleagues (Wells & Oakes, 1996) wrote notable reports on de-tracking efforts. The reports suggest that school reformers have not achieved their goal of improving American schools by eliminating tracking. Few schools have been able to eliminate tracking completely, and some of those that have eliminated tracking have suffered a loss in instructional quality as a result.

Gamoran and Weinstein's report (1998) provides concrete information on these points. These researchers conducted phone interviews with more than 250 schools nominated as being among the most restructured in the country. Although administrators at these schools reported that students spent most of their time in heterogeneous groups, the researchers determined that students spent substantial amounts of time in ability groups or tracks in more than half the schools. For example, almost all restructured high schools and middle schools assigned students to math classes based on test and school performance. Elementary schools varied in their grouping patterns. Some grouped children by ability into separate classes, and some grouped children by ability within classes.

Gamoran and his colleagues also made site visits to a sample of 24 of the nominated schools: 8 high schools, 8 middle schools, and 8 elementary schools. Their observations in these 24 schools confirmed findings from the larger study. Only three of the eight high schools had eliminated tracking, for example. One of the three untracked schools seemed to offer rigorous, academically challenging work in mixed-ability classes, but mixed-ability grouping appeared to lead to a loss of academic rigor in the other two schools. Among the eight middle schools, only one used mixed-ability grouping exclusively in all subjects. The site visitors reported that work in this school seldom called for higher-order thinking or deep analysis. Thus, of the 16 middle and high schools visited by Gamoran and Weinstein's team, only one provided evidence of consistently high-quality instruction in de-tracked classes. Gamoran and Weinstein drew few conclusions about elementary school de-tracking because the grouping situation in these schools seemed complex to them. Most children in these reformed elementary schools were in mixed-ability classes for most of the day, but pullout programs and within-class groups introduced some degree of differentiation in students' work in these schools.

Oakes and her colleagues visited 10 geographically diverse schools three times over a 2-year period to determine what happens to schools that decide to reduce ability grouping and tracking (Wells & Oakes, 1996). Reports on their project focus on the obstacles that de-trackers face. According to these observers, two obstacles are especially clear. One is the demand from parents for differentiation. Oakes and her colleagues found that many parents objected when their local schools proposed offering one set of undifferentiated classes for all. The parents argued that same-age children differ too much in their preparation, skills, and interests to fit into a single mold, and they demanded differentiated curricula in the schools. According to Wells and Oakes, the other major obstacle to de-tracking is the pressure for differentiation from higher education. Colleges and universities give preference to students whose course choices reflect strong academic motivation and good academic preparation. Overall, Wells and Oakes's de-tracking vignettes are stories of difficulty and failure rather than stories of unqualified success.

Although the first generation of ethnographic studies raised provocative questions about ability grouping, they do not provide scientific answers. The studies are simply too casual. Ethnographers documented some surface differences between tracks, but ethnographic conclusions about tracking effects are sometimes overstated and ethnographic interpretation of causes of low achievement are speculative at best. Ethnographers designed a second generation of studies to chart progress of de-tracking efforts, but the second-generation reports are largely accounts of unfulfilled expectations. The reports suggest that de-tracking is a complicated and difficult business. On the basis of their recent ethnographic observations, for example, Gamoran and Weinstein concluded that de-tracking is a goal that is often desired but rarely achieved. According to Gamoran and Weinstein, when de-tracking is achieved, it brings no guarantee of high-quality instruction for everyone but instead may bring a low-level equality to all.

DISCUSSION AND CONCLUSIONS

Grouping and tracking studies come in all shapes and sizes. They vary in methodology, quality, and interpretation. To find out what the research says about grouping and tracking, reviewers have to find their way through a cluttered landscape, and it is all too easy to get lost in the clutter. To keep on track, reviewers should distinguish carefully among ethnographic, correlational, and experimental studies of grouping and tracking.

The ethnographic studies of grouping, for example, are probably higher in rhetorical than scientific values. Ethnographers have reported that in low-track classes, the pace of instruction is slow, the curriculum is debased, and teachers are inexperienced. But careful scrutiny of the ethnographic evidence shows that the evidence for such charges is weak. When ethnographers quantify their observations, differences between upper and lower tracks usually turn out to be small. What is more important, no one can be certain of the factors that produce the surface differences found by ethnographers. For example, ethnographers often find a different instructional pace in higher and lower track classes, but the interpretation of this pace difference is not straightforward. The difference may reflect low teaching quality in lower track classes, as ethnographers suggest, but the slower pace may also be an appropriate teacher response to the needs of children who lack adequate background and preparation in a subject.

Findings from correlational analyses are also uncertain. Correlational analyses have consistently shown that the achievement gap between students in upper and lower tracks is due mostly to student self-selection. If the same students enrolled in collegiate and non-collegiate tracks at the beginning of high school, graduates of the two programs would differ in test scores by only a small amount at the end of high school. A second, less important factor that may contribute to track differences in achievement is the different number of advanced courses in core subjects taken by students in collegiate and non-collegiate tracks. A third factor may be the difference in the way that the same courses are taught for collegiate and noncollegiate students. Correlational analyses do not provide conclusive evidence on the second and third factors, however. The controls for self-selection in these analyses are usually inadequate, and so conclusions from correlational analyses are tentative at best.

Experimental studies still seem to be the best guide to the effects of grouping on children. Meta-analytic studies have shown that effects of grouping and tracking on learning vary by program and by student. XYZ grouping effects are clearly different from effects of other grouping programs. XYZ programs usually have negligible effects on the achievement of students in middle and low groups, and these programs have small effects at best on the achievement of students in high groups. Evaluation results are very different for programs in which groups follow curricula adjusted to their skill levels. Cross-grade and within-class grouping programs in reading and arithmetic, for example, adjust curricula to group skills, and these programs make important contributions to student achievement. Evaluation studies also show that enriched, accelerated, and advanced classes with high degrees of curricular adjustment are very beneficial in the education of gifted and talented learners.

Experimental evidence also shows that grouping arrangements affect student self-concepts but only by a small amount. Contrary to common expectations, grouping programs do not lead talented students to become self-satisfied and smug, nor do they cause a precipitous drop in the self-esteem of slower students. If anything, grouping programs have effects in the opposite direction. Grouping programs cause quick learners to lose a little of their self-assurance, and they cause slower learners to gain some badly needed self-confidence. Researchers from several laboratories have pointed out that social-comparison theory can explain these grouping effects on self-esteem.

My conclusions about grouping are obviously different from the well-known conclusions reached by Oakes (1985) in her book *Keeping Track*. Oakes concluded that students in the top tracks gain nothing from grouping and other students suffer clear and consistent disadvantages of grouping, including loss of academic ground, self-esteem, and ambition. My review of experimental, correlational, and ethnographic findings does not support Oakes's blanket indictment of tracking and grouping. Effects of grouping are far more variable than Oakes suggests. The findings depend on the type of grouping program examined, the group level, the outcome studied, the quality of the study, and perhaps other factors. Sweeping statements about the effect of grouping and tracking may make good rhetoric but they make poor science.

Recent accounts also suggest that Oakes's goal of de-tracking American schools may be easier to achieve in theory than in practice. Recent ethnographic studies show that school administrators who embrace de-tracking as a goal have seldom been able to implement it in their schools. Opposition from stakeholders and requirements of American colleges and universities are major obstacles to de-tracking. In addition, in schools where de-tracking has been achieved, the benefits are unclear. On the basis of site visits, for example, experts have concluded that de-tracking brings no guarantee of high-quality instruction for everyone but may instead lead all to a common level of educational mediocrity.

REFERENCES

Adams, G. L., & Engelmann, S. (1996). *Research on Direct Instruction: 25 years beyond Distar.* Seattle: Educational Achievement Systems.

Adler, M. J. (1983). *Paideia problems and possibilities*. New York: Macmillan.

Alexander, K. L., Cook, M. A., & McDill, E. L. (1978). Curriculum tracking and educational stratification. *American Sociological Review, 43*, 47–66.

Borman, G. D., Hewes, G. M., Overman, L. T., & Brown, S. (2002). *Comprehensive school reform and student achievement: A meta-analysis* (Report No. 59). Baltimore: Johns Hopkins University, Center for Research on the Education of Students Placed At Risk.

Boyer, E. L. (1983). *High school*. New York: Harper.

Braddock, J. H., II. (1990). Tracking the middle grades: National patterns of grouping for instruction. *Phi Delta Kappan, 71*, 445–449.

Cohen, J. (1977). *Statistical power analysis for the behavioral sciences* (Rev. ed.). New York: Academic Press.

Coleman, J. M., & Fults, B. A. (1985). Special class placement, level of intelligence, and the self-concept of gifted children: A social comparison perspective. *Remedial and Special Education, 6*, 7–11.

Coleman, J. S., Campbell, E., Hobson, C., McPartland, J., Mood, A., Wienfield, F., & York, R. (1966). *Equality of educational opportunity*. Washington, DC: U.S. Government Printing Office.

Cooper, H. M. (1984). The integrative research review: A systematic approach. *Applied Social Research Methods Series, Vol. 2*. Beverly Hills, CA: Sage.

Courtis. S. A. (1925). Ability-grouping in Detroit schools. In G. M. Whipple (Ed.), *The ability grouping of pupils, 35th Yearbook of the National Society for the Study of Education* (Part I, pp. 44–47). Bloomington, IL: Public School Publishing.

Gamoran, A., & Berends, M. (1987). The effects of stratification in secondary schools: Synthesis of survey and ethnographic research. *Review of Educational Research, 57*, 415–435.

Gamoran, A., & Mare, R. D. (1989). Secondary school tracking and educational inequality: Compensation, reinforcement, or neutrality. *American Journal of Sociology, 94*, 146–183.

Gamoran, A., & Weinstein, M. (1998). Differentiation and opportunity in restructured schools. *American Journal of Education, 106*, 385–415.

Garet, M. S., & DeLany, B. (1988). Student, courses, and stratification. *Sociology of Education, 61*, 61–77.

Getzels, J. W., & Dillon, J. T. (1973). The nature of giftedness and the education of the gifted. In R. M. W. Travers (Ed.), *Second handbook of research on teaching* (pp. 689–731). Chicago: Rand McNally.

Glass, G. V., McGaw, B., & Smith, M. L. (1981). *Meta-analysis in social research.* Beverly Hills, CA: Sage.

Goodlad, J. I. (1984). *A place called school.* New York: McGraw-Hill.

Gray, H. A., & Hollingworth, L. S. (1931). The achievement of gifted children enrolled and not enrolled in special opportunity classes. *Journal of Educational Research, 24*, 255–261.

Hansford, B. C., & Hattie, J. A. (1982). The relationship between self and achievement/performance measures. *Review of Educational Research, 52*, 123–142.

Hauser, R. M., Sewell, W. H., & Alwin, D. F. (1976). High school effect on achievement. In W. H. Sewell, R. M. Hauser, & D. Featherman (Eds.), *Schooling and achievement in American society* (pp. 309–341). New York: Academic Press.

Herman, R., Aladjem, D., McMahon, P., Masem, E., Mulligan, I., O'Malley, A., Quinones, S., Reeve, A., & Woodruff, D. (1999). *An educator's guide to schoolwide reform.* Washington, DC: American Institutes for Research.

Heyns, B. (1974). Social selection and stratification within schools. *American Journal of Sociology, 79*, 1434–1451.

Ingels, S. J., Scott, L. A., Taylor, J. R., Owings, J., & Quinn, P. (1998). *National Education Longitudinal Study of 1988 (NELS: 88), base year through second follow-up: Final methodology report.* Washington, DC: U.S. Department of Education, Office of Educational Research and Improvement, National Center for Education Statistics. (ERIC Document Reproduction Service No. ED 434 129)

Jencks, C. (1972). *Inequality.* New York: Basic Books.

Keliher, A. C. (1931). *A critical study of homogeneous grouping.* New York: Bureau of Publications, Teachers College, Columbia University.

Kulik, C.-L. C., & Kulik, J. A. (1982). Effects of ability grouping on secondary school students: A meta-analysis of evaluation findings. *American Educational Research Journal, 19*, 415–428.

Kulik, C.-L. C., & Kulik, J. A. (1984, August). *Effects of ability grouping on elementary school pupils: A meta-analysis.* Paper presented at the annual meeting of the American Psychological Association, Toronto. (ERIC Document Reproduction Service No. ED 255 329)

Kulik, J. A. (1992). *An analysis of the research on ability grouping: Historical and contemporary perspectives.* Research-based decision making series. Storrs: National Research Center on the Gifted and Talented, The University of Connecticut. (ERIC Document Reproduction Service No. ED 350777)

Kulik, J. A. (1998). Curricular tracks and high school vocational education. In A. Gamoran (Ed.), *The quality of vocational education. Background papers from the 1994 National Assessment of Vocational Education* (pp. 65–132). Washington, DC: U.S. Department of Education, Office of Educational Research and Improvement, National Institute on Postsecondary Education, Libraries, and Lifelong Learning.

Kulik, J. A., & Kulik, C.-L. C. (1984). Effects of accelerated instruction on students. *Review of Educational Research, 54,* 409–426.

Kulik, J. A., & Kulik, C.-L. C. (1987). Effects of ability grouping on student achievement. *Equity and Excellence, 23,* 22–30.

Kulik, J. A., & Kulik, C.-L. C. (1989). Meta-analysis in educational research [Monograph]. *International Journal of Educational Research, 13,* 221–340.

Kulik, J. A., & Kulik, C.-L. C. (1992). Meta-analytic findings on grouping programs. *Gifted Child Quarterly, 36,* 73–77.

Linchevski, L., & Kutscher, B. (1998). Tell me with whom you're learning, and I'll tell you how much you've learned: Mixed-ability versus same-ability grouping in mathematics. *Journal for Research in Mathematics Education, 29*(5), 533–554.

Loveless, T. (1998). *The tracking and ability grouping debate.* Washington, DC: Thomas B. Fordham Foundation. (ERIC Document Reproduction Service No. ED 422 445)

Loveless, T. (1999). *The tracking wars: State reform meets school policy.* Washington, DC: Brookings Institution.

Marsh, H. W. (1987). The big-fish-little-pond effect on academic self-concept. *Journal of Educational Psychology, 79,* 280–295.

Marsh, H. W., & Parker, J. W. (1984). Determinants of student self-concept: Is it better to be a relatively large fish in a small pond even if you don't learn to swim as well? *Journal of Personality and Social Psychology, 47,* 213–231.

Marsh, H. W., Chessor, D., Craven, R., & Roche, L. (1995). The effects of gifted and talented programs on academic self-concept: The big fish strikes again. *American Educational Research Journal, 32,* 285–319.

McPartland, J. M., Coldiron, J. R., & Braddock, J. H. (1987). *School structures and classroom practices in elementary, middle, and secondary schools.* Baltimore: Center for Research on Elementary and Middle Schools, Johns Hopkins University. (ERIC Document Reproduction Service No. ED 291 703)

Miller, W. S., & Otto, H. J. (1930). Analysis of experimental studies in homogeneous grouping. *Journal of Educational Research, 21,* 95–102.

Mosteller, F., Light, R. J., & Sachs, J. A. (1996). Sustained inquiry in education: Lessons from skill grouping and class size. *Harvard Educational Review, 66,* 797–842.

National Commission on Excellence in Education. (1983). *A Nation at Risk.* Washington, DC: U.S. Government Printing Office.

Oakes, J. (1985). *Keeping track: How schools structure inequality.* New Haven, CT: Yale University.

Otto, H. J. (1941). Elementary education—II. Organization and administration. In W. S. Monroe (Ed.), *Encyclopedia of educational research* (pp. 428–446). New York: Macmillan.

Otto, H. J. (1950). Elementary education—III. Organization and administration. In W. S. Monroe (Ed.), *Encyclopedia of educational research* (Rev. ed., pp. 376–388). New York: Macmillan.

Page, R. N. (1991). *Lower-track classrooms: A curricular and cultural perspective.* New York: Teachers College Press.

Petty, M. C. (1953). *Intraclass grouping in the elementary schools.* Austin: The University of Texas Press.

Rees, D., Argys, L. M., & Brewer, D. J. (1996). Tracking in the United States: Descriptive statistics from NELS. *Economics of Education Review, 15*, 83–89.

Rosenbaum, J. E. (1976). *Making inequality.* New York: Wiley.

Rosenbaum, J. E. (1980). Track misperceptions and frustrated college plans: An analysis of the effects of tracks and track perceptions in the National Longitudinal Survey. *Sociology of Education, 53*, 74–88.

Singal, D. J. (1991, November). The other crisis in American education. *The Atlantic, 268*, 59–62, 65–67, 70, 73–74.

Slavin, R. E. (1987). Ability grouping and student achievement in elementary schools: A best evidence synthesis. *Review of Educational Research, 57*, 293–336.

Slavin, R. E. (1990a). Ability grouping in secondary schools: A response to Hallinan. *Review of Educational Research, 60*, 505–507.

Slavin, R. E. (1990b). Achievement effects of ability grouping in secondary schools: A best evidence synthesis. *Review of Educational Research, 60*, 471–499.

Slavin, R. E., & Fashola, O. S. (1998). *Show me the evidence!* Thousand Oaks, CA: Corwin.

Slavin, R. E., & Madden, N. A. (2000). Research on achievement outcomes of Success for All: A summary and response to critics. *Phi Delta Kappan, 82*, 38–40, 59–66.

Slavin, R. E., Madden, N. A., Dolan, L. J., & Wasik, B. A. (1996). *Every child, every school: Success for All.* Thousand Oaks, CA: Corwin.

Tannenbaum, A. J. (1958). History of interest in the gifted. In N. Henry (Ed.), *Education for the gifted. 57th Yearbook of the National Society for the Study of Education* (Part II, pp. 21–38). Chicago: University of Chicago Press.

Wells, A. S., & Oakes, J. (1996). Potential pitfalls of systemic reform: Early lessons from detracking research [Special issue]. *Sociology of Education, 37*, 135–143.

Wylie, R. C. (1979). *The self-concept: Theory and research on selected topics* (Vol. 2). Lincoln: University of Nebraska Press.

CHAPTER 9

UNDERSTANDING RESEARCH ON THE CONSEQUENCES OF RETENTION

Lorrie A. Shepard

Current "no-social-promotion" policies reflect the urgent desire to improve the quality of education in America. Policymakers are dismayed by fast-food servers who cannot make change, the poor showing of U.S. seniors in the Third International Math and Science Survey (TIMSS), and complaints from business leaders about the inadequate skills of entry-level workers—and they attribute this poor performance to low standards and the willingness of educators to promote students to the next grade whether or not they have mastered requisite skills. For the sake of the nation's economy and for the good of low-achieving students themselves, no-social-promotion policies mandate retention in grade for students failing to meet grade level standards. Some no-social-promotion policies also provide early identification and intervention to prevent grade failure, but for those not helped enough, retention remains the remedy.

Like the majority of educators and lay citizens, policymakers are convinced that by ending social promotion they can improve student learning. But what if retention in grade is an ineffective treatment for low achievement? What policymakers may not realize is that the fast-food worker and the lowest scoring students in TIMSS were most likely retained, some of them more than once.

In this chapter, I summarize research on the consequences of grade retention, especially its effects on student achievement and school dropout rates. I begin with a brief overview of trends in retention rates as a context for examining outcomes. In particular, it is important to understand that retention rates and social promotion rates are only loosely coupled. Therefore, it is possible for both rates to be quite high. In fact, if as posited here, retention does not improve achievement, it is likely that many retained students will subsequently become social promotion "statistics" in the years following retention.

In the main section of the chapter, I summarize research findings showing the links between repeating a grade in school and dropping out. Although there is little controversy about causal interpretation of these data, I nonetheless explain the potential for invalid inferences and review how confounding variables have been addressed in the literature. Then I review comparative studies intended to evaluate the effect of grade repetition on student achievement. I consider the well-know meta-analysis by Holmes (1989) and several more recent large-scale studies including studies from Baltimore (Alexander, Entwisle, & Dauber, 1994), Chicago (Roderick, Bryk, Jacob, Easton, & Allensworth, 1999), Texas (Lorence, Dworkin, Toenjes, & Hill, 2002), and the *Prospects* reanalysis (Karweit, 1999). Given that interpretation of these studies has been controversial because of competing claims about which studies provided the most rigorous controls, I also restate the research design principles relevant to evaluating and comparing treatment effects.

In the concluding section of the chapter, I use the model of the Federal Drug Administration's requirements for safe and effective treatment to consider how evidence of effectiveness should be weighed in making decisions about retention policy.

RETENTION AND SOCIAL PROMOTION RATES

The most complete and up-to-date analysis of retention rates is provided in Heubert and Hauser's *High Stakes* National Research Council report (1999). Retention statistics are not collected nationally, rates have to be inferred from census data. What they show, however, is that "grade retention is pervasive in American schools" (p. 122). For the most recent cohort of 15–17 year olds, for example, the percentage who were either below the modal grade level or had left school was 36%.

Data documenting high rates of retention are surprising. If significant numbers of poor-performing students are being retained, then why does the rhetoric of social promotion imply that so many are being passed through the system? The key to understanding this apparent contradiction is to understand the difference between *annual* and *cumulative* percentages. The percentage cited by Heubert and Hauser is a cumulative rate, meaning that it accumulates for a given group of students across all of their K–12 years of schooling. By the time a cohort of same-age students has reached high school age, 36% are no longer in the appropriate grade. Some have dropped out without having been retained and some started school late, but most (somewhere between 20-25%) repeated at least one grade.

In contrast, data in Table 9.1 report the annual retention rates for North Carolina. North Carolina was chosen as an example from among the 27 states reported by Heubert and Hauser (1999) because it has the most complete data across grades and years and also has annual rates in the middle range compared to states like Mississippi, which retains 9–10% per year, or Indiana, which retains only 1.5% per year. Annual retention rates are the percentage of students retained in a grade in a given year out of the total number of students in that grade. For example, in 1987–1988, 7.4% of kindergartners in North Carolina were retained in kindergarten. Across all grades that year, 4.5% of students were retained. To see how annual retention rates relate to cumulative rates for a cohort, the 1987–1988 kindergarten class can be followed longitudinally, collectively adding the annual rate for successive grades. This calculation is shown by the underscored values. After 7.4% are retained in kindergarten, an additional 7.2% are retained in first grade, 2.1% more in second grade, and so forth. By the end of ninth grade, 41.6% have been retained at least once. These numbers are slightly inflated because they are not adjusted for double retentions or school dropouts. Nonetheless, they illustrate the very large cumulative effects of seemingly weak annual retention practices.

Table 9.1. Percentage of Students by Grade in North Carolina

						Grade Level								
	PK	K	1	2	3	4	5	6	7	8	9	10	11	12	Total
1979-80	NA	4.5	9.8	6.0	4.5	3.2	2.8	3.4	6.8	7.1	14.1	14.8	8.6	4.2	6.9
1985-86	NA	6.0	9.3	5.0	5.7	2.7	2.1	8.1	7.9	11.0	13.9	13.2	9.3	3.9	7.7
1987-88	NA	_7.4_	7.7	3.8	2.8	2.0	1.3	2.2	3.6	3.0	9.0	7.6	4.5	2.2	4.5
1988-89	NA	6.8	_7.2_	2.9	2.7	1.6	1.1	2.3	3.5	2.8	9.6	7.8	4.5	1.8	4.2
1989-90	NA	5.3	5.5	_2.1_	2.0	1.1	0.8	1.6	2.6	2.2	10.4	7.4	4.3	1.7	3.6
1990-91	NA	3.7	4.0	1.6	_1.4_	0.8	0.6	1.5	2.7	2.0	10.8	7.9	4.6	1.9	3.3
1991-92	NA	2.9	4.1	1.9	1.5	_0.7_	0.6	1.4	2.4	1.9	11.3	7.8	4.6	1.7	3.2
1992-93	NA	3.0	4.1	2.0	1.6	0.7	_0.5_	1.3	2.4	1.8	12.8	8.3	4.9	1.8	3.4
1993-94	NA	3.3	4.8	2.4	1.9	0.9	0.7	_1.6_	2.5	2.1	13.4	10.0	5.7	2.0	3.8
1994-95	NA	3.5	4.7	2.4	1.9	1.0	0.7	1.7	_2.6_	1.8	15.0	10.2	5.9	1.9	4.0
1995-96	NA	3.8	5.0	2.8	2.1	1.3	0.8	2.2	3.2	_2.3_	15.7	10.2	6.1	2.2	4.3
1996-97	NA	4.2	5.7	3.1	2.5	1.4	1.0	2.6	3.4	2.8	_15.8_	10.3	6.8	2.1	4.7

Source. Heubert and Hauser (1999).

Given the serious consequences of grade retention for dropping out of school, discussed next, many school systems have policies against double retentions or at least require that a second retention not occur within the same level of schooling—that is, within the primary, intermediate, or middle school grades. Following this same reasoning, it is the cumulative rate that is most relevant for policy analysis, because it reflects the proportion of students affected by retention at some time during their school career. The annual data, however, help to illustrate why there can be a high percentage of social promotion *decisions* at the same time that such a high proportion of *students* are retained. In principle, promotion-retention decisions are made 13 times in a student's career (14 times if they repeat a grade). Thus, as suggested earlier, it is very likely that a retained student will also be a social promotion statistic in years following retention unless retention provides a permanent improvement in achievement.

One additional point should be made regarding the adequacy of data on social promotion. Many reports lament the absence of national data, but none have attempted to define a passing standard and then calculate the implied retention rate if no-social-promotion policies were to be implemented fully. For example, the U.S. Department of Education report, *Taking Responsibility for Ending Social Promotion* (1999), uses data documenting poor achievement to infer that social promotion has occurred, but does not examine (or clarify) the extent to which retention may also be the cause or precursor of the observed negative outcomes. Only one potential passing standard is mentioned, which is the Basic level on National Assessment of Educational Progress (NAEP). This standard would fail from 32 to 40% of students each time the test is given. By comparing the rates of students judged to be incompetent (according to NAEP) with typical retention percentages in grades 4 and 8, it is possible to estimate, from the difference, a social promotion rate of 25 to 35%. If a less ambitious standard were used, such as the 20th percentile on norm-referenced tests, the social promotion statistic would be 15% annually. According to these standards, then, ending social promotion would mean providing massive interventions or retaining 20 to 40% of students annually. Given that most state legislative processes require an analysis of budgetary implications, it is surprising that no-social-promotion policies have been silent regarding the number of students affected and the necessary costs of ensuring attainment of standards.

GRADE RETENTION AND SCHOOL DROPOUT

A large number of studies have documented the link between retention and dropping out. However, given that a third variable, poor academic performance, predicts both retention and dropping out, the observed correlations should not automatically be interpreted to mean that retention directly causes an increase in dropout rates. Grissom and Shepard (1989) examined three large data sets from Austin, Chicago, and an affluent suburb using structural equation modeling. After controlling for background variables such as socioeconomic status, sex, ethnicity, multiple measures of achievement, and estimated errors of measurement, the unique effect of having been retained on dropping out was estimated. All other things being equal, repeating a grade increased the likelihood of dropping out by 20 to 30%. Thus, for a poor achieving student in Austin who might already have a 30% chance of dropping out, the risk would increase to 60% if that student had repeated a grade. In an affluent suburb where low achieving students might only have a 15% chance of dropping out, the risk was increased to 45% by having been retained.

In a more recent study, Roderick (1994) was able to provide more precise controls of students' prior achievement and attendance, as well as postretention grades and attendance. She found that "even after controlling for background and school performance through the sixth grade, youths who repeated prior grades were substantially more likely to drop out—particularly at age 16 when repeating one grade was associated with a doubling of the odds of school leaving" (Roderick, 1994, p. 747). More detailed analyses indicated that retention may work to place students at more risk for dropping out primarily by making them overage for their grade and, as a result, more likely to experience substantial disengagement during middle school.

Across all studies, in both the retention and dropout literatures, retention has been shown to substantially increase the rate of school dropout beyond what would be expected based on poor achievement alone. Direct effects of grade retention on increased dropout rates have also been documented in policy studies of previous no-social-promotion interventions such as the New York City Gates Program and Chicago's crackdown of the 1980s (Rice, Toles, Schulz, Harvey, & Foster, 1987). Therefore, as stated previously, these conclusions are not controversial among researchers. However, as I discuss in the concluding section of the chapter, the implications of these findings for educational policy depend on the viewpoint of policymakers and the underlying purpose of no-social-promotion policies. If grade retention is intended as an educational intervention primarily aimed at raising the achievement of retained students, then dropping out must be considered a serious negative side effect of such medicine. However, some policymakers may believe that an increased dropout rate is a necessary (or at least tolerable) corollary of raising standards. For example, when discussing increased dropout rates associated with the Massachusetts Comprehensive Assessment System exit exam, Massachusetts Board of Education member Abigail Thernstrom said, "Suppose the dropout rate goes up slightly, but the skills of the kids who stay become significantly stronger. We'll be better off" ("MCAS Opponents," 2000) Such a frame of reference would necessarily alter how evidence would be weighed to evaluate a policy's effectiveness in terms of its own goals; but as Heubert and Hauser (1999) have noted, there may also be issues of individual rights at stake given that low-SES and minority children are disproportionately subjected to the negative consequences of retention.

EFFECTS OF GRADE RETENTION ON ACHIEVEMENT

Major reviews of research on retention have consistently concluded that "there is no reliable body of evidence to indicate that grade retention is more beneficial than grade promotion for students with serious academic or adjustment difficulties" (Jackson, 1975, p. 627). However, two recent, large-scale studies of retained students in Baltimore and Texas have reported positive achieve gains for retained students. Moreover, authors of these studies, Alexander et al. (1994) and Lorence et al. (2002) raise questions about the adequacy of matching designs used in previous studies, claiming superiority for their own methods even though they are also quasi-experimental. Karweit (1999) provides perhaps the best overview of competing findings based on methodological differences and differences in valued outcomes, such as same-age versus same-grade comparisons.

Here I endeavor to extend Karweit's analysis both by clarifying policy perspectives that align with particular outcomes and by applying classic design principles from Campbell and Stanley (1966) to estimate the direction and magnitude of methodological artifacts. A goal would be to see if there are not some commonly agreed on criteria for weighing and evaluating study findings. For example, well-controlled studies should have greater weight than poorly controlled studies in forming conclusions; same-grade comparisons are more consistent with how grade retention is intended to work; and so forth.

Holmes's Meta-analysis

Holmes (1989) provided the most comprehensive synthesis of comparative studies of grade retention. He employed meta-analysis, now a widely used technique in medical research and the social sciences, to calculate and then aggregate standardized average differences between retained and low-achieving controls across 63 studies. Holmes found that 54 studies produced negative effects for retained students compared to controls, while only nine studies showed on-average, positive effects for retention.

For the 47 studies that measured academic outcomes, repeating a grade had a negative effect on the achievement of retained students (−.31 in standard deviation units) compared to students initially matched for equally low achievement. Chief criticisms of the Holmes analysis are that it relied on matched-control studies and mixed together same-grade and same-age comparisons.

While it is true that randomized experiments would provide a less equivocal basis for evaluating the effects of retention on achievement, it is not the case that sound inferences cannot be drawn from quasi-experimental studies. The conclusion that smoking causes lung cancer, for example, rests on quasi-experimental comparisons of smokers and nonsmokers, as well as tissue studies. As Campbell and Stanley (1966) outlined, it is important to know the likely threats to validity, and then to evaluate the strength of plausible rival hypotheses. As Jackson (1975) speculated, it is likely that matched studies favor the promoted group because retained students probably have more difficulties than just the achievement variables on which the groups were matched. For example, historically, retained students were more likely to have behavior problems than equally low-achieving students who were not retained. For the last 20 years, however, mainstreamed special education students could be the students in the class with the greatest difficulties, but they are often exempt from retention. If special education students or previously retained students are included in the control group, then the bias would favor the retained group. While such competing hypotheses (in this case, uncontrolled initial differences) cannot be ruled out when interpreting single studies, they may be less compelling over a large number of studies so long as the methodological biases are not the same across studies.

In addition to using a standardized metric for comparing effects, it is also customary that meta-analyses search for study features that may account for variation in study outcomes. For example, is the magnitude of effect associated with year of study, degree of control, publication outlet, characteristics of subjects, and so on? Indeed, in some literatures, there are marked differences in outcomes between poorly controlled and well-controlled studies. Holmes conducted these analyses and found that studies with greater controls (i.e., matching on prior achievement and IQ) still resulted in the same magnitude of negative effect. Also in keeping with the notion that not all studies share the same biases, Shepard and Smith (1989) selected matched controls from schools that did not practice retention, thus making it more likely that matching on multiple variables would ensure greater initial equivalence between groups. Consistent with other same-grade comparisons, this study found, on average, no difference between retained and promoted controls rather than harm to achievement.

Holmes (1989) found quite different results across studies depending on the timing of comparisons. In *same-age* comparisons, promoted controls are one grade ahead of retained students. If both groups were matched at the end of first grade, for example, then achievement results are again compared using the promoted group's second grade results and the retained group's second year of first grade results. In *same-grade* comparisons, data collection is staggered by one year to wait for the retained group to be in the same grade as the control group. The same-grade series typically begins by reusing the matching data from the control group in comparison to the results for the retained group at the end of their second year in the repeated grade.

The results of these comparisons are summarized in Table 9.2 for the retention year and several years post retention. Same-age comparisons portray a much more negative picture of retention effects. Typically, when evaluated on the same achievement scale, low-achieving, promoted controls do better because they have been exposed to more advanced curriculum. It should be noted, though, that usually both groups are performing below average. Same-grade comparisons provide a more favorable picture of the effects of retention on achievement; although it is important to recognize that retained students are being compared to younger students (a small benefit in grades K–2) and in the repeat year itself have the benefit of regression to the mean and retaking the same test, which cannot occur for the reused control data.

With one caveat discussed below, I agree with retention advocates that same-grade comparisons fit better with the logic of retention, which is intended to be a one-time adjustment in the student's academic pathway. To my knowledge, no one argues that low-achieving students should be retained every time they fall behind (perhaps because there is general awareness that retaining a student twice makes the likelihood of dropping out greater than 90%). Therefore, retention is intended as a one-time corrective to shore up deficient skills and ensure that a student has a sounder foundation. From this perspective, it is not how quickly students master

Table 9.2. Mean Effect Sizes for Academic Achievement

	1 Yr	*2 Yrs*	*3 Yrs*	*3+ Yrs*
Same age (different grades) comparisons				
Weighted by effect (# effects)	−.45 (178)	−.51 (32)	−.67 (22)	−.83 (18)
Weighted by study (# studies)	−.41 (28)	−.64 (5)	−.74 (3)	−.88 (3)
Same grade (different ages) comparisons				
Weighted by effect (# effects)	+.25 (107)	+.19 (61)	+.09 (33)	.00 (41)
Weighted by study (# studies)	.00 (10)	+.02 (7)	−.12 (5)	+.04 (6)

Source. Holmes (1989).

material, but whether they can learn more relative to grade expectation and then maintain that higher normative position in years following retention. I do not agree with Karweit (1999) and others that the data in Table 9.2 show a short-term positive benefit from retention. This is an example of a point where explicit consideration of evaluation criteria might lead to greater concurrence among researchers. Given the problem of correlated errors, I would argue that it is more reasonable to focus on the meta-analysis results averaged by study rather than single effects. As Holmes explained, the few positive studies he reviewed used more outcome measures than the negative studies, therefore, the effect size averaged across effects is more positive than the effect size averaged across studies. Weighted by study the same-grade comparisons show a .00 effect in the repeat year, a +.02 effect one grade after retention (which is year 2 of the study), a −.12 effect two grades after, and .04 three grades later. A fair reading of these data is one of no effect. In comparison to same-grade, low-performing peers, retained students experience neither a boost nor harm to what their achievement would have been without retention.

To follow up on the caveat mentioned earlier, there is a circumstance where it is essential to focus on same-age rather than same-grade learning outcomes, and that occurs in all those cases where retention ends in school dropout. For students who drop out because of retention, the issue *is* how fast they cover material and thus how far they get before leaving school. As shown in the same-age comparisons in Table 9.2, socially-promoted controls would know substantially more at the time of leaving school than retained students who have completed one less grade.

The Baltimore Study

The Baltimore study (Alexander, Entwisle, & Dauber, 1994) is widely cited both because of its positive findings regarding retention effects and for the high quality of the authors' longitudinal data set and painstaking analyses. The authors summarized their results as follows:

> Although the analysis in this book indicate retention has mainly positive consequences, this was not true for all repeaters under all circumstances. Positive effects are found mainly for youngsters held back only once, and for youngsters held back after first grade. Despite the preponderance of positive effects, retention does not cure children's problems. The distinction between "solution" and "some help" is critical, and glossing over it has created much of the confusion surrounding retention. The boost children get from repeating a grade, though real, is limited: most one-time repeaters realize some benefits, but remain far behind their agemates. (p. 214)

In a lengthy review, my coauthors and I (Shepard, Smith, & Marion, 1996) raised several methodological issues that call into question Alexander et al.'s summary of mainly positive effects. In his response, Alexander (1998) said, "Their treatment of our analysis is, in the main, fair and accurate" (p. 402). He objected primarily to our having painted him as an enthusiast for retention. Here I summarize four main methodological points that affect interpretation of achievement gains for retained students in Baltimore: scaling artifact, regression to the mean, testing effects, and the appropriate weight of 1st grade findings. Given the complexity of these issues, the reader may wish to refer to the original review article and response.

Alexander et al. (1994) were misled by the vertical score scale underlying the California Achievement Test. Because of the decelerating growth curves created by item-response-theory (IRT) scaling, it is always the case on these tests that students in a higher grade gain less on average than students in a lower grade. Yet these artifactually greater gains for retained students—who were a year behind—were interpreted to mean, incorrectly, that retained students were "closing the gap." Problems with interpreting vertical scale score gains are well recognized in the psychometric literature, and in recent years CTB has revised their IRT-based scales to produce more linear growth "curves."

As shown in Figure 9.1, we converted Alexander et al.'s data to within-grade standard scores to obtain a more accurate picture of reading achievement before, during, and after the repeat year. These more accurate trend lines show dramatic gains in the repeat year itself. However, once regression to the mean is taken into account for the extreme scores observed at the time of the retention decision, a more defensible summary of results is a loss in achievement for first grade retainees following retention, and no difference between achievement levels before and after retention for second, third, and higher grades retainees. Our inference about the likely magnitude of the regression effect is based on Alexander et al.'s own statistically adjusted comparisons which showed, except for first graders who did much worse, that retaineed students' level of achievement after retention was not significantly different from the level predicted on the basis of prior achievement.

We also criticized Alexander et al. because they seemed willing to believe that the large gains observed for retained students in the repeat year itself were real without considering either teaching to the test or practice effects on the identical test as possible influences. In our experience, the problem with what Campbell and Stanley (1966) called "testing effects" is nontrivial. Using randomized comparisons, Koretz, Linn, Dunbar, and Shepard (1991) found that performance on a familiar, taught-to test could be .33 to .5 standard deviations greater than performance on

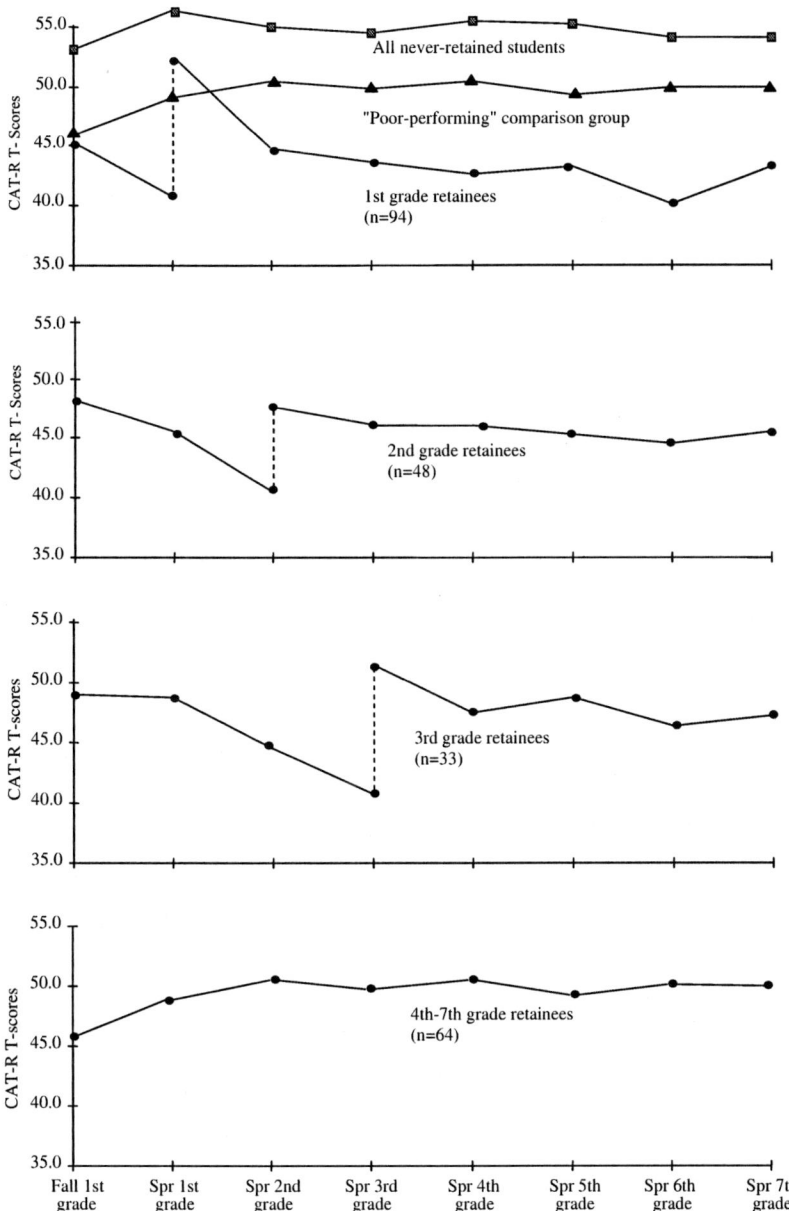

Figure 9.1. CAT reading comprehension scores in grades 1 through 7 converted to national-norm within-grade T-scores for first, second and third grade retainees, fourth through seventh grade retainees, all never-retained pupils, and the "poor-performing" comparison group. (Data from Alexander, Entwisle, & Dauber, 1994, p. 102; Figure from Shepard, Smith, & Marion, 1996, p. 255)

an equated unfamiliar test covering the same content. In a meta-analysis of studies on test practice, Kulik, Kulik, and Bangert (1984) found that one-time practice on the identical test produced on average a gain of .42, although the effect for low-ability students was only .17. Although Alexander et al. acknowledge that the real test of the meaningfulness of gains during the repeat year should be whether this apparent boost is sustained in subsequent years, at other times they speak of these gains as consequential and as a firm basis for considering retention to be an effective policy. "Instead of impeding their progress, repeating a grade helped retainees do better in their repeated year and for some years thereafter, although in diminishing amounts, until they made the transition into middle school" (Alexander et al., 1996, p. 214).

Finally, we fault Alexander et al. for acknowledging the detrimental effects of retention on achievement for first grade retainees but then forming a conclusion that emphasizes "mainly positive consequences." Given that the two samples where the authors see gains, that is, second and third grade retainees ($n = 48$, $n = 33$), had fewer students combined than the first grade sample ($n = 94$), a more defensible summary would have been either, like Jackson's (1975), that there is no evidence that retention improves achievement or that retention increases the risk of academic failure as often as it helps.

The Chicago Studies

On-going research by the Consortium on Chicago School Research (Roderick et al., 1999) provides a comprehensive evaluation of Chicago's highly visible, present-day effort to end social promotion. Strengths of the research design include the availability of comparable test score data in the years preceding the policy, on-going longitudinal comparisons, tracking of separate elements of the policy (such as regular school year gains versus Summer Bridge program gains), and attention by the authors to multiple rival hypotheses that might explain test score gains.

Both the first major report of findings from Chicago (Roderick et al., 1999) and the most recent follow-up (Roderick, Nagaoka, Bacon, & Easton, 2000) suggest dramatically different results for two different groups of students, creating what we might call "bifurcating" pathways. Those at-risk students who are threatened by retention but escape it are helped by the no-social-promotion policy. Not only are passing rates up, but in 1999 more sixth and eighth grade students are reaching the cutoff during the school year, rather than catching up during the Summer Bridge program. In addition, these gains seem to be real at least for an appreciable number of students who stayed on track (for grade level gains) two years after having met the promotion standard.

In contrast, students who did not meet promotion standards and who were retained under the policy have not been helped. Retention rates are up in kindergarten, first, and second grades in Chicago in anticipation of the third grade promotional gate, when students must pass a mandatory test to be promoted to the next grade; but in 1999, despite high exclusion rates (45%) of previously retained students, often due to special education placements, 33% of the remaining third graders were retained for a second time. For those students retained in the promotional gate grades—third, sixth, and eighth—approximately half fail to meet the promotional cutoff again after the repeated grade. Passing rates look especially bad for previously retained eighth graders (only 38% met the cutoff the second time through), because many retained students are dropping out at age 16. The authors are careful to point out that Chicago's overall dropout rates have not increased under the no-social-promotion policy, but more students are dropping out earlier. As to the achievement of retained students, the most important finding was one of no difference compared to "socially promoted" control students (identified as below the mandatory cutoff the year before the policy began).

The Texas Study

Lorence et al. (2002) used longitudinal data from the Texas Assessment of Academic Skills (TAAS) to evaluate the effect of retention for 781 third graders who were retained in 1994 and who also had a TAAS reading score below 70. By selecting this passing score, the authors could simulate in prior data the effect of the state-mandated retention policy that will go into effect in 2003. The control group was the remaining 30,140 third graders who had a test score below 70 but who were promoted to fourth grade. Strengths of the Lorence et al. study include the availability of data for four years post retention and the extensive efforts made by the authors to examine factors that might confound study results. For example, they estimated regression-to-the mean effects and made appropriate adjustments in reported gains. They used statistical adjustments to control for differences in demographic variables between the groups, and they checked for differential attrition between the retained and control groups.

In contrast to the existing literature and the similarly designed Baltimore study, the Texas study showed positive effects for retention even after accounting for regression. The gains for retained students were the most striking, of course, in the repeat year itself. At the end of the second year in third grade, reading test scores had risen 9.7 standard score points beyond what could have been expected due to regression; this translated to a large effect size of .65. The relative advantage in reading compared to controls was less in each successive year but still substantial until four years post retention. The corresponding effect sizes for grades 4, 5, 6, and 7 were, respectively, .52, .39, .28, and .14. An effect size of .52 in fourth grade, for example, means that retained students out-performed socially promoted controls in reading by half a standard deviation. For students starting at the 10th percentile, this would mean a boost of 12 percentile points compared to what their performance would have been had they gone directly on to fourth grade; in other words, their reading scores would rise from the 10th to the 22nd percentile as a result of retention. Lorence et al. attribute the benefits they found for retention in Texas, in contrast to findings elsewhere, to the intensive accountability pressures in Texas, which focus teachers' attention on low-performing students.

When I was asked by the Brookings Institution to provide a critique of the Lorence et al. paper, I noted several methodological concerns (Shepard, 2002). The authors have addressed some of these concerns very well in subsequent analyses—such as the problem of regression to the mean and disproportion of special education students. Two methodological or validity concerns remain, however, that may or may not be of sufficient magnitude to contradict the finding of positive academic benefits from retention. First, because of the need to match cases over time, the study necessarily suffered from attrition or what is referred to as "experimental mortality" in the research design lexicon. Forty-four percent of the retained group and 41% of the control group were lost because of incomplete data. As would be expected, the students leaving the study were lower performing than those who stayed. Based on their original scores in 1994, the retained students who stayed had an average score of 50.2 compared to 46.0 for the retained students who left the study. For control students, the means were 57.4 versus 52.6 for stayers and leavers, respectively.

I disagree with the authors that reading scores for leavers and stayers were similar enough for attrition not to be a problem. Indeed, this difference is an effect size of .28 for the retained group. However, I agree with them that both the rates and biases are similar enough between the retained and control groups for attrition not to threaten the validity of the comparison—with one caveat. Given the huge differences in sample sizes between the retained group and promoted controls (781 vs. 30,140) and the fact that retained students had already experienced grade failure, the study is vulnerable to differential *causes* of attrition. Control students are more likely to have left because of ordinary mobility factors, whereas retained students would be relatively more likely to leave because of additional school failure. (Note that leaving could include an additional retention or an exemption from testing due to special education placement.) What we have to avoid here is the tautological problem of studying the benefits of retention for only the 56% of retained students for whom retention was effective. A check on this hypothesis would be to examine not the initial scores of study leavers but their last score before leaving to make sure that they were not systematically lower than their initial scores would predict.

The second and more serious concern has to do with the validity of reported test score gains in Texas, especially for retained students and other low-performing groups. There is a substantial research literature (U. S. Congress, 1992) documenting the extent of test-score inflation that may occur under high-stakes conditions where teachers feel pressured to teach to the test. Basic-skills tests such as TAAS are especially vulnerable to such practices. In a recent study, RAND researchers Klein, Hamilton, McCaffrey, and Stecher (2000) found that gains in achievement reported on TAAS from 1994 to 1998 were not corroborated by gains for Texas on the NAEP. Hence there is strong evidence of test score inflation on TAAS. Instead of gains in effect sizes on TAAS of .31 to .49 for this period, the gains for Texas on NAEP were only .13 to .15. Indeed, the much-touted closing of the gap between majority and minority groups on TAAS was contradicted by NAEP data showing, in fact, that the gaps between groups had actually been widening. This last finding warns us that test score gains in Texas can be seriously misleading, especially for low-performing groups.

We lack an exact calculus for computing the amount of test score inflation that might affect the picture of gains for retained students in Texas. We do know, however, that retained students in the Lorence et al. study benefited differentially from the steadily rising scores in Texas because, for each grade level, their data were collected a year after that of control students. We also know that the amount of inflation suggested by the Klein et al. study for low-performing groups is of the same magnitude as the reported benefits of retention for all years except the repeat year itself and one year following. Viewed in this more cautious light, the findings in the Texas study are more consistent with the pattern reported in Baltimore.

Karweit's *Prospects* Study

Prospects was a nationally representative longitudinal survey conducted to provide data for a Congressionally mandated study of Chapter 1. Karweit (1999) studied the effects of retention using the first grade *Prospects* cohort because first grade is the grade with the highest incidence of retention and because this group had data from the fall preceding the retention decision, as well as two years of follow-up data. Of the original sample of 10,280 students who entered first grade in 1991, 7,341 had complete achievement data for three years; 250 of these students repeated first grade and 7,091 repeated no grades during the three years of the study.

Using same-grade comparisons, Karweit (1999) found positive benefits for retention. Given that the "control" group in this instance was the entire sample of students making normal grade-to-grade progress rather than a low-performing, promoted group, the initial difference between promoted and retained students at the end of first grade was quite large, an effect size of 1.25 standard deviation units on the Comprehensive Test of Basic Skills (CTBS) Reading Test. After statistical controls for differences between the groups in prior test scores, race and ethnicity, mother's education, income, and occupation, and other factors, the differences at the time of the retention decision were calculated to be .52. At the end of the second year in first grade, that difference had been reduced to only .13 standard deviations, and at the end of second grade, it had rebounded to only .24 standard deviations. Note that the effect size for the benefit of retention in this case is actually the difference between the before and after distance between the groups (e.g., .52 − .13 = .39).

The *Prospects* data are less vulnerable to some inferential threats than other studies, but some threats to validity remain. For example, the issue of teaching the test should be less of a problem in a national survey because an independent test, the CTBS, was used rather than the local accountability test. Two threats, however, are serious enough that they should be accounted for before relying on the positive findings. One is regression-to-the mean, but unlike the Baltimore and Texas studies, we lack sufficient information here to make the necessary adjustments. Some amount of the .39 effect above is certainly due to regression to the mean, which is exacerbated by the fact that the first grade scores for the promoted group were held constant from the previous comparison. This is a necessary feature of how same-grade comparisons must be calculated. In contrast, the second year of first grade results for retained students were free to bounce upward due to the imperfect correlation of test scores from one year to the next.

The second serious threat to the validity of inferences is the omission from the study of the 9.5% of students who were retained twice. As has been suggested previously, it is problematic to exclude from the comparison those students for whom retention was the most ineffective. Clearly, a second retention means that the first retention did not work. Given that these students are likely to have very low scores at the time they left the study, it is misleading to evaluate retention on the basis of scores for the 90.5% of students for whom retention was relatively more successful.

Karweit (1999) also conducted same-age comparisons, which are well known in the literature to produce more negative effects for retention. Same-age comparisons mean that retained students are compared to their age-mates who have gone on to the next grade. The first graders in this study, who started out .52 standard units behind promoted students (after adjustments), continued to be .57 standard units behind after one year, and .59 units behind at two years post retention. In prior studies, same-age comparisons have often shown harmful effects for retention where the gap may actually have widened between retained students and low-performing control students. This pattern most likely occurs because the promoted group, however low achieving, has gone on to the next-grade curriculum where they learn more advanced content than retained students who repeat the previous curriculum. In subsequent years, retained students continue to be one year behind in content covered. It is interesting that this pattern appears to hold true, even in reading, which is the skill area least affected by grade-specific curriculum. In the *Prospects* study, same-age comparisons did not show harm, only no benefit for the extra year spent in grade.

CONCLUSIONS

Grade retention is intended to cure (or at least to improve) poor achievement. If retention were evaluated by the Federal Drug Administration, would it be judged to be a safe and effective treatment? The FDA approval process asks two questions:

- Do the results of well-controlled studies provide substantial evidence of effectiveness?
- Do the results show the product is safe—which means that the benefits of the drug appear to outweigh its risks?

How should the evidence be weighed to make a final assessment about the effect of retention on achievement? Much hangs on the decision to focus on same-grade or same-age comparisons. Same-grade comparisons, where retained students are compared to their new, younger cohort of classmates clearly follows the logic of retention. But it is curious that this normative and relative comparison would be preferred in an era of standards that emphasizes the absolute level of student mastery. The same-age research on retention is unequivocal: Low-performing students who go on to the next grade learn more. So in a given year of their lives, low-achieving third graders are learning more math and language arts and reading at a higher level of proficiency than their initially equal counterparts who are held back in second grade. Focusing on same-grade rather than same-age comparisons is a large concession to the good intentions of retention policies, and it assumes that this one-time strong medicine will provide a significant boost to students' achievement in ensuing years.

Given the severity of a one-year disjuncture in a student's career and the known negative effect on dropping out, are even the same-grade comparisons sufficiently positive to argue for retention? The Holmes meta-analysis shows a zero effect when 10 studies are weighted equally. In other words, there is neither a gain nor a loss in achievement due to the extra year in grade. After taking account of regression to the mean, a defensible summary of the Baltimore study is that retention helped only in the repeat year itself. After that, there was a loss for first grade retainees, and no difference between achievement levels before and after retention for second, third, and higher-grade retainees. Chicago researchers found that the threat of retention helped the achievement of students just above the cutoff score who escaped retention, but it has not improved the achievement of students who actually repeated a grade. The most positive picture for retention comes from the same-grade comparisons in Texas and the *Prospects* data survey. Of these, the Texas study is the more rigorously controlled because it begins with a more comparable control group prior to the institution of an extensive retention mandate and implements controls for regression to the mean and attrition.

The positive Texas and *Prospects* studies do not outweigh the evidence from other negative or neutral studies and therefore do not meet the FDA's requirement to "provide substantial evidence of effectiveness." Forming such a conclusion may appear to some to make the standard of proof sterner for retention than for promotion. But this is precisely what the requirements are for a new drug to enter the market. In the education context as well, it is the stance that has been taken both scientifically and legally with respect to special education placements—a field that has also had to arrive at sensible policies given equivocal evidence of benefits and known negative side effects. In 1982, a panel of the National Academy of Sciences (Heller, Holtzman, & Messick) determined that the lack of clear evidence of benefit for special education placement and the potential for social stigma and ineffective instruction should place the burden of proof on those who argued for placement in a segregated setting. They would have to first document that a child could not learn under reasonable alternative instructional approaches before subjecting the child to the risks of referral, assessment, and placement. Similarly, retention should be shown to be effective—beyond the most favorable comparison or most favorable outcome measure—before it is administered routinely to low-achieving students.

As a final word, I should note, too, that other treatments for poor achievement have a much greater chance of success. After school programs, tutoring, summer school, and one-on-one reading instruction are more effective in raising achievement than repeating a grade, as shown by large positive results in their respective research literatures.

REFERENCES

Alexander, K. L. (1998). Letter to the editor. *Psychology in the Schools, 35*, 402–404.
Alexander, K. L., Entwisle, D. R., & Dauber, S. L. (1994). *On the success of failure: A reassessment of the effects of retention in the primary grades*. Oakleigh, Melbourne, Australia: Cambridge University Press.
Campbell, D. T., & Stanley, J. C. (1966). *Experimental and quasi-experimental designs for research*. Chicago: Rand McNally.
Grissom, J. B., & Shepard, L. A. (1989). Repeating and dropping out of school. In L. A. Shepard & M. L. Smith (Eds.), *Flunking grades: Research and policies on retention* (pp. 34–63). London: Falmer Press.
Heller, K. A., Holtzman, W. H., & Messick, S. (Eds.). (1982). *Placing children in special education: A strategy for equity*. Washington, DC: National Academy Press.
Holmes, C. T. (1989). Grade level retention effects: A meta-analysis of research effects. In L. A. Shepard & M. L. Smith (Eds.), *Flunking grades: Research and policies on retention* (pp. 16–33). London: Falmer Press.
Heubert, J. P., & Hauser, R. M. (Eds.). (1999). *High stakes: Testing for tracking, promotion, and graduation*. Washington, DC: National Academy Press.
Jackson, G. B. (1975). The research evidence on the effects of grade retention, *Review of Educational Research, 45*, 613–635.
Karweit, N. L. (1999). *Grade retention: Prevalence, timing, and effects*. (Report No. 33). Baltimore: John Hopkins University, Center for Research on the Education of Students Placed at Risk (CRESPAR).
Klein, S. P., Hamilton, L. S., McCaffrey, D. F., & Stecher, B. M. (2000). What do test scores in Texas tell us? *Educational Policy Analysis Archives, 8*(49). Available: http://epaa.asu.edu/epaa/v8n49/
Koretz, D., Linn, R., Dunbar, S., & Shepard, L. (1991, April). *The effects of high stakes testing on achievement: Preliminary findings about generalization across tests*. Paper presented at the annual meeting of the American Educational Research Association, Chicago.
Kulik, J. A., Kulik, C. C., & Bangert, R. (1984). Effects of practice on aptitude and achievement test scores. *American Educational Research Journal, 21*, 435–447.
Lorence, J., Dworkin, A. G., Toenjes, L. A., & Hill, A. N. (2002). Grade retention and social promotion in Texas, 1994–99: Academic achievement among elementary school students. In D. Ravitch (Ed.), *Brookings papers on educational policy: 2002*. Washington, DC: Brookings Institution Press.

MCAS opponents link tests to minority dropout rate. (2000, September 28). *Boston Herald* [On-line]. Available: www.bostonherald.com/new/local_regional/mcas09282000.htm

Rice, W. K., Toles, R. E., Schulz, E. M., Harvey, J. T., & Foster, D. L. (1987, April). *A longitudinal investigation of effectiveness of increased promotion standards at eighth grade on high school graduation.* Paper presented at the annual meeting of the American Educational Research Association, Washington, DC.

Roderick, M. (1994). Grade retention and school dropout: Investigating the association. *American Educational Research Journal, 31,* 729–759.

Roderick, M., Bryk, A. S., Jacob, B. A., Easton, J. Q., & Allensworth, E. (1999). *Ending social promotion: Results from the first two years.* Chicago: Consortium on Chicago School Research.

Roderick, M., Nagaoka, J., Bacon, J., & Easton, J. Q. (2000). *Update: Ending social promotion: Passing, retention, and achievement trends among promoted and retained students 1995–1999.* Chicago: Consortium on Chicago School Research.

Shepard, L. (2002). Comment. In D. Ravitch (Ed.), *Brookings papers on educational policy: 2002.* (pp. 56–63). Washington, DC: Brookings Institution Press.

Shepard, L. A., & Smith, M. L. (1989). Academic and emotional effects of kindergarten retention in one school district. In L. A. Shepard & M. L. Smith (Eds.), *Flunking grades: Research and policies on retention* (pp. 79–107). London: Falmer Press.

Shepard, L. A., Smith, M. L., & Marion, S. F. (1996). Failed evidence on grade retention. *Psychology in the Schools, 33,* 251–261.

U.S. Congress, Office of Technology Assessment. (1992). *Testing in American schools: Asking the right questions* (Publication No. OTA-SET-519). Washington, DC: U.S. Government Printing Office.

U.S. Department of Education. (1999). *Taking responsibility for ending social promotion.* Washington, DC: Author.

CHAPTER 10

RECOMMENDATIONS AND A PERSONAL VIEW

Herbert J. Walberg

The conferees, consisting of the chapter authors, other scholars, educators, parents, and policymakers did not reach consensus on all issues and interpretations of findings, but agreed that the major issues and views had been expressed in the papers and the work groups. Though not every participant agreed with each point, the generally consensual recommendations are as follows.

RETENTION

Although there is no magical cure for the possible harms of retention, it is critical to examine retention alternatives before students are retained, which suggests, among other things, quality preschools for children. Students who attend academically oriented preschools are less likely to be retained in later school years. In addition to preschool, full-day kindergarten might further benefit students. Such early programs provide children opportunities to build strong academic foundations. Even so, educators need provide remediation to meet students' academic needs, regardless of whether or not they have been well prepared or retained.

Even in the upper grades, steps can be taken that can reduce the need for retention. Advisor networks provide opportunities for faculty to exchange information and insights about course work and related matters. Such networks can help teachers and advisors understand the students' lives inside and outside school and their academic performance in all academic areas, not just the ones for which they are responsible.

Building students' interests into academic programs may help sustain their efforts. Many high schools emphasize college preparation, but not all students thrive under such a course of study. Giving some students the opportunity to experience a more career-based or project-based education may help them prosper.

In response to standards legislation, school districts are struggling to fit sufficient content and instruction into the school day. Expanding the school day or moving to year-round schooling and shorter summer vacations may help relieve some of this pressure and allow time for needed remedial work. Teachers would be able to structure longer and more intensive lessons and students would be able to continue learning without a long interruption.

If students are to succeed, they need well-prepared, effortful teachers who are able to meet their needs. School districts must not only recruit, retain, and motivate able teachers; they must also hold them accountable. If high expectations are placed on students, it seems reasonable to hold similarly high expectations of teachers.

Parents should also be involved in helping their children avoid grade retention and winding up in lower tracks. One way to increase parent involvement is to develop tip sheets that suggest how they can become more involved in their child's schooling. These sheets can offer suggestions for helping children with their homework, enriching educational projects to do at home, steps to take to prepare children for exams (and relieve test anxiety), and advice on interacting with teachers. They can also explain academic enrichment activities and institutions such as museums in their communities.

To accomplish such aims, schools can inaugurate parent education and outreach programs. Maintaining close relations of parents and teachers can help students' chances for school success. Teachers and parents need to be able to discuss all aspects of student performance—successes and lack of success alike. Waiting to talk to parents when a student is at risk of retention is too late. A wiser course is to draw parents into the educational process early and encourage them be key players in their child's academic life.

GROUPING AND TRACKING

Even if scholars may not have reached a consensus on the effects of grouping and tracking, what tentative recommendations can be made to policymakers and practitioners? School districts should consider multi-age classrooms in which students of similar achievement but different ages are grouped together, usually for certain subjects such as reading or mathematics. This helps remove the barrier of age and grade-level association and its accompanying stigma. Furthermore, research suggests that multi-age classrooms can enrich a student's learning and development.

It may also be beneficial to conduct individual conferences with students about where they might be best grouped. Students may have self-insights into how much effort they can expend. Some may be ready to reform and expend great effort to meet a high standard. Others may feel ill prepared but profit from encouragement. Still others may know enough about their present status to conclude that they presently cannot muster the effort and time that may be required. Individual conferences with students can inform both educators and students themselves to make better-informed decisions.

Group placement should not be permanent. In theory, grouping is the placement of students into groups of like-ability students. However, students are individuals with individual learning rates and phases of development. Extramural factors can profoundly influence how much they can learn at any given time. Grouping should allow students to move between groups when appropriate. On a similar note, all students—regardless of achievement level—should receive the same high level of quality instruction and performance expectations. Academic groups should not be a caste system.

A PERSONAL VIEW

As a student of education but not a scholar specialized in retention, grouping, or tracking, I asked myself what—in addition to the chapter authors' and the consensual recommendations—I might take away from the conference and the revised contributions, which constitute the chapters in the main body of this book. I was reminded of the deep scholarship of the contributors and their sincere efforts to bring focused evidence and practical recommendations in a book and conference that for the first time brought to bear three domains of research on the question raised in the book's title, *Can Unlike Students Learn Together?*

I was also reminded of the concerted efforts of the conferees to bring some closure to the question raised and their success in achieving a partial degree of consensus on the recommendations even though the three main topics seem inherently controversial. These features of the book and conference as a whole are entirely in keeping with one of the original premises of the Laboratory for Student Success—not necessarily to achieve consensus on education policy and practice issues but to bring scholars and educators together in a neutral setting to discuss possibly controversial questions.

Thus, research questions remain open since research on the three conference issues is inherently difficult, or at least difficult on which to achieve a consensus. Why?

Often preferred by sociologists, "statistically controlled" studies depend on inclusion of students' abilities, attitudes, and achievement as well as the many conditions within and outside the school that may affect their success. Although a researcher might set forth a reasonable list, another may disagree that the list is complete or that each possible cause is well measured. Preferred by psychologists, "experimental studies" randomly assign students to one of the policies in question, say tracking, but this may be difficult to achieve. Students and parents, for example, may object to such random assignment. Even if possible to achieve this feat, the results may be affected by a "hothouse" or other extraneous causes that may not be found in less contrived situations.

For these evidentiary reasons and because of the consequential lack of scholarly and educator consensus, efforts to bring like children together for teaching and learning seem likely to continue in most American schools. Loveless (1998), for example, reviewed the research literature with respect to the prevalence of ability grouping and tracking. Loveless finds that no national survey of ability grouping has been done. On the basis of local surveys, however, he writes:

> Ability grouping for reading instruction appears nearly universal, especially in the early grades. Schools seek to create teachable groups of children within classes containing a broad range of skills, from students who independently breeze through children's novels to those who have yet to learn basic letter sounds. (p. 2)

Loveless also summarized national, randomly drawn surveys of tracking. In the middle school survey, the percentage of tracked students rose from 63% in fifth grade to 73% in eighth grade in some or all subjects. The high school survey showed that 86.5% of U.S. high schools practice mathematics tracking. Although some education theorists object to these methods, surveys "show solid support for tracking among parents, teachers, and students" (Loveless, 1998, p. 1).

Such practices seem likely to continue until a greater degree of scholarly consensus can be achieved. In the meantime, the consensus recommendations seek, where possible, avoidance of retention, grouping, and tracking largely by nipping problems in the bud before they are necessary. But their possible inevitability may be reflected in the title in the dilemma and question raised by the title of John Gardner's book of four decades ago, *Excellence: Can We Be Equal and Excellent Too?* That would require bringing all children to an equally high level and keeping them there during the school years—a formidable challenge and the subject of other forthcoming books in the present Laboratory-Information Age series.

REFERENCES

Gardner, J. W. (1961). *Excellence: Can we be equal and excellent too?* New York: Harper.

Loveless, T. (1998). *The tracking and ability grouping debate.* Washington, DC. The Thomas B. Fordham Foundation.

ABOUT THE CONTRIBUTORS

ABOUT THE EDITORS

Arthur J. Reynolds, Ph.D., is a professor of social work, educational psychology and human development at the University of Wisconsin-Madison. He directs the Chicago Longitudinal Study, which since 1985 has been tracing the impact of the Chicago Child-Parent Center Program and other government-funded early childhood educational programs in 25 Chicago public schools. He and his team have tracked the experiences of more than 1,500 children from preschool to early adulthood. Reynolds' research focuses on children's social adjustment and academic success, with special emphasis on how environmental conditions affect development. His many published findings include *Success in Early Intervention: The Chicago Child-Parent Centers* (2000). Most recently, he coedited *Early Childhood Programs for a New Century*; the 2003 book examines preschool education and care, early school-age programs and practices, and national investment.

Herbert J. Walberg, Ph. D., is University Scholar and Emeritus Professor of Education and Psychology at the University of Illinois at Chicago and Distinguished Visiting Fellow at Stanford University (1999–2004). Dr. Walberg has served on numerous boards, as well as, national and international advisory committees. He has also written and edited more than 55 books and written about 350 articles on topics such as educational effectiveness and exceptional human accomplishments. Among his latest books are the *International Encyclopedia of Educational Evaluation* and *Psychology and Educational Practice*. He is also a fellow of five academic societies including the American Association for the Advancement of Science, the International Academy of Education, and the American Psychological Society.

ABOUT THE CHAPTER AUTHORS

Karl L. Alexander, Ph.D., is the John Dewey Professor of Sociology at Johns Hopkins University. His interests center on problems of educational stratification that can be addressed via organizational, social-psychological, and life course perspectives. The Beginning School Study (BSS) has been his primary research activity since the project commenced in 1982. He presently is directing fieldwork on an extension of the BSS to reinterview the original study group at ages 27–28. The second edition of his research monograph on grade retention, *On the Success of Failure: A Reassessment of the Effects of Retention in the Primary Grades,* coauthored with Doris Entwisle and Susan Dauber, was published in fall 2003 by Cambridge University Press. Ongoing research is examining the early adult transition through the lens of the BSS; one focusing on mode of high school exit.

Susan L. Dauber, Ph.D., is a Senior Program Officer at the Spencer Foundation in Chicago. She has conducted research on middle school tracking, parent involvement, school reform, contextual influences on achievement, and retention. With Karl Alexander and Doris Entwisle, she coauthored the book *On the Success of Failure: A Reassessment of the Effects of Retention in the Primary Grades.* She received her Ph.D. in sociology from Johns Hopkins University in 1994.

Doris R. Entwisle, Ph.D., Research Professor of Sociology, Johns Hopkins University, has been involved with the BSS since its inception. Her interests center on the sociology of child development especially on how socioeconomic background affects the transition to first grade and cognitive growth more generally. In 1977 she received the Society for Research in Child Development (SRCD) award for Distinguished Scientific Contribution to Child Development. Her current research concerns how youth in the Beginning School Study manage to juggle their work and school roles as they make the transition to adulthood.

Adam Gamoran is Professor of Sociology and Educational Policy Studies at the University of Wisconsin-Madison. His research has focused on stratification and inequality in school systems and the organizational contexts of teaching reform. Gamoran was a Fulbright Scholar at the University of Edinburgh in 1992–1993, and a Visiting Professor at Tel Aviv University in 1998. He has published numerous studies of tracking and ability grouping, including an article with William Carbonaro in the Winter 2002 issue of the *American Educational Research Journal*. Gamoran has edited two books and is the lead author of *Transforming Teaching in Math and Science: How Schools and Districts Can Support Change* (Teachers College Press, 2003). In 2001, Gamoran was elected to membership in the National Academy of Education.

Maureen T. Hallinan, Ph.D., is the White Professor of Sociology and director of the Center for Research on Educational Opportunity, Institute for Educational Initiatives at the University of Notre Dame. Dr. Hallinan's research is primarily in sociology of education. She is currently examining the determinants and consequences of the organization of students for instruction, as well as the effects of school characteristics on student achievement and social development. Dr. Hallinan is the principal investigator of the project, *Comparative Analysis of Best Practices in Public and Private Elementary and Secondary Schools,* a five-year study funded by the U.S. Department of Education.

With over 100 articles in professional journals, Dr. Hallinan is also the author or editor of seven books and has chapters in several edited volumes. Recently, she edited *The Handbook of the Sociology of Education* (2000) and coedited *Stability and Change in American Education: Structure, Process and Outcomes* (2003).

Dr. Hallinan was president of the American Sociological Association in 1995–1996 and president of the Sociological Research Association in 2000. She was elected to the National Academy of Education in 1999 and is currently vice president for fellowships. She is the recipient of the University of Notre Dame's Presidential Award Citation (1997) and the Research Achievement Award (2003).

Robert M. Hauser, Ph.D., is Samuel A. Stouffer Professor of Sociology and Vilas Research Professor of Sociology at the University of Wisconsin-Madison. His current research interests include trends in educational progression and social mobility in the United States among racial and ethnic groups, the uses of educational assessment as a policy tool, the effects of families on social and economic inequality, and changes in socioeconomic standing, health, and well-being across the life course. He has worked on the Wisconsin Longitudinal Study since 1969 and directed it since 1980. Recently, he chaired the National Academies Panel on the Appropriate Use of High Stakes Tests (National Research Council, Committee on Appropriate Test Use 1999. *High Stakes: Testing for Tracking, Promotion, and Graduation*, edited by Jay Heubert and Robert M. Hauser. Washington, DC: National Academy Press).

At the University of Wisconsin, Professor Hauser has directed the Center for Demography and Ecology and the Institute for Research on Poverty. He currently directs the Center for Demography of Health and Aging, which is supported by the National Institute on Aging. He is a member of the National Academy of Sciences and is a fellow of the American Statistical Association, the Center for Advanced Study in the Behavioral Sciences, and the American Academy of Arts and Sciences. He has served on the National Research Council's Committee on National Statistics, Commission on Behavioral and Social Sciences and Education, and Board on Testing and Assessment. He is cochair of the National Academies Panel on Performance Levels in Adult Literacy.

Shane R. Jimerson, Ph.D., is a Professor of Counseling, Clinical, and School Psychology, and Professor of Child and Adolescent Development in the Gevirtz Graduate School of Education at the University of California, Santa Barbara. Dr. Jimerson is the Associate Dean for Research in the graduate school, and is also the Associate Director of the Center for School-Based Youth Development. Dr. Jimerson has served on numerous boards and advisory committees at the state, national, and international levels. His scholarly publications and presentations have provided further insights regarding outcomes associated with early grade retention, the development of high school dropouts, achievement trajectories, the efficacy of early intervention programs, reading assessment, children's grief and adaptation in response to a loss, and school crisis prevention and intervention. The quality and contributions of his scholarship are reflected in the numerous awards and recognition that he has received. Dr. Jimerson received the *Best Research Article* of the year award from the *Society for the Study of School Psychology* in 1998 and then again in 2000. He also received the 2001 *Outstanding Article of the Year Award* from the National Association of School Psychologists' *School Psychology Review*. Dr. Jimerson's scholarly efforts were also recognized by the *American Educational Research Association* with the 2002 *Early Career Award in Human Development*. He and his UCSB research team received the 2003 *Outstanding Research Award* from the *California Association of School Psychologists*. Also during 2003, Dr. Jimerson received the *Lightner Witmer Early Career Contributions Award* from *Division 16 (School Psychology) of the American Psychological Association*. His scholarship continues to highlight the importance of early experiences on subsequent development and emphasize the importance of research informing professional practice to promote the social and cognitive competence of children.

Nader Kabbani, Ph.D., is an Assistant Professor in the Department of Economics at the American University of Beirut. He is also a research consultant for the Making Wages Work website, managed by the Finance Project with support from the Annie E. Casey Foundation. Previously, he worked as an economist with the Economic Research Service of the U.S. Department of Agriculture. He received his Ph.D. in Economics from Johns Hopkins University in 2001. His current research interests include youth employment and training programs, food assistance and food security issues, and income assistance programs.

James A. Kulik, Ph.D., is Director and Research Scientist at the University of Michigan's Office of Evaluations and Examinations. Dr. Kulik received his Ph.D. in psychology in 1966 from the University of California at Berkeley and was a faculty member at Wesleyan University in Middletown, Connecticut, before joining the University of Michigan faculty in 1968. Since 1976, Dr. Kulik has been using meta-analytic methods to summarize research findings in various areas of social science research. His meta-analytic projects have resulted in approximately 75 publications, including dozens of journal articles, numerous presentations at scientific meetings, and a comprehensive monograph on meta-analytic findings and results in educational research.

Suh Ruu Ou, Ph.D., is a Research Scientist at the Waisman Center, University of Wisconsin-Madison. Dr. Ou received her Ph.D. in Social Welfare from University of Wisconsin-Madison. Her areas of specialization are program evaluation, research methodology, educational attainment, and the effects of early childhood intervention.

Devah I. Pager, Ph.D., is an Assistant Professor in the Department of Sociology and a Faculty Fellow at the Institute for Policy Research at Northwestern University. She received her Ph.D. in Sociology from the University of Wisconsin-Madison (2002). Her research focuses on racial stratification in education, employment, and the criminal justice system. Dr. Pager's recent research has focused on the consequences of incarceration for labor market inequality. The findings of this project, which used a large-scale experimental audit design to test the effects of race and criminal records on employment opportunities among Milwaukee employers, are reported in the *American Journal of Sociology* (2003). Other recent publications include a study of the effects of racial composition on perceptions of neighborhood crime, coauthored with Lincoln Quillian (*American Journal of Sociology,* 2001) and an article investigating the relationship between occupational placement and Black-White earnings inequality, coauthored with Eric Grodsky (*American Sociological Review,* 2001). Dr. Pager spent the 2002–2003 academic year in Paris on a Fulbright grant where she conducted research on changes in criminal justice interventions in

France and their relationship to increasing immigration and ethnic conflict.

Lorrie A. Shepard, Ph.D., is Professor and Dean of the School of Education at the University of Colorado at Boulder. Her research focuses on psychometrics and the use and misuse of tests in educational settings. Technical topics include validity theory, standard setting, and statistical models for detecting test bias. Her studies evaluating test use have addressed identification of learning disabilities, readiness screening for kindergarten, grade retention, teacher testing, and effects of high-stakes accountability testing. Books include: *Flunking Grades: Research and Policies on Retention* (with M. L. Smith) and *Methods for Identifying Biased Test Items* (with G. Camilli). Her current interest is the use of classroom assessment to support teaching and learning.

Dr. Shepard is past president of the American Educational Research Association and past president of the National Council on Measurement in Education. She was elected to the National Academy of Education in 1992 and served as vice president of the NAE. She has been editor of the *Journal of Educational Measurement* and the *American Educational Research Journal*. In 1999, she won the National Council on Measurement in Education's Award for Career Contributions to Educational Measurement. Dr. Shepard currently serves on the National Research Council's Board on Testing and Assessment.

Solon J. Simmons is completing his dissertation in Sociology at the University of Wisconsin-Madison in the intersection of the fields of social stratification, economic sociology and politics. His research focuses on political interpretations of economic inequality and economic opportunity. His recent work examines the enduring influences of class-based and economy-based themes in presidential campaigns in the United States, and the relationship between party ideology in campaign materials and party image in the population.

Judy A. Temple, Ph.D., is Associate Professor of Economics at Northern Illinois University. Her research interests are in the areas of public sector economics, including the economics of education and cost-benefit analysis. She is an investigator with the Chicago Longitudinal Study. With Arthur Reynolds, she recently completed the first cost-benefit analysis of a federally-funded early intervention program by comparing program costs to the longer-term benefits of increased educational attainment and reduced delinquency observed at age 21.

Temple has received funding from the National Science Foundation, the National Institutes of Health, and the U.S. Department of Education for her research on the longer-term effects of early intervention. She was a National Academy of Education/Spencer Foundation postdoctoral fellow, and is an associate at the Institute for Research on Poverty at UW–Madison. Temple is a former president of the Illinois Economic Association. She received her Ph.D. in economics from Michigan State University.